Thérèse of Lisieux: Secrets of Joy

Thérèse of Lisieux

Secrets of Joy

Fr. Pierre Descouvemont

Translated by
A Benedictine Oblate

THE CENACLE PRESS
AT SILVERSTREAM PRIORY

First published in French as
Thérèse, quelques secrets de la joie (Cerf, 2006)
© Les Éditions du Cerf, 2006

First published in English by The Cenacle Press 2023
© 2023 by Silverstream Priory

The Cenacle Press at Silverstream Priory
Silverstream Priory
Stamullen, County Meath, K32 T189, Ireland
www.cenaclepress.com

ppr 978-1-915544-67-4
ebook 978-1-915544-75-9

Book design by Nora Malone
Cover design by Julian Kwasniewski
Cover art: "Therese at fifteen"
© Archives du Carmel de Lisieux.

Contents

Part 3
When I Consider God

Abbreviations used in this book

A, B, C	The three autobiographical manuscripts of Thérèse, published as *The Story of a Soul*
BT	La Bible avec Thérèse de Lisieux
CG	*Correspondance Generale*, letters of Thérèse's correspondents
DE/G	Dernieres Entretiens, collected by Sr. Genevieve, published in *Novissima Verba*
DE/MSC	Dernieres Entretiens, collected by Sr. Marie du Sacre-Coeur, published in *Novissima Verba*
DLTH	*Thérèse et Lisieux*, volume of photographs and documents
DLVI	*Thérèse de Lisieux: La vie en images*, volume of charts and images
LT	Letters from Thérèse, published in two volumes
MSST	*Conseils et souvenirs* of Sr. Genevieve, published in English as *My Sister St. Thérèse*
NPPA	Notes prepared by the Carmelites for the Apostolic Process
NV	*Novissima Verba*, publication of the Dernieres Entretiens

PA	Apostolic Process, 1915-1917
PN	Poems of Thérèse
PO	Proces de l'ordinaire (The Bishop's Process), 1910-1911
Pr	Prayers of Thérèse
RP	Plays of Thérèse
TLMT	*Une Novice de Sainte Thérèse*, Pierre Descouvement, published in English as *Thérèse of Lisieux and Marie of the Trinity*, (Alba House, 1997).
YN	Yellow Notebook of Mother Agnes of Jesus, published in *Novissima Verba*

All Bible quotations are taken from the RSVCE, unless otherwise noted.

Introduction

In St. Paul's first letter, addressed to the Christians of Thessalonica, he wrote: "Rejoice always!"[1] How hard it is to obey this command! Almost every day reasons for feeling sad pile up: the mail brings us bad news, people become a burden or irritate us, their success makes us jealous, their problems upset us or make us feel guilty.

When we look at ourselves, things are no better. We aren't proud of our failures to love or our boasting; we are afraid of the future; we lament our lack of courage or our extreme weakness; or quite simply we must admit that we have caused others pain with our mistakes and that our past hasn't always been glorious. It can even happen that we feel overwhelmed by the terrible sense that our life is useless.

When we think about heaven, it proves to be similar. Prayer seems very dry to us; even the simplest prayer—the rosary—is burdensome. God seems far away; He doesn't answer our cries. Our participation at Mass doesn't appear to be fruitful. And the thought of heaven, far from making us rejoice, may give rise to the painful question: "Does heaven exist and if it does, will I reach it?"

---

[1] 1 Thess 5:16.

1

The saints experienced all these problems and temptations, often more than we do. How did they conquer them? What convictions allowed them to remain joyful against the odds? Perhaps we could ask St. Thérèse of Lisieux to tell us some of the secrets of her joy, the reasons for her smile.

All who were lucky enough to know her are unanimous in testifying that her smile was an essential feature of her face: *her countenance was radiant with joy.* No photograph succeeded in capturing her marvelous smile. Instant photos didn't exist in her day—at least seven or eight seconds were required. Thérèse's face was very mobile, and she was obliged to keep it still during those long poses if the picture was to come out well. This discrepancy between her photos and the reality was so great that for years the Carmelites of Lisieux didn't want to show the public the photos Céline had taken of her sister, and especially the third photo taken on June 5, 1897, when Thérèse was burning up with fever. When she sent this photo to her spiritual brother, Maurice Bellière, Thérèse wrote, "The novices complained that I had put on my 'solemn face'; normally I smile more." In fact, it wasn't until 1961 that the photos were removed from their drawer and the world could finally see the true face of the nun who had been canonized in 1925, thirty-six years earlier.

In this book we hope to show *the deep reasons for this smile.* Thérèse's smile was a reflection of the profound joy which inhabited her heart. This joy was rooted in an unshakable *faith* in every facet of Christian revelation. Thérèse had the audacity to take seriously *everything* the Bible says about God's mystery. To remain joyful at all times, and to counteract her many reasons to be sad—which Thérèse had, just like everyone else, and certainly many more than some—she went to the Bible to find the reasons Jesus gave us to remain joyful nevertheless.

We should keep in mind that joy *often co-existed with sadness in her soul.* And Thérèse didn't feel bad about this. She had realized in childhood that a certain kind of sadness wasn't necessarily sinful, since Jesus had experienced it in the Garden of Gethsemane. When Mr. Martin entered the mental asylum in Caen, she frequently repeated what she wrote to Céline and what Fr. Pichon liked to say in his retreats: "Jesus suffered with sadness…without sadness what would the soul be suffering?" "We wish to suffer generously, grandly." In her letter she added, "Céline! What an illusion!"[2]

We shouldn't forget that, for Christians, joy is *a fruit of the Holy Spirit.*[3] Thérèse knew this, but she also knew that the Spirit only produces the fruits of peace, joy, and love in our hearts by causing them to retain the words of the Word. Jesus didn't say to His apostles, "You can forget everything I told you. To remain joyful, it will be enough for you to remain attentive to the Spirit whom I will send you." No. That isn't the way the Holy Spirit acts. Jesus declared: "The Spirit will bring back to your mind all that I have told you… He will lead you into the whole truth."[4]

For the saints, invoking the Holy Spirit never replaces *ongoing meditation on Holy Scripture.* (We could collect into a book the many Biblical texts which shaped Thérèse's spiritual life.[5]) We will show throughout this work that it was by studying Scripture, by seeking to discover in it, as she said, "the character of the Good God," that Thérèse was able to remain joyful—whatever the situation in her life. And likewise she draws after her many little souls who, following her footsteps, endeavor in their turn to live in the joy the Good News offers.

2 LT 89.
3 Gal 5:22.
4 Jn 14:26; 16:13.
5 See *La Bible avec Thérèse de Lisieux* (Paris: Editions du Cerf-DDB, 1979).

Instead of offering general teaching based on the fundamental axioms of Thérèse's spirituality,[6] we hope to help our readers by showing her way of responding, and her way of helping her novices respond, to the inevitable difficulties of every human life, as found in Thérèse's life and writings.

Additionally, we shouldn't assume that a cloistered nun's problems have nothing to do with the problems we experience in the world. Some are inclined to think a Carmelite's temptations are much less severe than the temptations experienced by celibates who haven't chosen their celibacy or by mothers of families burdened by domestic cares and anxieties. Taking this view means forgetting that life in Carmel requires sacrifices which are often heroic: in particular, religious life brings constant frictions we can hardly imagine since we don't have to endure anything like them. (This is why some people who demonstrate wonderful courage in the world find themselves unexpectedly disconcerted by the trials of enclosed life.) Hence, we should assess the victories Thérèse gained over her problems at their true worth. Let's place ourselves in her school so we can overcome them too.

To help the reader live supernatural joy in every situation, we include the temptations to sadness everyone experiences sooner or later in three areas: our own life, in relationships with other people, and when we turn our eyes to heaven. Furthermore, to show that St. Thérèse's teaching is in harmony with the tradition of the Church, in each chapter we have included excerpts from another saint or spiritual author which communicate the same insights.

---

[6] This is what we have done in *Thérèse de Lisieux: docteur de l'eglise, guide de lecture* (Paris: Editions du Cerf, 1997).

Part 1

When I Consider My Life

1

The Pain of Living

"You fill me with joy with all that you do."[7]

There are moments in life when, without being really depressed, we feel that life isn't very interesting. The ancient spiritual masters gave a name to this strange malady of the soul with no taste for anything: *acedia*. It was part of the list of the eight capital sins drawn up by Evagrius of Pontus, a Greek monk of the fourth century, from Pontus in Asia. In the Renaissance, *acedia* gradually disappeared from the list, and was replaced by sloth. Actually, sloth is only one consequence of *acedia*. Usually, a slothful person does only what is interesting (rather than nothing at all), and then the backlog of mail piles up and critical tasks are constantly put off. The slothful person doesn't accept the kind of life God is offering him. Instead, he throws himself into a multitude of projects causing him to forget the essential activity to which he should be devoting himself, particularly prayer. Long ago, the Desert Fathers noted that it's easier to spend oneself in many external works than to remain in one's hermitage to pray.

---

[7]   C 7r; see Psalm 92.

"Distraction" is what Blaise Pascal called the attitude whereby a person refuses to reflect on the meaning of his life, to see what he is, or look where he is going. As one comedian quipped, "This inscription could be put on the tomb of many people: 'here lies someone who never knew why he was alive.'" This is the malaise of many of our contemporaries; they try to compensate for the emptiness of their lives in front of their screens. They plod through life, getting up in the morning and going to bed in the evening without recognizing why they should carry on. They live to work; life is nothing but commuting, working, and sleeping.

Christians, having received the grace to believe that God is really speaking in the Bible, discover in it powerful weapons for fighting this feeling of distaste toward life.

Love the life God has given me

A Catholic should think that his or her life is interesting since God declares it's the one He chose for us. St. Thérèse affirms this at the beginning of her first autobiographical manuscript: "Just as the sun shines simultaneously on the tall cedars and on each little flower as though it were alone on the earth, so Our Lord is occupied particularly with each soul as though there were no others like it. And just as in nature all the seasons are arranged in such a way as to make the humblest daisy bloom on a set day, in the same way, everything works out for the good of each soul."[8]

Indeed, from all eternity God is thinking of each one of His children. He loves us with a particular and entirely free love. All of us are unique stars in the heaven of His creation. The Jewish Talmud explains our creation in God's image and likeness in this way:

---

[8]   A 3r.

"Man was created unique and it is in this that he resembles God."[9] In the charming witticism of the convert André Frossard: "God only counts up to one."[10]

In the morning, even before we get out of bed, what a joy to consider that God has loved us with an infinite love! We had done nothing, yet we were the object of a boundless paternal affection. The Alps hadn't yet risen, the rocks weren't yet solidified, and God had already thought of each one of us and loved us with an inexhaustible tenderness.[11] When we are lucky enough to hold a baby in our arms, in some way we are participating in the joy with which the Father embraces and protects each of us, all the time bringing us out of nothingness. The difference is that His love is infinite! How He wishes that we would believe in it without any doubt!

Obviously, this isn't a reason to stay in bed, but a spectacular reason for joy, for celebrating, from the very beginning of the day, the infinite love which never ceases creating us, which protected us during the night, which will accompany us throughout our day, and which will always make "everything work for our good."[12]

Why are we sometimes tempted to have a negative view of our life? The answer is that we are inclined to gauge success in terms of the nature and number of the activities in our days rather than frequently recalling the absolutely gratuitous love the Lord grants every one of His children. The person who thrives most in life, whether in a family or in a religious community, isn't necessarily the one who accomplishes the most. It's the person who believes the most in the unconditional love at the origin of his existence and remembers that

9   J. Eisenberg and A. Abecassis, in *Bible Ouverte* (Paris: Editions Albin Michael, 1978), 109.
10   André Frossard, *Il y a une autre monde* (Paris: Fayard, 1976), 26.
11   See Ps 119:156.
12   Rm 8:28.

it's intended to be the object of his eternal contemplation and the main cause of his joy.[13]

St. Thérèse believed wholeheartedly in the Lord's completely gratuitous love. While reading the New Testament, she was fortunate to have found a clear phrase from St. Paul on this subject. The Apostle declares, "For he says...'I will have mercy on whom I have mercy, and I will have compassion on whom I have compassion.' So, it depends not upon man's will or exertion, but upon God's mercy."[14] Thérèse quoted these verses from the Letter to the Romans at the beginning of her first manuscript and in a letter to Fr. Bellière.[15]

As her four brothers and sisters who had died in childhood had done,[16] she wished to go to heaven, not because she had earned it, but simply in virtue of the Lord's mercy. She wanted to come before the Lord "with empty hands," as she wrote in her *Act of Offering*. From childhood, she had the aim of refusing God nothing, but she didn't want to rely on her own generous actions to attain heaven. She explained this one day to Sr. Genevieve (her sister Céline):

> We must do all in our power to give without counting and deny ourselves constantly. We must prove our love by all the good works of which we are capable and which, after all, are of little worth...Even when we have done all that we think we should have done we are to consider ourselves, 'unprofitable servants,' hoping at the same time that God will, through His grace, give us all that we desire.[17]

---

[13] In the next chapter, we will see that God is asking us to respond generously to His love in our lives.

[14] Rm 9:15–16.

[15] A 2r; LT 224.

[16] Pr. 6.

[17] Sr. Genevieve of the Holy Face, *My Sister Saint Thérèse* (Rockford: TAN Books, 1997) [MSST], 57.

Thérèse understood God's love even more fully at twenty-one, when she found, in a small notebook belonging to Céline, a Bible verse which her sister had recopied before entering Carmel: "As one whom his mother comforts, so I will comfort you...you shall be carried upon my hip and dandled upon my knees."[18] Thérèse wrote, "Never had words more tender, more melodious, come to rejoice my soul."[19] Thanks to these two verses from Isaiah, she realized more deeply that God is a father who loves us like a mother and that the primary thing we need to do is believe in that love with all our soul, and abandon ourselves to it with a wholly childlike trust.

A few weeks later, having been asked to write an account of her life, Thérèse had no trouble seeing in it the infinite tenderness the Lord had had toward her: "The flower about to tell her story rejoices at having to publish the totally gratuitous gifts of Jesus. She knows that nothing in her was capable of attracting the divine glance, and His mercy alone brought about everything that is good in her."[20]

One day Céline entered the cell where her little sister was busy sewing. She was struck by the profound recollection on her face: "What are you thinking about?" she asked Thérèse. "I am meditating on the Our Father. It is so sweet to call God our Father!" she replied.[21]

Let's see ourselves as treasured children too, just as Thérèse did. For we are loved beyond measure; we are cherished, accompanied, and protected. Then when the doldrums try to get hold of us, they will melt like snow under the sun's heat. Indeed, we will take a very different view of our lives when we accept every minute of our day as a marvelous gift from the Father who specially arranged them for

---

[18] Is 66:13, 12.
[19] C 3r.
[20] A 3v.
[21] MSST 109.

us from all eternity. Our souls and bodies, the air we breathe, the food we eat, the people we meet, the friends we see—all this should be welcomed as coming from the hand of the most loving of Fathers. This makes sense of St. Paul's exhortation to live every moment of our lives "in thanksgiving."[22]

How can we still disparage our lives when we have the right, and the duty, to call *Abba* the One who brought us into being and who is specially watching over each step we take. "Even though I walk through the valley of the shadow of death, I fear no evil; for thou art with me, thy rod and thy staff, they comfort me."[23]

Be happy that God is happy

There is another truth which should cause us to remain deeply joyful, whatever our mood might be. It's the fact of God's infinite happiness. As the saints always have, Thérèse rejoiced at the thought that, while being extremely "sensitive" to His children's troubles, God is infinitely and eternally happy. "Oh my God, happy Blessed Trinity!" is the opening of her well-known Offering to Merciful Love, from June 1895. She reflected that after having suffered enormously under Pontius Pilate, Jesus entered forever into the Father's glory and henceforth He rejoices with all the blessed in heaven, with supreme happiness. (This is why she preferred crucifixes which represented Jesus as already dead, because then, "I remember that He is no longer suffering," she said.[24])

When another cause of sadness arises in our minds, we should rejoice, like Thérèse, like Charles de Foucauld, at the idea that nothing prevents God—our beloved God—from being infinitely happy. Indeed, we are invited to rejoice in His joy, to marvel at it, and be

---

[22] 1 Thess 5:12.
[23] Ps 23:4 KJV.
[24] YN August 19, n. 3.

happy about it! A Carmelite said once: "When I feel depressed, I find a chair, I take a seat, and I think, following Thérèse and all the saints, that, in my soul, God is infinitely happy. Then peace returns to my heart."

God is happy

St. Charles de Foucauld said frequently that one of the greatest sources of his joy was the thought that Jesus is now happy forever. "When we are sad, discouraged about ourselves, about others, about things in life, let us reflect that Jesus is in glory, seated at the right hand of the Father, eternally blessed, and that if we love Him as we should, the happiness of the infinite Being's happiness should always outweigh the sadness of finite things in our souls. After considering the idea of our God's infinite happiness, our soul should become jubilant and the pains pressing it should disappear like clouds before the sun: our God, our All, is happy. We should rejoice continually, for all creaturely troubles are but an atom compared to the Creator's blessedness."[25]

Similarly, Brother Charles loved the feast of the Ascension above all others because it was the celebration of Christ's definitive entry into His glory.

"Most blessed of days! Most beautiful of days! There is no sweeter feast in the year to my heart. Christmas is a gift you gave me at the cost of your painful future! In my mind, Easter is the manifestation of the happiness into which your

[25] Charles de Foucauld, *La Dernière Place, Retraite en Terre Sainte* (Bruyères-le-Châtel: Nouvelle Cité, 2002), 89.

soul entered at the hour of your death and the beginning of your bodily glorification. Today your happiness is complete, absolute; today you receive your reward at the Father's right hand. Now I have nothing to desire for You, my God, *Rabboni*. I can only give thanks. 'I give you thanks for Your great glory.' I can only say, 'Amen, Amen, Alleluia!' Amen, all is accomplished. I have only to pray for your Church, your mystical body, for souls, your spiritual members. But for You, it is done, there is nothing to ask. I am content, I am happy. I have nothing to say but Amen, Amen. Amen endlessly. And thank you, thank you. Thank you endlessly!"[26]

Rejoice at the idea that God is waiting for me in heaven

As a final point, we should remember that we are all called to immerse ourselves, starting in this life, in a limitless ocean of blessedness and love.

> Therefore, my heart is glad, and my soul rejoices;
>   my body also dwells secure.
> For thou dost not give me up to Sheol,
>   or let thy godly one see the Pit.
> Thou dost show me the path of life;
>   in thy presence there is fulness of joy,
>   in thy right hand are pleasures for evermore.[27]

The sense of incompleteness we often feel at the end of a very enjoyable party comes precisely from the fact that our hearts cannot

---

[26] Charles de Foucauld, *Considérations sur le fêtes de l'année* (Bruyères-le-Châtel: Nouvelle Cité, 1987), 400–401.
[27] Ps 16: 9–11.

be satisfied by any reality in this world. Our hearts are made for an infinite joy which we will only experience after death. The vision of God alone can fill hearts constantly longing for a happiness infinitely more intense than any we experience on earth.

Thérèse used the word "heaven" 709 times in her writings and almost always used it to designate the paradise where her brothers and sisters who had died in childhood had already arrived; she hoped to join them one day. (Curiously, the word "heavens" was the first word she managed to read on her own.[28]) The feast days of earth are "never as ravishing as those of heaven," she wrote two days before her vestition as a Carmelite, on January 8, 1889.[29] And the next day she wrote, "How I thirst for heaven, there where I will love Jesus without reserve!"[30]

At the end of her life, even as she desired "to spend her heaven doing good on earth,"[31] she continued to long just as much to enter into God's joy for all eternity. "How I need to see the marvels of heaven! Nothing touches me here on earth."[32] And two days later, "Oh! yes, I desire heaven! Rend the veil of that sweet encounter, oh my God!"[33]

Here then, are three reasons quite sufficient to drive away the painful feelings which often prevent us from being joyful in the way the Lord asks. We should savor the simple joys the Lord strews in our lives and remember that these are the manifestations of His completely

---

[28] A 13v.
[29] LT 77.
[30] LT 79.
[31] YN July 17, n.1.
[32] YN August 31, n.8.
[33] YN September 2, n. 8.

undeserved and entirely personal love. We should also rejoice in the thought that God is immeasurably happy, that nothing is lacking to His joy, and that we are called to join Him and share in His joy forever.

In the next chapter, we will see that Thérèse believed also in the wonderful power God gives us for increasing, in some way, His infinite joy by offering Him our smiles and our acts of love. This is another reason—and not a small one—to rejoice always.

2

Lack of Motivation
My life benefits no one

"I want to work for your Love alone with the one
purpose of pleasing you, consoling your Sacred Heart,
and saving souls who will love you eternally."[34]

How many people are sad because they feel they are useless? They say, "My life isn't good for anything…Why doesn't God come and put an end to my existence? I'm a burden to others and myself. If I disappeared, the world wouldn't be any worse for it: I wouldn't be inconveniencing others with my presence anymore!" I am thinking especially of single people who really wanted to be married, those who are out of work, or who are forced to take a job they don't like, those who have some disability and can live only by depending on others, all the elderly people who, after living their lives in service of others, go on with the tremendously painful feeling that they no longer have anything to offer those around them. What should you say to these people? Is there anything in the Bible that would encourage them and help them grasp the fruitfulness of their life?

[34] Pr 6.

They need to be reminded of the amazing possibility we all have, whatever our way of life, whatever our successes or failures, whether familial, professional or apostolic, of pleasing God. *Here we encounter one of the great Gospel paradoxes which Thérèse understood perfectly and illuminated her whole life.* From all eternity God loves us freely: if He created us, it's not because He needed us. Yet He loves us so much that He desires to receive something from us. He doesn't need it for His essential happiness, but He asks for it. St. Thérèse says He "begs" for it.

From childhood, she was truly fascinated by this aspect of the Gospel, and her life is completely incomprehensible if we forget her deep-seated conviction that she could, through her generosity, give joy to God and make Him loved. In September 1896 she wrote:

> See, then, all that Jesus lays claim to from us; He has no need of our works but only of our love, for the same God who declares He has no need to tell us when He is hungry did not fear to beg for a little water from the Samaritan woman. He was thirsty. But when He said: "Give me to drink," it was the love of His poor creature the Creator of the universe was seeking. He was thirsty for love.[35]

In other words, Thérèse didn't *always* go before God with empty hands. She was equally interested in coming to Him *with hands full of the flowers of her love.* "With the unique goal of pleasing Him and saving souls" as she put it in her *Act of Offering.*

To please Jesus

The desire to please Jesus becomes a real leitmotif in Thérèse's sayings and writings. As a child, she offered Him sacrifices, which she kept track of on her "chaplet of good deeds," following the custom of the

---

[35] B 1v.

period.[36] On the day before her first communion, during her confession with Fr. Domin, chaplain of her Benedictine boarding school, she asked him, "Father, do you think that Jesus is happy with me?"[37]

However before her conversion at Christmas in 1896, she couldn't bear the idea that others weren't *equally* pleased with her very small acts. For instance, when she did a little housekeeping "to please the good God," she cried when Céline didn't give her the impression of appreciating her services.[38] On Christmas Eve she received the grace of no longer being consumed by whether or not others were content with what she did. She felt "the need to forget myself, and to please others; since then, I've been happy!"[39] From that time on, the desire to please Jesus and others was her focus. It hardly mattered if events didn't meet her expectations or if she wasn't pleased; what was essential was that Jesus was happy.

To symbolize her joy in abandoning herself with trust to Jesus' "good pleasure," for a while Thérèse used the image of the "little ball" or little toy, which lets itself be used by a child according to his whim. This idea appeared first in a letter from Sr. Agnes, written on November 8, 1887, and was used by Thérèse during her trip to Rome in a letter from 14 November.[40] She continued to employ it in the following months to show she accepted the disappointments preventing the realization of her desires: namely, entering Carmel as soon as possible,[41] and her reception of the habit on 9 January 1889, exactly nine months after her entry into the monastery.[42]

---

36 A 8v, 11r.
37 PA 35.
38 A 44v.
39 A 45v.
40 LT 34.
41 LT 36.
42 LT 76.

For St. Thérèse, Jesus always remained "the little divine beggar of Christmas"; this is the title of a play she wrote and put on in Christmas 1895.[43] It includes an expression which summarizes one of her deep convictions quite well: Jesus is begging for our love. He needs it so that souls redeemed by His Blood may be effectively saved.[44]

In her darkest hours, Thérèse continued to offer her smiles to the Lord with the simple goal of pleasing Him, of making Him smile. This is what she celebrates in a poem composed in the depths of her spiritual night and entitled *My Joy*. Giving it to Mother Agnes as a present for her feast day, she said, "My whole soul is there."

> If sometimes I shed tears,
> My joy is to hide them well.
> Oh! how many charms there are in suffering
> When one knows how to hide it with flowers!
> I truly want to suffer without saying so
> That Jesus may be consoled.
> My joy is to see him smile
> When my heart is exiled...
>
> My joy is to struggle unceasingly
> To bring forth spiritual children.
> It's with a heart burning with tenderness
> That I keep saying to Jesus:
> "For you, my Divine Little Brother,
> I'm happy to suffer.
> My only joy on earth
> Is to be able to please you.[45]

---

43 RP 5.
44 See Col 1:24.
45 PN 45, st 5, 6.

Along with St. John of the Cross, Thérèse was filled with wonder at the idea that the bride of the Song of Songs could please her God with one glance of her eyes or one hair.[46] She commented on what this verse means: "With the greatest thing and with the smallest... What a mystery!"[47] Living as a child before God isn't merely a matter of expecting everything from Him; for Thérèse, it also means considering oneself as the King's child who can please Him through loving actions.

This desire to please Jesus so filled Thérèse's heart that she stated she would willingly suffer secretly to give Him joy, even if He didn't know she was the source of that joy. On July 16, 1897, a few hours before repeating her hope of spending her heaven doing good on earth, she told her sisters:

> If God were to say to me: "If you die right now, you will obtain great glory; if you die at the age of eighty, your glory will be far less, but it will please me much more," I would not hesitate to answer: "My God, I want to die at eighty, for I am not seeking my own glory, but I only want to please You. The great saints have worked for God's glory, but I, who am only a very little soul, work only for His pleasure, His whims. And I would be happy to bear the greatest sufferings—even without God's knowing it, if this were possible—not for the purpose of giving Him a passing glory, but if only I knew that in this way a smile would rise to His lips."[48]

The only reward Thérèse wanted in heaven was the possibility of loving Jesus as she desired: with a love that had no limits. "How

---

[46] See Song 4:9.
[47] LT 164.
[48] DE/MSC 16 July.

I thirst for heaven, there where I shall love Jesus without reserve!" she wrote two days before receiving the habit.[49] A few months later, she wrote also, "One act of love will make us know Jesus better… it will bring us closer to Him during the whole of eternity!"[50] This was the same conviction that made her say two months before her death: "I've never given Him anything else besides love, and so now He gives me love, and that's not all. Very soon He'll give me more love."[51] The only reward the bride expects is the boundless love with which, in heaven, she can finally love her Bridegroom.

Our life is truly completely transformed when we firmly believe that we are called to give joy to God's heart. Churches would be full to bursting if the people of our parishes, both young and old, had the boldness to believe, as Thérèse did, that by their prayerful presence before the Eucharist, they could really make God happy! Imagine the answers a child returning from Mass, filled with this conviction, would give to his father, if he asked, "Why did you go? Didn't you find it a little long?" "Yes, Papa! The priest forgot the three essential qualities of a sermon: short, brief, and not long." "But then why did you stay?" "Oh, it was to make God happy, Papa!"

I also imagine the response we might make to an elderly woman asking, "What good is it to live a day longer?" "To make God happy, dear lady."

To make Jesus loved and to save souls

By loving Jesus wholeheartedly, by increasing her acts of love, Thérèse knew she was contributing in a very real way to making Him loved. Up to her death, she considered herself responsible for "earning a living

---

[49] LT 79.
[50] LT 89.
[51] YN July 22, n. 1.

for her children," for the poor sinners whose *sister* she was. Seated at their table, she called divine mercy down on them; but she was also their *mother*, responsible for obtaining their salvation through her steadfast love. In a single paragraph in her last manuscript, she went from one position to the next, one right after the other.[52]

Therefore, it's a mistake to think that at the end of her life Thérèse rejected the idea that we can *merit* something before God. Certainly, she knew that eternal life is an absolutely gratuitous gift from the Father, something to be received with empty hands; and she remembered that her acts of love were treasures which God placed in His child's hands.[53] However, even on her death bed she was galvanized by the idea that on the last day, when Jesus came in His glory, He would say, "Now it is My turn. I will pay in God! I recompense a hundredfold!"[54] (She discovered this expression in 1887 in the *Conferences* of Canon Arminjon and used it to encourage herself to bear the long *via crucis* of her tuberculosis patiently.)

THÉRÈSE FORGOT TO START A NEW PARAGRAPH!

Often St. Thérèse didn't take the trouble to begin a new paragraph when stating a new idea. Speaking of her prayer to the Lord on behalf of her unbelieving brethren, she begins by saying that, seated at their table, she prays in solidarity with them, "Have pity on us, O Lord, for we are poor sinners!…Oh! Lord, send us away justified." Sometimes people have commented that in praying this way, Thérèse no longer considered herself a just soul capable of saving sinners—which she had

---

52 C 6r.
53 YN August 6, n. 8.
54 YN August 5, n. 1.

said ten years earlier when praying for Pranzini's salvation. They claim she was so conscious of her condition as a sinner that she no longer prayed *for* "poor sinners" but *with* them. She was their *sister*.

How true this is! Thérèse understood better and better that in allowing herself to have the infinite torrents of God's mercy poured over her, she was allowing many other hearts to be inundated with it and purified in their turn.

In spite of this, immediately afterward—and without taking the trouble of starting another paragraph—simply writing an ellipsis before the words "O Jesus," Thérèse reveals another aspect of her intercessory prayer. She wrote, "O Jesus! if it is needful that the table soiled by them be purified by a soul who loves You, then I desire to eat this bread of trial at this table until it pleases You to bring me into Your bright Kingdom. The only grace I ask of You is that I never offend You!"[55]

What audacity! Thérèse presents herself before Jesus here with the soul of *a bride* and with all her love as *a mother* and hopes to purify the table of sinners in this fashion. She doesn't refer to the blood of the Lamb, which alone is capable of cleansing us from all sin, as she knew quite well. In this sentence she is not praying *with* them, but *for* them. She is not their *sister*, but their *mother*. Without forgetting her sinful condition, she prays like a king's daughter, as someone especially pleasing to the Lord and able to merit the salvation of her unbelieving brethren, *through perseverance in steadfast faith and love.*

---

[55] C 6r.

In view of this, it's evident that Thérèse's "little way" isn't a sentimental spirituality. The roses she wanted to shower on earth after her death were obtained by means of sacrifice and renunciation. Similarly, Thérèse didn't fall into the error of "pure love," which maintains that it's possible to arrive at a love so disinterested that a person forgets the whole idea of a reward. Until her death she retained the desire which made her enter Carmel so young: to save many sinners and to help priests become holy. She renounced marriage but she wanted to live a fruitful life. Like the bride in the Song of Songs, she rejoiced in the idea of loving her Lord, of being drawn by the fragrance of His anointing oil, and drawing many souls after her.[56]

In her last letter to Father Roulland, Thérèse affirmed her desire to go to heaven clearly—both to finally love Jesus as she wished, and to make Him loved by many souls: "What attracts me to the homeland of heaven is the Lord's call, the hope of loving Him finally as I have so much desired to love Him, and the thought that I shall be able to make Him loved by a multitude of souls who will bless Him eternally."[57]

"The smallest movement of pure love is more useful to the Church than all other works put together." St. John of the Cross.[58]

The copy of the *Spiritual Canticle* Thérèse used reads: "is more profitable to His Church." Thérèse quoted these words

---

[56] C 34r.
[57] LT 254.
[58] *Spiritual Canticle*, st 29.

on several occasions.[59] She wrote it in calligraphy in the center of her "Consecration to the Holy Face."[60]

Do we need to add that Christians also experience the joy of serving others in their various activities during the day? They don't profess to be more generous in this area than their unbelieving brethren, but they approach others with the certainty that, by doing an act of service, it is Jesus they are honoring and serving. Further, when they have the dreadful feeling that their services are scarcely appreciated or that they aren't achieving the expected results, they don't become overly upset. If they don't succeed in making others smile, they are still giving Jesus joy. That's an incredible motivation!

Accordingly, in Thérèse's school, let's rejoice that we are royal children, capable of pleasing our God and King. Life is transformed when we are convinced that God truly appreciates His children when they try to please Him. So often Christians imagine that God is content to put up with them in the way they put up with particularly difficult neighbors. No, says the prophet Zephaniah, God dances with joy because of His children.[61] He rejoices at their progress, as a father does when seeing his child become braver. He regards us, says the Song of Songs, with the admiration that a bridegroom feels for his beautiful beloved.

---

[59] B 4v, LT221, LT 245.
[60] Pr 12.
[61] The Hebrew root typically translated as rejoice literally means to spin or dance, under the influence of great emotion. See Zeph 3:17.

Let me see your face,
    let me hear your voice,
for your voice is sweet,
    and your face is comely.[62]

And as the bridegroom rejoices over the bride,
    so shall your God rejoice over you.[63]

We must not continue telling the Lord that we are nobodies and that we can't do anything. Would a father be happy to hear one of his children constantly saying, "Papa, I'm a failure"? We know the answer God would give us if we were foolish enough to say such a thing: "My precious child, you may not be brilliant, but you are unique in the world. Hold your head up. Catch your breath, and then run on your path with courage. I am with you."[64] Indeed, the more we joyfully appreciate that God alone is the King of kings and Lord of lords, the more He tells us that we are His beloved royal children and that we should hold our heads up with dignity.

When I prepare young people for the sacrament of reconciliation, I advise that they gladly ask the Lord's pardon for two things they aren't doing enough: we must *kneel* and *stand* upright before God. However, I note that even if they were acrobats, they couldn't do both at the same time![65]

---

[62] Song 2:14.
[63] Is 62:5.
[64] See Is 43:4, Ps 119:32, Mt 28:20.
[65] In the past, the standing posture was a symbol of Christian prayer. From the start, the Church exhorted the faithful to favor it in their Sunday liturgies in order to express their faith in Christ's resurrection and their certainty of already being resurrected with Him. The first Council of Nicaea (315) even forbade the faithful to kneel during the Paschal season!

3

Trials

"Everything is grace."[66]

There are times when we really have the feeling God is asking too much of us: problems pile up and we can't help but exclaim, "Too much! It's too much, Lord! You need to arrange it so that things don't keep turning out like this! In these circumstances, how can I still obey the Apostle's commandment to rejoice always?" For more than a century, St. Thérèse has been helping millions of Catholics answer this question, since in the midst of many trials she offered God numberless smiles. By studying Scripture and meditating on *The Imitation of Christ*, she discovered the secret to remaining at peace in all situations, in spite of wounded feelings and physical sufferings.

Descend into the center of my heart

To see how it's possible for both suffering and joy to exist in the souls of the saints, we have to remember that this joy—though it may be more helpful to use the word peace[67]—is experienced at the

---

66 YN 5.6.4.
67 See Phil 4:7.

level which the Bible calls the heart. This is a deeper level than 1) the physical sphere, which at such times may be completely immersed in very painful physical suffering, and 2) the realm of emotion, which at times may be assailed by pain we can't ignore. The peace Jesus promised His disciples is not "that of the world."[68] It isn't the tranquility that the absence of all personal or familial care affords, but the profound peace of heart which the certainty of God's presence gives; the certainty that He loves us, and that our generous acceptance of suffering will contribute to the world's salvation.

Like all the saints, Thérèse again and again experienced both great disappointment and great peace in her soul at once. For example, on October 31, 1887, she went to Bayeux with her father to meet with Msgr. Hugonin and ask him for permission to enter Carmel two months later. The negative answer she got from the bishop didn't affect her profound peace. "My soul was plunged into bitterness but into peace too, for I was seeking God's will."[69] She had the same experience on November 20th, after her failed request to Pope Leo XIII. "In the bottom of my heart I felt a great peace, since I had done everything in my power to answer what God was asking of me. This *peace*, however, was in the *depths* only; bitterness *filled* my soul, for Jesus was silent."[70]

A year and a half later, when it was time for Thérèse to receive the Carmelite habit with the name Sister Thérèse of the Child Jesus and the Holy Face, she learned that her dear father was to be committed to the mental asylum of Bon Secours in Caen. She experienced then even more intensely than at Bayeux or in Rome that peace is still possible, even while great sadness filled her soul. She wrote to Céline

---

[68]   Jn 14:27.
[69]   A 55v.
[70]   A 64r.

on April 4, 1889, "I admit that this word *peace* seemed a little strong to me, but the other day, when reflecting on it, I found the secret of suffering in peace...The one who says peace is not saying joy, or at least, felt joy...To suffer in peace, it is enough to will all that Jesus wills..."[71] Three weeks later she penned something similar, "Let us suffer the bitter pain, without courage!... (Jesus suffered in sadness! Without sadness would the soul suffer!...) And still, we would like to suffer generously, grandly!... Céline! what an illusion!"[72]

In this passage, Thérèse repeats word for word a formula Fr. Pichon, her spiritual father, liked very much: "Jesus suffered with sadness...without sadness, is the soul suffering?" Thérèse had read this in the notebook into which Sr. Marie-Joseph had copied the outline of talks given by this Jesuit during the retreat he preached in October 1887.

While still a child, Thérèse realized that it was entirely possible to be both sad and at peace. Later she was happy to discover in her copy of *The Imitation of Jesus Christ* a reflection from Felicité de Lamennais affirming that Jesus experienced in His soul this coexistence of suffering and joy: "Our Lord in the Garden of Olives enjoyed all the delights of the Trinity and nonetheless his agony was no less painful." Quoting this, Thérèse added on July 6, 1897, "This is a mystery, but I assure you that I understand something of it through what I am experiencing in myself."

In his letter from January 6, 2001, *Novo millenio ineunte*, Pope John Paul II quoted this reflection from Thérèse to remind us that the unspeakable suffering Christ faced in bearing the world's sins didn't prevent Him from always being joyful in the depth of His soul. "Not infrequently the saints have undergone something akin to

---

[71] LT 87.
[72] LT 89.

Jesus' experience on the Cross in the paradoxical blending of bliss and pain. In the *Dialogue of Divine Providence*, God the Father showed St. Catherine of Siena how joy and suffering can be present together in holy souls:

> Thus the soul is blissful and afflicted: afflicted on account of the sins of its neighbor, blissful on account of the union and the affection of charity which it has inwardly received. These souls imitate the spotless Lamb, my Only-begotten Son, who on the Cross was both blissful and suffering.[73]

St. Thérèse's smile, as with all the saints, shouldn't give us any illusions. Only in her heart's core she could be joyful while she experienced physical and moral hardships. Two months before her death, on July 30, 1897, she said everything by holding up a glass that contained very bitter medicine, but looked like a delicious currant liqueur. "This little glass, it is the image of my life. To the eyes of creatures, I drank exquisite liqueurs…but it was bitterness. I say 'bitterness,' but no, my life has not been bitter, because I knew how to make my joy and sweetness out of every bitterness." On August 15 she said something similar to her sister. Mother Agnes had repeated the words of St. John of the Cross about the death of souls consumed by love, and Thérèse responded with: "You will have to say that the joy and transports were in the depth of my soul. It wouldn't encourage souls very much if they didn't think I had suffered a great deal."

All the same, it's not enough simply to descend into our heart's depth for us to experience the peace that Christ promised. We need to preserve in our hearts everything He revealed to illuminate the mystery of our suffering. We can never say it enough: the Holy Spirit

---

[73] *Novo millenio ineunte*, 27.

only produces His fruits of peace in us by causing us to appreciate the Biblical texts which help us live our trials not as absolute evils, but as providential means for us to grow in faith, hope, and charity. What aspects of the Gospel did Thérèse meditate on to remain peaceful when she was faced with trials?

Dare to believe that "all is grace"

While she knew that many events which happen in this world are contrary to God's will—and they are often caused by the "prince of this world"—Thérèse believed unwaveringly that God only permits these to happen for the sake of a greater good, since He makes everything work together for the benefit of His children.[74] It's true that most of the time we definitely don't see the benefits which might result from massacres or all the violence filling human history. However, without a single exception, the saints always believed they would discover in heaven the reasons for these divine "permissions." This was true for Thérèse too. She surrendered herself with complete trust to the Father's holy will, to the incomprehensible designs of Providence. With Joan of Arc, whom she liked to call her older sister in heaven, Thérèse knew that we must "take all in good part."

What is more, on the last page of the Gospel book which she wore over her heart, she wrote out a verse from Psalm 91 which expressed her desire to make her life a perpetual song of thanksgiving: "Lord, you fill me with joy by *all* that you do." She underlined the word *all*, convinced as she was that "all is grace."

Everything is grace. Georges Bernanos made this phrase famous by placing it at the conclusion of his novel *The Diary of a Country Priest*. St. Thérèse said it on June 5, 1897, reflecting that she might

[74] Rm 8:28.

die without receiving last rites.[75] We know Thérèse used this expression regularly to show her faith in the mystery of divine providence, thanks to the testimony Céline gave in the process for Thérèse's canonization.[76] In her manuscripts Thérèse used the word grace ninety-nine times and in her other writings one hundred and seventy times. We will see that, while she thanked God for the happy events of her life, she gave thanks even more for the trials she went through.

Luminous hours

Thérèse took up her pen in 1895, obeying her sister (who was Prioress), to recount her life and especially some items from her childhood. She wrote that she was doing so to sing "the mercies of the Lord,"[77] as she would do eternally. She thanked the Lord for having surrounded her with a boundless affection in her family, for having very early had the desire to refuse Jesus nothing, to consecrate her life to Him and become a great saint like Joan of Arc. She thanked Him for having given her, in youth, the experience of silence and prayer and a hunger for the Eucharist.

She thanked Him for the grace she had received on Christmas Eve 1886 specially—the grace to definitively leave the swaddling bands of childhood. She thanked Him for the graces she had been granted since then: Pranzini's conversion[78]; reading the works of Canon Arminjon[79]; the graces of prayer received with Céline in the Belvedere of Les Buisonnets[80]; the victory over her timidity at her

---

[75] In that era, it was common to wait until a person was dying to give them what is known now as "the sacrament of the sick."

[76] PA 293.

[77] A 2r.

[78] A 46v.

[79] A 47v.

[80] A 48v.

meeting with Msgr. Hugonin and the Bishop's "yes"[81]; the graces of generosity received during the three months she prepared before entering Carmel[82]; the grace of having known Mother Genevieve, foundress of the Lisieux Carmel[83]; the great graces received on the day of her profession[84]; her meeting with Fr. Alexis[85]; the floods of grace received following her Offering to Merciful Love[86]; the grace to receive as a gift, in October 1895, Fr. Maurice Bellière, her first spiritual brother[87]; the grace not to fear the war; of not hesitating to make certain remarks to her novices[88]; the grace of understanding and living better the demands of genuine fraternal charity[89]; the abundant graces received during her personal retreat of September 1896[90]; the grace of discovering how to bring all her brothers and sisters into her prayer.[91] And so on!

Dark days

Thérèse's thanksgiving was just as fervent when she recalled the trials she hadn't been spared, but which had caused her faith, hope, and love to mature. For example, even more painful than Mrs. Martin's death was Pauline's entry into Carmel. Thérèse felt this departure very keenly, as a separation from her second mother. And it's known that the sorrow resulting from it was the cause of the illness she suffered

[81] A 53v.
[82] A 68v.
[83] A 69v.
[84] A 77r.
[85] A 80v.
[86] A 84r.
[87] C 31v.
[88] C 23v.
[89] C 11v.
[90] B 2v–5v.
[91] C 33v.

for many weeks and from which she was delivered by the Virgin's smile on Pentecost, in May 1883.

In 1885 Thérèse went through a terrible bout of scruples that lasted fifteen months; she only defeated it in November 1886, after invoking her brothers and sisters who had died in childhood. That was another reason to bless God. "I knew then that if I was loved on earth, I was also loved in heaven... Since that moment, my devotion for my little brothers and sisters has grown and I love to hold dialogues with them frequently."[92]

The next year, she fought a long battle against the many obstacles preventing her from realizing her deepest longing: to enter Carmel just before she turned fifteen. She hoped to do this so she could celebrate the first anniversary of her Christmas transformation in the convent. Disappointments arose, but Thérèse remained peaceful, since her faith allowed her to discern Jesus' hand in all the delays imposed on her. She offered herself to Jesus as His "little ball"; He was free to play with it as it seemed good to Him: to leave it in a corner, or press it to His heart. The essential thing was to joyfully adhere to His will, to His "childish whims," by not doubting His love or predilection for a moment.[93]

Upon entering Carmel, Thérèse was immediately subjected to the unkind comments of a converse sister (Sr. St. Vincent de Paul) who didn't like the new postulant's *petite bourgeoise* demeanor. Thérèse answered her with a smile, since she viewed the hand which inflicted these "pinpricks" with love. "I am, however, *very happy* to suffer what Jesus wants me to suffer. If He doesn't directly puncture His little ball, it is really He who guides the hand that

---

[92] A 44r.
[93] A 64r.

is puncturing it!"[94] A month later, on February 12, her father, Louis Martin was admitted to the asylum of Bon-Secours in Caen. Thérèse immediately took this trial as coming from Jesus' hand: "It is His divine hand that is adorning His spouse for the day of her wedding..."[95]

By contemplating the Holy Face, the name she had taken January 10, Thérèse found the courage to rejoice that her father was participating in the Savior's passion so intimately. Changed due to his illness, Mr. Martin's face mysteriously resembled the disfigured face of Jesus. Disfigured as the Lord had been, her father would be transfigured one day to the likeness of the Risen One. Having drunk "the most bitter and most humiliating of all chalices," he would receive from God "a most magnificent throne in the kingdom of heaven."[96] This is what Thérèse wrote to her father on November 25, 1888, when he was recovering after his second stroke. "God always tries those whom He loves."[97] Furthermore, Thérèse regarded this painful trial as a "priceless treasure" given to her family by the Lord. Below her coat of arms on the last page of the manuscript she wrote, "Our greatest treasure: February 12, 1889." This date was an essential part of the "days of grace granted by the Lord to His little bride."[98]

Life will be definitely revolutionized when we dare to believe, with Thérèse and all the saints, in the awesome mystery of providence. The Bible continually proclaims it: God isn't simply the creator of the world—He watches over the course of history with special attention and over the life of every creature.

[94]   LT 74.
[95]   LT 82.
[96]   A 73r.
[97]   LT 68.
[98]   A 86r.

Our God is in the heavens; he does whatever he pleases.[99]

She [Wisdom] reaches mightily from one end of the earth to the other, and she orders all things well.[100]

Offer the rose of a smile amid life's thorns

Another fact that helped Thérèse to remain at peace amid trials was her profound faith in the immeasurable value of the cross. "Suffering alone can give birth to souls for Jesus" she wrote to Céline on July 18, 1891.[101] She reiterated this certainty in letters that followed and wrote in the same vein to her sister Léonie: reunited in heaven, "We shall be happy for having suffered for Jesus."[102] To her she also wrote, "Let us suffer in peace, the hour of rest is approaching, the light tribulations of this life of a moment are preparing us for an eternal weight of glory... how much God loves you and is granting you His graces...He finds you worthy of suffering for His love, and it is the greatest proof of affection that He may give you, for suffering makes us like Him..."[103]

Do we need to add that for Thérèse it's always a matter of suffering offered with love for the conversion of sinners? Of winning souls for Jesus, so that He may be loved? "Jesus wills to make their salvation depend on one sigh from our heart...What a mystery! If one sigh can save a soul, what can sufferings like ours not do?...Let us refuse Jesus nothing!"[104]

In her poems Thérèse often celebrates the mysterious fecundity of suffering—a suffering lived out of love for Jesus, for the sake of saving souls for Him.

[99]   Ps 115:3. See also Luke 12:16.
[100] Wis 8:1.
[101] LT 129.
[102] LT 170.
[103] LT 173.
[104] LT 85.

> If sometimes bitter suffering
> Should come to visit your heart,
> Make it your joy:
> To suffer for God...what sweetness!...[105]

And in her very last poem, she even said:

> Yes, to suffer while loving is the purest happiness![106]

St. Catherine of Siena on Providence

The Dialogue of Catherine of Siena contains a whole treatise on Providence (chapters 135 to 153). The saint encourages the reader to take seriously the words of the Gospel: "Do not worry about tomorrow, sufficient for each day its own troubles."[107]

"So, first of all, we must ask for 'heaven' (that is, a good and holy life), for I your heavenly Father know well enough that you need these lesser things. That is why I made the earth and commanded it to give you its fruits."

Unfortunately, many people don't recognize that the Father's will is always good. "My will they neither understand nor judge rightly, except when it seems to hold some worldly advantage or pleasure for them. But if this fails them, because it was there that they had set their whole will and hope, they think that they have neither felt nor received my providence or any kindness. They think they have been deprived of everything good. They are blinded by their selfish

---

[105] PN 10, st 8.
[106] PN 54, st 16.
[107] See Mt 6:34.

passion, they do not recognize the wealth within, nor the fruit of true patience.[108]

The more Thérèse comprehended the absolutely free gift of God's love for us—a crucial feature of her "little way"—the more she realized the essential attitude we ought to have before God: receive His love; rejoice in it; love Him; give Him love for love.

What counts, what pleases the Lord, isn't the number of sacrifices we offer Him, but the love in our hearts. Even so, it's not necessary to suffer in order to love. Thérèse explained this clearly toward the end of her first manuscript.

> And now I have no other desire except to love Jesus unto folly...Neither do I desire any longer suffering or death, and still, I love them both; it is love alone that attracts me, however. I desired them for a long time; I possessed suffering and believed I had touched the shores of heaven, that the little flower would be gathered in the springtime of her life. Now, abandonment alone guides me. I have no other compass!...I can no longer ask for anything with fervor except the accomplishment of God's will in my soul without any creature being able to set obstacles in the way...Now my every act is LOVE.[109]

She expressed this again in her second manuscript more concisely, "I desire to suffer for love and even to rejoice through love."[110]

---

[108] Catherine of Siena, *The Dialogue*, ch. 141, trans. Suzanne Noffke, OP (New York: Paulist Press, 1980), 291.
[109] A 82v–83r.
[110] B 4v.

Nonetheless, until the end of her life *Thérèse insisted that to save souls, we must pay the price and endure Calvary.* She quoted Jesus' words many times: "Truly, truly, I say to you, unless a grain of wheat falls into the earth and dies, it remains alone; but if it dies, it bears much fruit."[111] A few days before her death, she said also to her sister, "It is true that I wanted to suffer much for God's sake, and it's true that I still desire this."[112] On the day of her death, she declared, "All I wrote about my desires for suffering. Oh! it's true just the same!" And "I am not sorry for delivering myself up to Love." "Never would I have believed it was possible to suffer so much! never! never! I cannot explain this except by the ardent desires I have had to save souls."

Share in my guardian angel's serenity

We should think more often of the one whom Padre Pio called his "twin brother," namely, our guardian angel. Thérèse thought of hers and frequently invoked him. Our guardian angels are present, very near to us. They are utterly serene, ever contemplating the joy with which the three Persons of the adorable Trinity regard each other and how they lovingly watch over us. Like all the blessed in heaven, our angel perceives that all our trials are permitted by a God who knows what He is doing and is making everything work together for the benefit of His treasured children. Our angel wishes to help us here on earth to share in his peace, even as he awaits the day when we will be immersed in the ocean of God's joy, as he is.

As surprising as it may seem, along with Thérèse, we can also consider that the angels aren't as happy as we are, since they cannot suffer and share in Christ's redemptive suffering as we can.[113] As

---

[111] Jn 12:24.
[112] YN September 25, n. 2.
[113] See YN August 16, n. 4.

St. Margaret Mary was invited to do in one of the courtyards of Paray-le-Monial, we can unite ourselves to the perpetual adoration the Seraphim offer the Lord also, and invite them to share in the merits of the acts of love we offer Him in our afflictions.

St. Margaret Mary:
A marvelous exchange with the seraphim

As I was employed in the community work with flax, I withdrew to a little corner, close to the Blessed Sacrament. There, at work on my knees, I felt myself suddenly recollected interiorly and exteriorly. At the same time, I saw before me the loveable Heart of my adorable Jesus, shining brighter than the sun. It was in the midst of the flames of its pure love, surrounded by seraphim who were singing in wondrous harmony: love triumphs, love delights, the love of the Sacred Heart gives joy!

These blessed spirits invited me to join with them in the praises of that divine Heart, but I did not dare to do so. But they reproached me, saying that they had come "in order to join with me to render It a continual homage of love, adoration, and praise. And thus, for this purpose they would take my place before the Blessed Sacrament, so that I might love Him without interruption through their mediation, and likewise, they would participate in my love, suffering in my person as I was rejoicing in theirs." At the same time, they inscribed this partnership in the Sacred Heart, in indelible golden letters of love. This lasted for approximately two or three hours. I have felt its effects my whole life as much by the aid I have received from it as by the sweetness it produced and produces in me, from which I remain very humbled and confounded; in praying to them, I simply called them my heavenly associates. This grace gave me a great desire for purity of intention and such a high idea of it which one must have to converse with God that everything seems impure for that to me.[114]

May Thérèse's example help us maintain our peace of heart even when there's a new trial in our lives. As she did, we should dare to believe that God is watching over us so carefully that not a hair of our heads falls without His permission,[115] that He makes everything work for our good, and that in our hearts and our bodies we make up what is mysteriously lacking in the passion of Christ.[116]

As Thérèse did, let's joyfully sing while scattering the roses of our smiles before the Lamb's throne. As she did, let's do our best to tell Him that our song will be even more lovely as the thorns among which we gather those roses are "long and sharp."[117] And let's bear in mind, as Thérèse recognized perfectly, that what pleases Our Lord isn't the length of the thorns wounding His children, but the joy with which they are singing before Him.

[114] Marguerite-Marie Alacoque, *Vie et Oeuvres de Ste Marguerite Marie*, vol. 1 (Editions St. Paul: Paris, 1990), 129.
[115] Mt 10:30.
[116] Col 1:24.
[117] B 4r.

St. Francis de Sales:
Adore God's will in every situation

Submit your will frequently to that of God; be prepared to adore it when it sends you tribulations just as you do during times of consolation.[118]

---

[118] St. Francis de Sales, *Oeuvres Complètes*, (Paris: Religieuses de la Visitation d'Annecy, 1929), vol. XXI, p. 18.

4

The Heavy Burden of the Past
My past is unbearable

"We are not saints who cry over our sins; we take delight in
them because they serve to glorify the mercy of God."[119]

One reason for being sad that seems entirely legitimate is the
memory of all our failures. It was our own fault! Sooner or
later, we all have to admit that we have too often squandered the
gifts we received or that we haven't helped others develop theirs.
Such sadness isn't bad: there is even a prayer asking for the gift of
tears. King David received this gift, the one who sang:

> For I know my transgressions,
>   and my sin is ever before me.
> Against thee, thee only, have I sinned,
>   and done that which is evil in thy sight.[120]

Yet immediately afterward, he asks the Lord to give him "the joy of
Thy salvation," since a Christian doesn't spend all his time weeping

---

[119] TLMT 75.
[120] Ps 51:3–4.

for his sins after sincerely asking for the Lord's pardon. Instead, he should rejoice at the thought of the infinite mercy God has granted him. St. Thérèse can help us make our entire past (understood here as the less than glorious moments of our life) "sing the mercies of the Lord" just as she helped her "dear little brother," Maurice Bellière, to do.

Having finished her last manuscript on her sick bed, Thérèse suddenly asked herself if it wouldn't be exposed to a horrible misinterpretation when the story of her life became known. Wouldn't some readers imagine that her trust in God depended upon the fidelity with which she had responded to her vocation during her life? If that were the case, then sinners who read her story wouldn't dare to approach God with the simplicity of a child throwing himself into his father's arms to ask for pardon because they had done something foolish again.

So that her future readers could avoid these misunderstandings, Thérèse began to write again, one last time, to express her confidence in the Lord's mercy. "Yes, I feel it; even though I had on my conscience all the sins that can be committed, I would go, my heart broken with sorrow, and throw myself into Jesus' arms, for I know how much He loves the prodigal child who returns to Him. It is not because God, in His prevenient Mercy, has preserved my soul from mortal sin that I go to Him with confidence and love."[121]

On July 11, 1897, she said something similar to Mother Agnes:

One could believe that it is because I haven't sinned that I have such great confidence in God. Really tell them, Mother, that if I had committed all possible crimes, I would always have the same confidence; I feel that this whole multitude of offenses would be like a drop of water thrown into a fiery

---

[121] C 36v.

furnace. You will then tell the story about the converted sinner who died of love; souls will understand immediately, for it's such a striking example of what I'm trying to say. However, these things cannot be expressed in words.[122]

Note that Thérèse doesn't speak here about "sins," but "crimes."

For more than a century there have been thousands of sinners astonished by these words from Thérèse. Some regard this as her "last will and testament." Indeed, this is one of the surprising paradoxes of our saint. Here is a girl who was careful her whole life to obey God in everything. She told her cousin a few weeks before her death "It seems to me that from the age of three onwards, I have refused nothing to the Good God."[123] Yet one of her charisms is specifically to reconcile great sinners with Him.

That God uses great converts, like St. Augustine or St. Charles de Foucauld, to lead sinners to Himself seems normal. That He also uses little Thérèse, entirely pure, to reconcile great sinners with Himself defies logic! But God has a sense of humor! Prison chaplains can tell you: a photo of Thérèse often holds the most important place in the cells of prisoners.

To really benefit from Thérèse's teaching on this topic, we need to remember that, despite her exceptional generosity in refusing God nothing, displayed from childhood, she recognized that to conquer her deep-seated pride she needed the Lord's mercy continually. If we

---

[122] YN July 11, n. 6.

[123] We know about this confidence of St. Thérèse's thanks to a letter that Sr. Marie of the Eucharist wrote to her cousin, Céline Maudelonde, on July 20, 1897. She wrote: "I asked her, 'Have you sometimes refused something to God?' She answered, 'I can't remember having done so. Even when I was very small, from the age of three, I started refusing nothing that God was asking of me.' That says everything, doesn't it?" (DE, 717).

follow her example, we can learn to accept our condition as sinners and let our entire past "sing the mercies of the Lord."

Accept my condition as a pardoned sinner

Thérèse recalled the sadness affecting her in childhood at the end of the month when she didn't win the school prize awarded for math and handwriting—which weren't her strongest subjects! She cried bitter tears and then cried about having cried.[124] What pride! So, she had no trouble accepting what Fr. Pichon told her after hearing her general confession in Carmel, in May 1888: "Before the good God, the Blessed Virgin, and all the saints, I declare that you have never committed a single mortal sin…[but] thank God for what He has done for you, for if He had abandoned you, instead of becoming a little angel, you would have become a little devil." After describing her confessor's "declaration" she added: "I had no difficulty in believing it; I felt how weak and imperfect I was."[125]

Thérèse was so aware of how fragile she was that on August 7, 1897, just a few weeks before her death, she was still begging the Lord to prevent her from falling into pride. It's vital that we don't imagine her as capable of resisting the temptations she faced against faith, or practicing this or that virtue, through her own strength. She admitted, "When we do that, we run the risk of falling into the abyss."[126]

All the same, her profound perception of her weakness didn't cause her to panic. Quite the contrary! Every time she realized once again that she might slip into pride, she threw herself with complete confidence into Jesus's arms so He could save her from the danger. She didn't count on her good will but on God. On Him alone!

[124] See A 44v.
[125] A 70r.
[126] YN August 7, n. 4.

Readers of *The Story of a Soul* often pass too quickly over the final important text Thérèse sent to her godmother in September 1896; it has the form of a spiritual testament. Addressing Jesus, Thérèse says, *"I feel that if You found a soul weaker and littler than mine, which is impossible, You would be pleased to grant it still greater favors, provided it abandoned itself with total confidence to Your Infinite Mercy."*

What did she mean when she spoke about a soul "weaker, littler" than hers? What weakness is intended here? What weakness did she confess? It's not a question of weakness of will, since she admitted with great simplicity that she never failed to make an effort.[127] Hence, it can only be a question of that deep-seated weakness of her creaturely liberty, the liberty she didn't cease placing in Jesus' hands so that He might maintain her in genuine humility. *Like all the saints in history, Thérèse knew she was part of that long procession of "anonymous proud people,"* as Fr. Molinié would put it, *who never stop converting.*

The "little souls" Thérèse calls to walk on her "little way" aren't naturally humble souls! They are souls who never stop asking the Savior for the grace of humility. Georges Bernanos understood this well, as a good disciple of St. Thérèse. The day of his first communion at Aire-sur-la-Lys, he asked the Lord for three things: "First, humility; second, humility; third, humility."[128]

Reviewing her life, Thérèse was even happy to discover in it *obvious signs of her weakness and of the Lord's kindness to her.* A case in point: she considered it a great grace that she hadn't made even one lasting friendship with her classmates. (Jeanne Raoul, whom she had liked a lot and with whom she gladly chatted during recess, simply gave her an indifferent glance after the several months of summer

---

[127] YN August 8, n. 3.

[128] Jean-Loup Bernanos, *Georges Bernanos a la merci des passants*, (Paris: Plon, 1986), 40.

vacation.) "How *small* and *fickle* are the hearts of creatures!" Thérèse concluded. As a result, she thanked Jesus for having had mercy on her weakness. "Jesus knew I was too feeble to be exposed to temptation... for I encountered only bitterness where stronger souls met with joy, and they detached themselves from it through fidelity. I have no merit at all, then, in not having given myself up to the love of creatures. I was preserved from it only through God's great mercy! I know that without Him, I could have fallen as low as St. Mary Magdalene."[129]

Thérèse devised the story of the doctor who removes the stone from the road to prevent his child from being hurt. He would have lovingly cared for his son if he had fallen, but preferred to preserve him from a fall. Thérèse identified herself with this child whom God surrounded with a very special protection, and this, without her having deserved it in any way. She added that she could love the Lord still more than if she had fallen. Similarly, she refutes anyone who says this passage means that we must have sinned much to love the Lord much. It's true that Jesus said, "He who is forgiven little, loves little."[130] However, Thérèse admits, "He *forgave* me, not much, but *all*."[131]

Does this mean that Thérèse imagined herself to have been preserved from all sin...like the Virgin Mary? Absolutely not! On the page before, she comically observes the vanity with which she showed off her good memory during a catechism class: "In my *profound humility* this was what I was waiting for; and rising with great assurance I said everything that was asked of me, to the great astonishment of everybody."[132]

Thérèse interpreted the fact of her very early entry into Carmel in a similar way. If she entered before Céline, it was because she was

---

[129] A 38v.
[130] Lk 7:47.
[131] A 39r.
[132] A 37v.

"weaker" than her sister. The Lord hid her in Carmel so that she would be preserved from temptations found in the world. On July 23, 1888, Thérèse explained to her sister the reason for this: "One [lily] was weak, the other was strong; Jesus took the weak one, and He left the other."[133]

We should keep in mind that Thérèse's awareness of her weakness wasn't at all unhealthy. It had nothing to do with the attacks of scruples she endured in her youth and from which she had been freed after having confidently invoked her four brothers and sisters who died in childhood. Instead, it was a deep awareness that every free person is fundamentally weak as long as he doesn't entrust himself to the Creator's care. That is why, on the day of her first communion, prompted by the Holy Spirit, Thérèse had the idea of placing her liberty into God's hands. "Her liberty frightened her. She felt so feeble and fragile that she wanted to be united forever to the divine Strength!"[134]

ELIZABETH OF THE TRINITY: GOD'S ABYSSES OF MERCY

Dear little sister,

He [Jesus] is the unchanging One, He who never changes. He loves you today as He loved you yesterday, and will love you tomorrow. Even if you have caused Him pain, remember that abyss calls to another abyss and that the abyss of your misery, little Guite, calls to the abyss of His mercy.[135]

---

[133] LT 57.
[134] A 35r.
[135] Elizabeth of the Trinity, *Complete Works*, vol. 2, trans. Anne Englund Nash (Washington, DC: ICS Publications, 1995), 305.

Making everything in my past sing the Lord's mercies

St. Thérèse can teach us also the art of singing the Lord's mercies when we are overwhelmed at the memory of our past sins. She explained this in the letters she wrote to Fr. Bellière (June 21-August 10, 1897), to encourage him to walk the path of complete trust and abandonment.

A spiritual brother

On October 17, 1895, Mother Agnes received a letter from a seminarian with the White Fathers asking for a Carmelite to specially support his spiritual progress and future missionary apostolate. The Prioress immediately thought of Thérèse. She found her in the laundry and entrusted the seminarian to her. His name was Maurice Bellière.

St. Teresa of Avila's feast had been celebrated only two days before and Thérèse couldn't help but see a marvelous gift from her patron saint in this combination of events. She had always dreamed of having a brother who was a priest. It was an impossible dream since her two brothers had died in childhood. But now, at age 22, heaven had given her a brother her own age, a future priest and what was more, a future missionary! "Not for years had I experienced this kind of happiness. I felt my soul was renewed; it was as if someone had struck for the first-time musical strings left forgotten until then."[136]

Thérèse redoubled her fervor, offering all her prayers and acts of renunciation for her missionary brother. But the young seminarian didn't bother to write to his Carmelite sister. He only sent a card in November to tell her of his departure for military service. Only in July did he get in touch with Carmel again. He wrote to Mother Agnes:

---

[136] C 32r.

Mother, I am a soldier and this time has been worthless for the seminarian. I had many falls, unbelievable stupidities, in the midst of the world, which took me over again. I have just made the biggest of all [we don't know what this was], but it is quite certain that it will be the last, since it has cured me. I am in a deplorable situation—and it is necessary that my dear Sister Thérèse of the Child Jesus get me out of it—she must lay siege to heaven, which will let itself be moved by her prayers and her penance." [137]

The news that came in October to Mother Marie de Gonzague was much more positive. "The storm has passed; calm has returned and the poor soldier has again become the seminarian as before." [138]

May he become a saint!

Thérèse wrote immediately in answer to Maurice, expressing her joy at hearing that her "poor prayers" had been heard. She stated her desire frankly: that he become "a saint completely on fire with the love of God and of souls." [139]

On December 26, after the required epistolary silence of Advent, Thérèse encouraged Bellière in his path toward missionary life: "The greatest honor God can give a soul is not to give it much but to ask much from it! Jesus is treating you then as a privileged one. He wills that you already begin your mission and that through suffering you may save souls." [140] She said, he shouldn't be surprised at suffering from the thought of leaving his family soon. Jesus Himself experienced this trial: "To save our souls He

[137] CG II, 871.
[138] CG II, 902.
[139] LT 198.
[140] LT 213.

left His Mother; He saw the Immaculate Virgin standing at the foot of the Cross…"

In February, before the epistolary silence of Lent, she sent him some of her poems and asked him to pray for her each day by saying: "Merciful Father, in the name of our gentle Jesus, the Virgin Mary, and the Saints, I beg You to enkindle my sister with Your Spirit of Love and to grant her the favor of making You loved very much."[141]

I am just a very little soul!

On April 25, 1897 she didn't start her letter by addressing "*Monsieur l'abbé*," but instead dared to write "My dear little brother." She explained: "Our good Mother told me I could use when writing to you the name I always use when I speak of you to Jesus."[142] Then she compared their friendship to that uniting blessed Margaret Mary and venerable Fr. Claude de la Colombiere. However, she insisted. "I beg you to believe me. God has not given you as a sister a great soul but a very little and a very imperfect one."

On June 7, Maurice Bellière told his "Good and very dear sister" about the grace he had recently received on the feast of Pentecost. His spiritual director had assured him that he truly had a missionary vocation and that after his holidays with his family he could, on October 1, begin his novitiate with the White Fathers in Algiers.[143]

I am entering into life

Two days later, on June 9, Thérèse's health was much worse. She was expected to die imminently. She took advantage of a moment when the infirmarian was absent to send her "dear little brother" a word of

---

[141] LT 220.
[142] LT 224.
[143] CG II, 1011.

farewell. "I am not dying, I am entering into life and all that I cannot say to you here below I will make you understand from the heights of heaven…"[144] Then Thérèse's health improved slightly and this note from June 9 was not sent. Taking up her pen again on June 21, Thérèse felt she needed to return to a passage in the letter that Bellière had sent to her on June 7. It referred once again to his "wasted" youth. This letter and the three which followed, are in fact a small treatise on mercy which Thérèse directed to her spiritual brother.

Abysses of mercy in Jesus's Heart

Thérèse wanted her brother to become accustomed to celebrating the "abysses of mercy of the heart of Jesus," as she was. She wanted him to have the loving boldness of Mary Magdalene toward Jesus. Though Mary Magdalen had sinned greatly she understood that "this Heart of love was not only disposed to pardon her but to lavish on her the blessings of His divine intimacy, to lift her to the highest summits of contemplation."[145]

Thérèse explained to Maurice that he should make his entire past sing God's mercy—even and especially the parts he wasn't proud of. *The Lord wants to use these to reveal His immeasurable love to us.* "The remembrance of my faults humbles me, draws me never to depend on my strength which is only weakness, but this remembrance speaks to me of mercy and love even more."[146] Thérèse imparted the same idea to Sr. Marie of the Trinity, her youngest novice: "We are not among the saints who are weeping over our sins: we are delighted with things that serve to glorify the mercy of God."[147] Apologizing for perhaps

---

[144] LT 244.
[145] LT 247.
[146] LT 247.
[147] TLMT 75.

not explaining this idea well, Thérèse ended her letter with this wish: "that one day Jesus will make you walk by the same way as myself."

Maurice Bellière answered her on July 15:

No, dear little sister, you did not explain yourself poorly. You are right. I understood your theories well […] you are opening up new horizons for me […] I find the insights on the mercy of Jesus, on the familiarity he encourages, on the simplicity of the soul's relations with this great God which has little touched me until the present because undoubtedly it had not been presented to me with this simplicity…[148]

"Punished" with a kiss

Thérèse was pleased that her little brother was beginning to understand. On July 18 she wrote another message to him. In it, she returned to the parable she had used a few months before to help Léonie understand that faults of weakness shouldn't prevent her from maintaining complete confidence in the Lord's mercy.[149] When a father finds one of his children in the process of doing something foolish again, he would be happy to see the child throw himself into his arms saying, "Papa, punish me with a kiss." He much prefers this response to that of a child who would go and cower in a corner from fear of punishment. St. Thérèse concluded, this is what we should always do: take Jesus "by the heart."[150]

Jesus rejoices every time we receive His forgiveness

Three days later, Bellière replied objecting that in the seminary they had been told that "the divine Heart is much more saddened by the

[148] GC II, 1144.
[149] LT 191.
[150] LT 258.

thousand little acts of cowardice, indelicacies that His friends commit than by sins, even grave ones" committed by worldly people. [151] Having received more graces, they are less excusable. Thérèse had no trouble answering him, writing on July 26. She said that this concept was only condemning the *carelessness* of consecrated persons, when they are resigned to their falls and don't make any effort to overcome them. When it's a question of faults or weakness, like the prodigal son, we should unhesitatingly throw ourselves into Jesus' arms and so fill His Heart with joy. She concluded, "Ah! how little known are the goodness, the merciful love of Jesus, Brother!...It is true, to enjoy these treasures one must humble oneself, recognize one's nothingness, and that is what many souls do not want to do; but, little Brother, this is not the way you act, so the way of simple and loving confidence is really made for you." [152]

The saints' hearts are full of compassion for us

Maurice Bellière's last objection was this: you are going to leave for heaven soon, "My very good and very dear sister, and there you will perceive how wretched I am. Will you be able to love me with the same affection as now?" [153] On August 10, Thérèse answered her brother that in heaven she would participate not only in the Lord's justice and holiness, but also in His *infinite mercy*. "I believe the Blessed have great compassion on our miseries, they remember being weak and mortal like us, they committed the same faults, sustained the same combats, and their fraternal tenderness becomes greater than it was when they were on earth." [154]

---

[151] CG II, 1045.
[152] LT 261.
[153] CG II, 1059.
[154] LT 263.

Allow myself to be kissed by Jesus

Thérèse continued her letter by telling Maurice that after her death he would receive as his inheritance her little crucifix, the one which she brought on her pilgrimage to Rome, and which she was almost always holding in her hand on her sickbed. "When looking at it, I think with joy that, after having received my kisses, it will go to claim those of my little brother."

What she didn't say here was the way which she liked to venerate the crucifix. She explained this to Sr. Genevieve: "It is good to kiss the feet of the crucifix; it is better to kiss His Face; but it is even better to place the crucifix on one's cheek and allow ourselves to be kissed."[155] Thérèse frequently repeated the thought that we have the opportunity to delight Jesus' Heart by allowing Him to pardon our faults "with a kiss"!

He is only love and mercy

At the end of her letter—the last letter she wrote—she also told Bellière that he would receive the last image she had painted. The text she wrote on it in calligraphy proclaims one last time the boundless trust her brother's heart needed to develop. "I cannot fear a God who made Himself so little for me...I love Him!...For He is but love and mercy."[156]

FYODOR DOSTOEVSKY: GOD'S MERCY

In *Crime and Punishment*, Dostoevsky puts in the mouth of Marmeladov, a drunk who has just finished off a liter of wine

---

155   See MSST 53.
156   LT 266.

with money stolen from his daughter, this marvelous hymn to the mercy of God: "Do you suppose, you that sell, that this pint of yours has been sweet to me? It was tribulation I sought at the bottom of it, tears and tribulation, and have found it, and I have tasted it; but He will pity us Who has had pity on all men, Who has understood all men and all things, He is the One, He too is the judge. He will come in that day and He will ask: 'Where is the daughter who gave herself for her cross, consumptive stepmother and for the little children of another? Where is the daughter who had pity upon the filthy drunkard, her earthly father, undismayed by his beastliness?' And He will say, 'Come to me! I have already forgiven thee once...I have forgiven thee once...Thy sins which are many are forgiven thee for thou hast loved much...' And He will forgive my Sonia, He will forgive, I know it...I felt it in my heart when I was with her just now! And He will judge and will forgive all, the good and the evil, the wise and the meek...And when He has done with all of them, then He will summon us. 'You too come forth,' He will say, 'Come forth ye drunkards, come forth, ye weak ones, come forth, ye children of shame!' And we shall all come forth, without shame and shall stand before Him. And He will say unto us, 'Ye are swine, made in the Image of the Beast and with his mark; but come ye also!' And the wise ones and those of understanding will say, 'Oh Lord, why dost Thou receive these men?' And He will say, 'This is why I receive them, oh ye wise, this is why I receive them, oh ye of understanding, that not one of them believed himself to be worthy of this.' And He will hold out His hands to us and we shall fall down before Him…and we shall weep…and we shall understand all things! Then we shall understand all![157]

The memory of all our past sins shouldn't make us yield to a sadness contrary to the spirit of the Gospel. We should remember Jesus' extremely clear statements: "Truly, I say to you, the tax collectors and the harlots go into the kingdom of God before you."[158] And "I came not to call the righteous, but sinners."[159] This was a gospel text that Thérèse especially liked.[160] Instead of letting ourselves become discouraged by the burden of our sins, we should allow their whole weight to sink into the Lord's Heart. We must bear in mind that the conversion to which we are all called consists in transforming the bewilderment of having sinned into the bewilderment of being loved so much!

FROM ST. FAUSTINA'S DIARY: "FIRST ACCESS TO MY MERCY"

When a soul sees and has realized the gravity of its sins, when the whole abyss of the misery into which it immersed itself is displayed before its eyes, let it not despair, but with trust let it throw itself into the arms of My mercy, as a child into the arms of its beloved mother. These souls have a right of priority to My compassionate Heart, they have first access

---

[157] Fyodor Dostoevsky, *Crime and Punishment*, trans. Constance Garnett, (Mineola: Dover Publications, 2001), 18.
[158] Mt 21:31.
[159] Mt 9:13.
[160] See A 39r; B 5r; Pr. 7.

to My mercy. Tell them that no soul that has called upon My mercy has been disappointed or brought to shame. I delight particularly in a soul which has placed its trust in My goodness.[161]

5

Temptations Are Too Strong
I am so weak

"My Beloved, my weakness is extreme.
Ah, I'm far from being an angel from heaven!"[162]

"God has forgiven my sins, all my sins! It's true! I believe it and it's marvelous! But how fragile I still am! What trouble I have not repeating the offense, not falling again into the old ruts where I was so often stuck in the past! My complete conversion is so slow in coming!" How can someone be joyful if they have this kind of ball and chain? I want to answer this question; it's one that comes up frequently.

Or, to put it better, I wish to communicate the message Thérèse addressed to all the prodigal children who haven't yet started rejoicing at the liberty of their return to the Father because of their various relapses.

At first glance, it may seem surprising that Thérèse has a message for "repeat offenders." She was so generous in her will to refuse God nothing, even from her youth! That's true. Yet, as we saw in the preceding chapter, she had a vivid awareness of her deep-seated weakness as

---

[162] PN 17, st 7.

a creature marked by original sin. She knew for certain that her pride was always ready to surface and that she would have been extremely proud if God hadn't kept her very close to Himself. But in the final analysis, she didn't experience the sadness of the prodigal children who have trouble definitively checking their bad habits and adopting once and for all habits in harmony with God's kingdom.

While Thérèse proclaims loud and clear the deep-seated fragility of her liberty, she is still obliged to acknowledge that by dint of effort she became stronger and stronger, more and more courageous. Hence, she didn't suffer from the particular form of frailty experienced by those who must make almost superhuman efforts to resist temptations of every type which surface in their hearts. How can a person remain joyful, how can someone avoid discouragement when faced with this difficulty? How can we not be jealous of people who don't have this sort of turmoil because they had good habits from childhood? Let's assemble the advice Thérèse gave her novices. It is specifically tailored for these "repeat offenders."

Never become discouraged

One day Céline was very sad and thoroughly disheartened. Thérèse had just shown her all her faults. She was thinking, "I will never make any progress." Fortunately, that evening during her prayer time, she read the answer St. Gertrude received from Our Lord after she experienced a temptation to discouragement.

> In all things and above all things, hold on to your good will, for this disposition alone will impart to your soul the splendor and the special merit of all the virtues. He who possesses this good will, this sincere desire to advance My Glory, to thank Me and to compassionate My Sufferings, to love and to serve Me as much as all creatures combined, will, without

any doubt, receive a reward compatible with My Infinite Goodness. Furthermore, it may sometimes happen that one soul derives more profit from such a desire than some other soul might gain from the performance of good works.

Filled with joy at her discovery, Céline told this to Thérèse. She went further:

> Do you know that the Life of Father Surin contains a striking passage on this subject of good will? He had just performed an exorcism and the demons confessed; "We are victorious on all sides, yet, when it comes to this little watch-dog whose name is good will, we must always yield." And so, even if you are without virtue, you at least have "a little watch-dog" who will save you from all danger. Be consoled, for it will eventually bring you to heaven!—Ah! Where is the soul who does not desire with all her heart to possess the virtues? This longing is common to us all. On the other hand, how very few there are in the spiritual life who are willing to fail, to stumble and fall, to be happy when others find them prostrate on the ground![163]

As a matter of fact, nobody manages to kick out in just a few days the bad habits he allowed to move in with him. Time is required for that. St. Francis de Sales frequently restated the necessity of having patience when we begin, or begin again, walking the path of virtue. He said "Illnesses of the heart as well as those of the body come on horseback and post haste, but they leave on foot, with little steps."

In advising her novices, Thérèse returned frequently to the perseverance with which they needed to begin once again "raising your little foot to climb the difficult staircase of perfection." She declared:

[163] MSST 24.

one day the Lord will be so moved by your good will that He Himself will come to take you to bring you in a single bound to the top of the staircase. Yet while waiting for that blessed moment, you must continue to raise your little foot without giving up!

Rejoice in my weakness

Thérèse taught that we ought to do more than persevere. She learned from St. Paul how to glory in her weakness.[164] Sr. Genevieve recalled: "The foundation of her teaching on this subject was that we should not lose heart at the sight of our weakness but rather glory in our infirmities. 'It is so sweet to feel our weakness and littleness,' she often told us."

Thérèse was speaking from experience. She wrote in July 1890 to Marie Guérin:

> You are mistaken...if you believe that your little Thérèse walks always with fervor on the road of virtue. She is weak and very weak, and every day she has a new experience of this weakness, but...Jesus is pleased to teach her, as He did St. Paul, the science of rejoicing in her infirmities. This is a great grace, and I beg Jesus to teach it to you, for peace and quiet of heart are to be found there only. When we see ourselves as so miserable, then we no longer wish to consider ourselves, and we look only on the unique Beloved!..."[165]

On November 16, 1896 she wrote to her aunt: "It will soon be nine years since I am in the Lord's house. I should, then, be already advanced in the ways of perfection, but I am still at the bottom of the ladder. This does not discourage me, and I am as happy as a cicada, always singing."[166]

---

[164] 2 Cor 12:15.
[165] LT 109.
[166] LT 202.

The Devil's Best Tool

It was announced that the devil was going to give up his trade and offer his tools to anyone who wanted to pay his price for them. On the day of the sale, they were laid out in an attractive manner: malice, hatred, envy, jealousy, sensuality, deceit. All the instruments of evil were there, each one with the price marked.

Apart from the others, there was a harmless looking device, very worn, but its price was far higher than that of anything else. Someone asked the devil what it was. "It's DISCOURAGEMENT," came the reply.

"Well! Why have you put such a high price on it?"

The devil answered, "Because it's so useful to me that the others hardly matter. With this, I can get into anyone. And once on the inside, I can maneuver it in the way that's most convenient for me. This tool is so worn out because I use it with almost everybody and very few people know it belongs to me."

Needless to say, the devil's asking price for DISCOURAGEMENT was so high that the tool never sold. The devil is still in possession of it and he continues to use it!

Thérèse stated the same thing in her last manuscript: "Now I am astonished at nothing. I am not disturbed at seeing myself to be weakness itself. On the contrary, it is in my weakness that I glory, and I expect each day to discover new imperfections in myself."[167] And a little later: "You can see that I am a *very little soul* and that I can offer God only *very little things*. It often happens that I allow

---

[167] C 15r.

these little sacrifices which give such peace to the soul to slip by; this does not discourage me, for I put up with having a little less peace and I try to be more vigilant on another occasion."[168]

She also told Mother Agnes three days before moving down to the infirmary: "I have my weaknesses also, but I rejoice in them... Then I enter into myself, and I say: Alas, I'm still at the same place as I was formerly! But I tell myself this with great gentleness and without any sadness! It's so good to feel that one is weak and little!"[169]

It's true that Thérèse hoped her weaknesses didn't actually offend the Lord. She shared this hope with Sr. Anges during her profession retreat in September 1890: "It seems to me, that Jesus can give me the grace of no longer offending Him or committing faults that *don't offend* Him but serve only to humble and to make love stronger."[170]

During a retreat preached to Carmel in October 1891, Fr. Alexis Prou confirmed her in this opinion. "He launched me full sail upon the waves of confidence and love which so strongly attracted me, but upon which I dared not advance. He told me that my faults caused God no pain, and that holding as he did God's place, he was telling me in His name that God was very much pleased with me...I felt at the bottom of my heart that this was really so, for God is more tender than a mother..."[171]

Yet this didn't prevent Thérèse from experiencing her weakness up to the end of her life. On July 29, 1897, she failed to suppress a reaction of annoyance quickly enough when Sr. Martha brought a small music box to the infirmary, hoping to entertain her in this way. She said to Sr. Martha later, "Oh, I beg you to pardon me. I

---

[168] C 31r.
[169] YN July 5, n. 1.
[170] LT 114.
[171] A 80v.

acted through selfishness. Please pray for me." Shortly after, she told Mother Agnes, "Oh, how happy I am to see myself imperfect and to have such need of God's mercy at the moment of my death!"[172]

"I experience a very deep joy not only when I discover I'm imperfect, but especially when I feel I am. All this surpasses all praise, which only bores me."[173]

Offer my efforts

St. Thérèse reminds all the world's prodigal children likewise that, even if they haven't succeeded in promptly eradicating the pernicious habits that enslaved them for so long, they ought to rejoice at the thought that the Lord is genuinely pleased to see their efforts to free themselves from them. When they are made with love, such efforts mysteriously draw other sinners to the Lord. This is so true that these children, though still very weak, may exercise a real spiritual paternity with regard to other sinners; they will thank them eternally for having helped them in their turn to be converted. They will even perceive that the acts of love done by all of history's Mary Magdalenes have played a part in the Maria Gorettis' preservation of their chastity!

Yes, poor sinners that we all are, we shouldn't hesitate to "live on love," even if we have to admit that we still fail very frequently.

> Living on Love is keeping within oneself
> A great treasure in an earthen vase.
> My Beloved, my weakness is extreme.
> Ah, I'm far from being an angel from heaven!...
> But if I fall with each passing hour,
> You come to my aid, lifting me up.

---

[172] YN July 29, n. 3.
[173] YN August 2, n. 6.

At each moment you give me your grace:
I live on Love.[174]

This joy is an essential feature of Thérèse's "little way." Thérèse knew quite well that by asking us to become like children to enter the kingdom of heaven, Jesus wasn't asking us to become "innocents." (While romanticism exalts the innocence of childhood, as did Victor Hugo in his poem "The Poor Children," Catholics bear in mind that their hearts are deeply wounded by original sin.) Thérèse understood unambiguously that when Jesus asks us to become like little children, it's a question of going to the Lord with a child's simplicity, like a child who doesn't hesitate to throw himself into his father's embrace to ask his pardon for his latest blunder. This is the joy Thérèse was trying to impress upon her sister Céline when she told her:

> Whenever you are lacking in virtue, you should not excuse yourself by throwing the blame on physical causes, on the weather, or some other trial. Instead, you should make it a means of self-humiliation, and then go to take your place in the rank and file of *little souls*, since you are so weak in the practice of virtue. Your soul's urgent need at present is not to practice heroic virtue, but to acquire humility. For this end, your acts of self-conquest themselves must have some admixture of imperfection so that you will not be able to dwell on them with any degree of self-complacency. Rather just to recall them will humble and remind you that you are not holy. There are some souls who, as long as they live, will find that they are never appreciated. This makes it impossible for them to think that they possess those virtues which they admire in others.[175]

[174] PN 17, st 7.
[175] MSST 24; CSSG 22–23.

ST. FRANCIS DE SALES: HAVE PATIENCE WITH YOURSELF

Your miseries and weaknesses should not surprise you. God has seen many more and his mercy does not reject the wretched, but works to their good, making their misery the throne of his glory. Have patience with all, but primarily with yourself. I mean that you should not be distressed about your imperfections and that you should always have the courage to rise again. I am glad that you begin anew every day; there is no better means for succeeding in the spiritual life than always beginning again and never thinking that you have done enough.[176]

Offer my sorrow

With marvelous audacity, Thérèse even dared to offer God the pain she felt after committing some fault. She understood that God wants to make use of *all our sufferings* for the redemption of the world—here understood as those caused by our blameworthy failures: a peevish action, a sharp word, an impulsive decision.

Thérèse expressed her thinking on this marvelously one day when Mother Agnes told her younger sister about the feelings of discouragement and sadness that overwhelmed her after a fault. Thérèse answered her:

> You don't act like me. When I commit a fault that makes me sad, I know very well that this sadness is a consequence of my infidelity, but do you believe I remain there? Oh! no,

---

[176] St. Francis de Sales, *Oeuvres Complètes*, (Annecy: Visitandines d'Annecy, 1964), vol. XVII, p. 161; XIV, p. 22.

I'm not so foolish! I hasten to say to God: My God, I know I have merited this feeling of sadness, but let me offer it up to You just the same as a trial that You sent me through love. I'm sorry for my sin, but I'm happy to have this suffering to offer to You.[177]

Let's note that this attitude is entirely correct: Thérèse calls sin by its name; she acknowledges it; she asks pardon of God for it. Nevertheless, she follows up with a properly Christian boldness—offering to God the feelings of sadness which followed the fault, as a sacrifice pleasing to Him, and one which helps in the world's salvation. This boldness harmonizes with the words of St. Paul, "We know that in everything God works for good with those who love him"—"even our sins," observes St. Augustine.[178]

A few days later, Thérèse returned to the same thought in another conversation with Mother Agnes: "I have my weaknesses also, but I rejoice in them. I don't always succeed either in rising above the nothings of this earth; for example, I will be tormented by a foolish thing I said or did. Then I enter into myself, and I say: Alas, I'm still at the same place as I was formerly! But I tell myself this with great gentleness and without any sadness! It's so good to feel that one is weak and little!"[179]

Remain vigilant

When we are very weak—and even when we aren't—it's essential to hear the Lord telling us what told His Apostles in Gethsemane: "Watch and pray that you may not enter into temptation; the spirit indeed is willing, but the flesh is weak."[180] Thérèse advised Sister Marie

---

[177] YN July 3, n. 2.
[178] Rm 8:28.
[179] YN July 5, n. 1.
[180] Mt 26:41.

of the Trinity to be vigilant, when the latter told Thérèse about the fervor she felt animating her after a retreat. Thérèse added also that Marie shouldn't become discouraged if she lost the initial skirmishes.

> Watch yourself! I have always noticed that hell is loosed against a soul who has just finished a retreat. The demons get together to make us fall as soon as we take the first steps, in order to discourage us. In fact, once fallen, we say: "How can I hold onto my resolutions since, as of this moment, I have lost them?" When we reason like that, the demons are already the victors. It is necessary then, that each time they throw you down, you pick yourself up without surprise and humbly say to Jesus: "Even though he has just now made me fall, I'm not conquered. Here I am again at the beginning, ready to commence the fight of love for you." Jesus, who is touched by your good will, will Himself be your strength.[181]

Jesus warned us about this: when the devil is driven out from a house, he tries to get back into it with the help of seven other devils.[182] The prodigal children so happy to be reunited with their Father therefore have every reason to remain on their guard, that is, they should take many precautions to prevent a new incursion of the evil one into their life. They must be careful about what they read; they should not think it doesn't matter what movies they watch! They must remember the sophisticated slogans by which they previously let themselves be ensnared: "You can't deny yourself everything!" "Get with the times!" "In order to help others, you have to know what they are watching," and so on. In short, *to rebuild yourself, it's essential to give yourself an environment that makes it easier to practice virtue.*

---

[181] TLMT 85.
[182] Mt 12:43–45.

Throw myself into the arms of Jesus

No matter how watchful I am, I am still weak. And so, I have to throw myself into the arms of Jesus, the Good Shepherd over and over again. I am safe from the evil one's attacks there. Thérèse knew she could rely on Him alone to achieve her desire of becoming a saint. "The elevator which must raise me to heaven is Your arms, O Jesus! And for this I had no need to grow up, but rather I had to remain little and become this more and more."[183]

Thérèse was delighted to discover in the Bible that the Lord "has a weakness" for the weak; He likes to bend down to the small and humble. He is happy to care for the sheep who are most wounded in His flock. "*Whosoever is a little one, let him come to me.*"[184] Thérèse concluded: therefore, the littler I am, the more I acknowledge my littleness, my fundamental powerlessness to succeed by my own abilities to love as I should, the more the Lord will hasten to me to carry me in His arms and communicate His love to me. Isaiah declared it long ago: "*He will gather the lambs in his arms, he will carry them in his bosom.*"[185]

Surely Francis de Sales had this verse in mind when he wrote: "We shouldn't worry about feeling weak, knowing that God is strong and kind to us. Why should we lose heart? Quite the contrary, my daughter, I prefer to be feeble rather than strong before God, since He carries the weak in His arms, and He leads the strong by the hand."[186] Mother Yvonne-Aimée de Jesus, a disciple of St. Thérèse, and Prioress of the Malestroit convent of Augustinian Hospitallers, wrote in

---

[183] C 3r.

[184] Prv 9:4 DRA.

[185] Is 40:110.

[186] St. Francis de Sales, *Oeuvres Complètes*, (Paris: Religieuses de la Visitation d'Annecy, 1929), vol. XXI, p. 164–65.

the same vein: "Let us remain very little so that the Good Shepherd may keep us on His Heart…that is the privilege of the little ones."[187]

Thérèse liked to collect images that depicted Jesus holding children in His arms; with these she could visualize herself in the arms of Jesus. She was particularly fond of one picture given to her in her childhood, which showed Jesus taking little children in His arms and holding them on His knees. Below a picture of the same scene, she glued some verses taken from a journal:

> Come, He is calling you, He wants to welcome you
> Throw yourself into His arms and do not be afraid
> Happy little children, rest your head
> on the Heart of Jesus.

Similarly, she loved the theme of the Good Shepherd gathering His lost sheep and taking them on His shoulders or into His arms. She ended her last manuscript by declaring that she would maintain the same trust even if she had committed "all the sins that can be committed." She wrote: "I would go, my heart broken with sorrow, and throw myself into Jesus' arms, for I know how much He loves the prodigal child who returns to Him."[188]

A few weeks earlier, on May 9, she wrote to Fr. Roulland:

> My way is all confidence and love. I do not understand souls who fear a Friend so tender… When I take up Holy Scripture all seems luminous to me; a single word uncovers for my soul infinite horizons, perfection seems simple to me, I see it is sufficient to recognize one's nothingness and to abandon oneself as a child into God's arms.[189]

---

[187] Paul Labutte, *Mere Yvonne-Aimee de Jesus*, (Paris: OIEL 1997), 497–98.

[188] C 36v.

[189] LT 226.

This shows how much Thérèse liked to contemplate the Gospel passage in which Jesus obliges His disciples to let the little children come to Him, saying to them: "Let the children come to me, and do not hinder them; for to such belongs the kingdom of heaven."[190] She frequently commented on this text to her novices and often wrote it in calligraphy on images. In fact, Thérèse was convinced that to follow the "little way" without falling down on the path, it's absolutely essential to abandon oneself with confidence into Jesus' care.

Call on the Virgin Mary and my guardian angel

In the spiritual combat we wage against our adversary, it's wise to seek refuge under Mary's virginal mantle. Thérèse told Céline that she "virginizes" us.[191] Thérèse invoked the Blessed Virgin quite frequently, particularly starting on the day in July 1889 when she felt she was covered by Mary's mantle.[192] To be sure, with all her maternal love, Mary helps us to stay in Jesus' arms.

Thérèse also asked her guardian angel to watch over her. She acknowledged having a "very special attraction to pray to the blessed spirits of heaven, particularly to the one whom God gave as the companion of my exile."[193] Thérèse encouraged Céline to rely heavily on her guardian angel's protection: "Do not fear the storms of earth...Your guardian angel is covering you with his wings, and Jesus, the purity of virgins, reposes in your heart. You do not see His treasures; Jesus is sleeping and the angel remains in his mysterious silence. However, they are there with Mary, who is hiding you also under her veil!..."[194]

---

[190] Mt 19:14.
[191] LT 105.
[192] See Chapter 20, p. 233
[193] A 40v.
[194] LT 161.

One day Thérèse made a large bookmark for her breviary from two images glued together back-to-back. One was an image of Our Lady of Perpetual Help and the other showed a guardian angel accompanying a child on the road. In this way she demonstrated the equal confidence with which she placed herself under the protection of her guardian angel and under the protection of Mary's mantel.[195]

Surrender unconditionally to the fire of love

Finally, why was Thérèse so happy to have continual recourse to the Lord's mercy? It was because she understood that He is infinitely happy to pour out its streams on us. That was His mission. He didn't come "for the just, but for sinners"[196]—a Gospel verse Thérèse quoted liberally.[197] In fact, Thérèse realized that by purifying our hearts from sin, God is accomplishing a work more miraculous than creating them. As St. John of the Cross explains in his *Maxims* (which Thérèse always had to hand): "When He purifies a soul of its disordered affections, God in some way does a work greater than when He drew it forth from nothingness, since nothingness is not opposed to His majesty, while the creature's disordered desire resists him."[198]

To celebrate the profession of Sr. Marie of the Trinity, Thérèse set to verse a poem by John of the Cross on which she frequently commented to her. She presents the idea that the Lord can turn everything to our benefit, both the good and the bad He finds in us, since He is purifying our hearts in the fire of His love.

> Love, I have experienced it,
> Knows how to use (what power!)

---

195 DLVI 288–89.
196 Mt 9:13.
197 See A 39r; B 5r; RP 2, 3bis.
198 *Maxims*, no. 68.

The good and the bad it finds in me.
It transforms my soul into itself.[199]

Hence, our condition as sinners shouldn't prevent us from handing ourselves over to love's purifying fire unreservedly. To be an offering pleasing to the Lord, there is no need to be a pure and spotless victim, as were the victims in the old covenant. It's enough to cast oneself with complete trust into the living Flame of Love which transforms everything into itself. "In order that Love be fully satisfied, it is necessary that It lower Itself, and that It lower Itself to nothingness and transform this nothingness into fire."[200]

These are the primary reasons for remaining joyful in spite of her weakness that Thérèse drew from Scripture. One day when she had again experienced her fragility, she told Sr. Genevieve: "It fills me with joy to have been imperfect. Today the Lord has granted me great graces; it has been a profitable day indeed." And when Sr. Genevieve was astonished by this idea, she added, "My little method consists in this—*rejoicing always and continually smiling—in times of defeat as well as victory.*"[201]

This idea complements what she wrote at the end of her first manuscript: "True, one can fall or commit infidelities, but knowing how to draw profit from *everything*, love quickly consumes everything that can be displeasing to Jesus; it leaves nothing but a humble and profound peace in the depths of the heart."[202]

---

[199] PN 30, st 3.
[200] B 3v.
[201] MSST 25.
[202] A 83r.

6

Lack of Courage
I'm not brave enough

"Let us suffer the bitter pain, without courage!...
(Jesus suffered in sadness! Without sadness would
the soul suffer!...) And still, we would like to suffer
generously, grandly!...Céline! what an illusion!...”[203]

My courage fails me

Sometimes this is our reaction when we are suddenly faced with a situation that is especially difficult: bereavement; emotional, professional, or political defeat; a difficult task to carry out; dangerous battles to fight; tedious work to finish, and so on. Profound exhaustion grips us: we don't face the problem as we should. This discouraging feeling is especially painful since up until then we had the sense that we were courageous. We didn't give anyone—and especially ourselves—the impression of being cowardly! Then suddenly all that changes. In fact, we are obliged to admit that we aren't what we imagined. Our mainsprings of action go completely slack; they may even seem to be broken.

In these conditions, far from helping us, faith now adds to our distress. We feel guilty for not being braver, for being unable to give

---

[203]   LT 89.

the Lord the faithfulness He expects in this kind of situation. "It doesn't do much good to pray," say certain friends to us, "since you are no more courageous than anyone else!" We don't need to be told this for us to think it. Prayer seems completely fruitless.

Let's ask Thérèse to reveal what she did when she felt a lack of courage. What kept her from giving up?

Ponder Jesus in the Garden of Olives

Thérèse had a special devotion to the sixteen Carmelites of Compiegne who were martyred on July 17, 1794. In 1894 she joined in celebrations commemorating the centenary of their martyrdom. While making banners in their honor she said to Sr. St. Augustine, whose patroness was the Prioress of the Compiegne Carmelites, "What an honor if we were to have the same destiny, the same grace!"

Fr. de Teil, in charge of their beatification process, had come to the Lisieux Carmel in September 1896. He gave a conference on their magnificent story. Thérèse really appreciated this presentation; it awakened in her heart the desire for martyrdom. The conference definitely highlighted the enthusiasm with which the Carmelites had gone to their ordeal. On the night before their execution, July 16, the feast of Our Lady of Mt. Carmel, they had enthusiastically sung in their prison a song composed by Sr. Julie, who had an extreme fear of the guillotine.[204] Here is the first stanza:

> Let our hearts be giv'n to joyfulness
> The day of glory now is here!
> Let us banish all of our weakness,
> We can see that the cross now is near!
> Let's prepare ourselves for the victory!
> Let us each as a conqueror go forth!

---

[204] It used the tune of the Marseillaise, the French national anthem.

Under the cross, God's great banner,
Let's all run, let's all fly toward glory!
Let our ardor be enflamed!
Let's give our bodies in his Name!
Let's climb, let's climb, the scaffold high!
We'll give God the victory![205]

Even though she admired their courage, Thérèse also realized that such enthusiasm is by no means essential...For the very simple reason that Jesus, King of Martyrs, had no such feeling when He was tortured on Calvary. Even before this, Thérèse was familiar with a phrase Fr. Pichon often repeated in his retreats: "The martyrs suffered with joy; the King of martyrs suffered with sorrow." Indeed, while there are many martyrs who received the charism of suffering with a certain panache—such as Thomas More making jokes at the scaffold or young Théophane Vénard smiling as he died—Jesus was fearful when His hour, the hour of His sacrifice, arrived.

St. Mark tells us: in Gethsemane Jesus "began to be greatly distressed and troubled."[206] Thus, to please God, we don't have to go through our sufferings like heroes, giving the impression that we feel nothing. At sixteen, during her father's mental illness, Thérèse perceived this. On April 26, 1889, she explained to Céline that to do this wouldn't be suffering like Jesus. In the Garden of Gethsemane, He suffered "sorrowfully." He even asked His Father that the chalice of suffering might be taken from Him. So, Thérèse concluded, we must accept to suffer "without courage"![207]

[205] William Bush, *To Quell the Terror* (Washington DC: ICS Publications, 1999), 36–37.
[206] Mk 14:33.
[207] LT 89.

Someone reading quickly risks seriously misinterpreting certain texts from Thérèse. In this case, we have in mind the fervent pages written in September 1896 where she expresses desires "which reach to infinity."[208] Thérèse wished to be a missionary, to have been one for all the ages, and to plant Christ's cross everywhere. She particularly wished to undergo every possible martyrdom to prove her love to Jesus. We can understand her godmother's (her sister Marie) reaction on receiving that letter: "You are possessed by the good God the way the wicked are possessed by the devil."[209] Her godmother felt discouraged. She had the sense that she could never achieve the holiness her goddaughter had reached.

Marie of the Sacred Heart's misunderstanding is lucky for us since it resulted in Thérèse's wonderful letter from September 17, 1896. Thérèse puts things in perspective there. No, her passionate desire to be a martyr isn't what is pleasing to God in her soul. What pleases Him is seeing her love her littleness; it's the profound awareness of her weakness since Jesus likes to work on poor material of that kind.

When we feel overwhelmed by the awareness that we aren't of the same caliber as the saints, reading this letter from Thérèse should rekindle our hope. God doesn't choose athletes who have lots of courage from the start to fill heaven. He prefers to choose what is "weak in the world to shame the strong."[210]

Contemplate the Holy Face

Long and frequent contemplation of Jesus on the cross and especially of His Holy Face aroused in Thérèse's soul the desire to be generous.

---

[208] B 2v.
[209] GC II, 997.
[210] 1 Cor 1:27.

Two months before her death, she said: "I recall how much it cost me to ask our novice mistress' permission to perform acts of mortification in the refectory, but I never gave in to my repugnancies; it seemed to me that the Crucifix in the courtyard, which I could see from the linen-room window, was turned towards me, begging for these sacrifices."[211]

Thérèse wrote to her sister in March 1889, "Jesus has done foolish things for Céline...Let Céline do foolish things for Jesus..."[212] She developed this line of thinking further in 1894 to help her sister to enter Carmel, since many around her were telling her that a strictly contemplative life wasn't compatible with her exuberant character. "What a joy to suffer for Him who loves us unto folly and to pass as *fools* in the eyes of the world." She continued:

> But, after all, we are not the first; the only crime with which Jesus was reproached by Herod was that of being *foolish*, and I think like him!...Yes, it was *folly* to seek out the poor little hearts of mortals to make them His *thrones*, He, the King of Glory, who is seated above the Cherubim...He, whom the heavens cannot contain...He was *foolish*, our Beloved, to come to earth in search of sinners in order to make them His friends, His intimates, His *equals*, He, who was perfectly happy with the two adorable Persons of the Trinity!...We shall never be able to carry out the follies He carried out for us, and our actions will never merit this name, for they are only very rational acts and much below what our love would like to accomplish.[213]

---

[211] YN July 13, n. 18.
[212] LT 85.
[213] LT 169.

This passage explains the desire for martyrdom in the hearts of the great lovers of Christ. We shouldn't see it as masochism, or the sign of an exceptional temperament, but the manifestation of a desire to give Jesus "love for love." Thérèse wrote in September 1896: "Martyrdom was the dream of my youth and this dream has grown with me within Carmel's cloisters. But here again, I feel that my dream is a folly, for I cannot confine myself to desiring one kind of martyrdom. To satisfy me I need all."[214]

Yes, Thérèse remained faithful her entire life to the motto she wrote in calligraphy under her "coat of arms": *love is paid only by love.* Contemplation of Christ's passion profoundly influenced her life just as it revolutionized that of St. Teresa of Avila. For St. Teresa it was gazing for a long time at a small statue representing the flagellated Christ which caused the Spanish Carmelite to renounce her worldly parlor conversations and begin to reform her order.

"He loved me too much." Elizabeth of the Trinity would frequently repeat this verse from St. Paul's letter to the Ephesians, using the translation she had available.[215]

Schooled by the saints' examples

Over the centuries, it has often happened that hearts are converted by reading the life of a saint. The young knight Ignatius, whose leg had been wounded in the Siege of Pamplona, asked his surgeon to operate again since it was absolutely necessary that he have full use of both legs so he could dance. In order to amuse himself during his recovery, he opened *The Golden Legend.* This book recounts with vivid details stories such as St. Francis of Assisi's feats or the achievements of St. Dominic. Little by little the desire to imitate them took hold

---

[214] B 3r.
[215] See ch 2 v. 4.

of the young officer's heart. Similarly, three centuries earlier, a young Portuguese man marveled at the account of five Franciscan friars recently martyred at Marrakesh. He resolved to enter the Friars Minor in order to go to Morocco to preach the gospel and be a martyr himself. God had a different plan for him. He became a brilliant preacher and ended his days in Padua: the well-known St. Anthony.

Doesn't every calling have its origin in the desire to resemble a person one begins to admire deeply? The future orchestra conductor thinks, "I, too, will direct concerts." After visiting a museum for the first time, the future painter thinks, "I, too, will create paintings." Likewise, it's contact with the saints, past or present, which often sounds in someone's heart the first call to holiness.

"I, too, will be a saint," thought little Thérèse when she first read the story of Joan of Arc. "It seemed I felt within me the same burning zeal with which they were animated, the same heavenly inspiration. [...] I considered that I was born for glory."[216] God placed in her heart then a desire to become a "great saint," but one whose glory wouldn't be evident in the world's eyes. Certainly, Thérèse couldn't have imagined that after her death many hearts in turn would be revolutionized by the account of her life...or that she would become the secondary Patroness of France, on a par with Joan of Arc.

It isn't simply the example of the saints in heaven which encourages us. The generosity of Catholics we meet every day can enkindle our desire to take the demands of the Gospel more seriously. For example: seeing adults take charge of youth who are preparing for their Confirmation; seeing people of every age and station dedicate a week of their vacation to making a retreat; seeing friends fast or spend a whole night in prayer, we want to do the same.

[216] A 32r.

Equally marvelous is the collaboration that can occur between husband and wife. They can help each other enormously in their Christian life, and this gives their love an astonishing depth.[217] Raoul Follereau wouldn't have undertaken his initiative on behalf of lepers[218] without the affection and support of his wife Madeleine, whom he met at age 15. More recently, the world discovered all that King Baldwin of Belgium had found in the love uniting him to Queen Fabiola, and what they both owed to their friendship with Sr. Veronica O'Brien.[219] And of course, there is also the example of Louis and Zélie Martin!

Similarly, beautiful spiritual friendships can spring up between two devout souls, helping them both advance and become "twin stars" of holiness. It's enough to remember the very strong and very pure bonds that united Clare and Francis of Assisi, Teresa of Avila and John of the Cross, Jane de Chantal and Francis de Sales, or Charles de Foucauld and his cousin Marie de Bondy, and many others. Adopting as spiritual brothers Maurice Bellière and Fr. Adolphe Roulland, Thérèse didn't suspect all that their friendship would bring her. We also know the benefits of her deep camaraderie with two other nuns in her community: her sister Céline, and Sr. Marie of the Trinity, the youngest of her novices.

---

[217] TN: An obvious example in this context is St. Thérèse's parents, recently canonized.

[218] TN: Little known outside of the French speaking world, writer and philanthropist Raoul Follereau devoted his life to serving those suffering from Hansen's Disease, especially in Africa. Referring to his wife, he said, "It's only with two that one is invincible."

[219] TN: King Baldwin was a devout Roman Catholic and a Knight of the Holy Sepulcher. He and his wife were involved in the Charismatic movement and made regular pilgrimages to Paray-le-Monial.

CHARLES DE FOUCAULD: GIFTS FROM HEAVEN

Here, in a meditation written at Nazareth, Charles de Foucauld recalls the influence of his cousin Marie de Bondy. Her affection and example, as well as the guidance of Fr. Huvelin, were crucial in his conversion.

At the beginning of October 1886, after six months of home life, I was filled with admiration, I desired virtue, but I did not know You…by what means, God of mercy, did you become known to me?

What routes did You use? What sweet and strong external means?

A beautiful soul aided You, but by her silence, her sweetness, her goodness, her perfection; she let herself be seen, she was kind and spread her attractive fragrance, but she was not the one acting. You, my Jesus, my Savior, You did everything within and without! You have drawn me to virtue through the beauty of a soul whose virtue appeared to me so lovely that it irrevocably won my heart.

You have drawn me to the truth through the beauty of this same soul. You gave me four graces:

The first was to inspire me with this thought: since this soul is so intelligent, the religion that she believes cannot be a folly, as I suppose it to be.

The second was to inspire me with this further thought: since religion is not folly, maybe the truth, which is not on earth in any other [religion], nor in any philosophical system, is here?

The third was to say to myself: "Therefore, study this religion: find a teacher of Catholic religion, priest instructor, and let's see what's in it, and if we should believe what it says."

The fourth was the incomparable grace of addressing myself to Fr. Huvelin.

By making me enter his confessional, at the end of October (I think between the 27th and 30th), You gave me every good, my God: if there is joy in heaven at the sight of one sinner converting, there was some when I entered the confessional!

What a blessed day, what a day of benediction!

You placed me under the wings of this saint, and I am staying there. You carried me through his hands and it has been grace upon grace. I asked for lessons in religion: he made me kneel down and make my confession, and sent me to receive communion immediately."[220]

Have faith in the Communion of the Saints

While the ability to share with others plays an important role in a Catholic's dynamism, his faith in the mystery of the communion of the saints frequently boosts his courage too. He knows that the least of his actions has an impact throughout the entire Church, and ultimately, throughout the whole world. How many Catholics discouraged by trials have found in this certainty the strength to continue the battle against despair: they were sure of helping their brethren to gain the same victory. We will see in Chapter 9 what great faith Thérèse had

---

[220] Charles de Foucauld, *La Dernière Place: Retraite en Terre Sainte*, (Bruyères-le-Châtel: Nouvelle Cité, 2002), 117–18.

in the communion of the saints and how much strength she found in this. By the same token, she remembered how much she owed to the prayers and generosity of all the saints, both in heaven and on earth.

Allow myself to be carried by Jesus

This is the ultimate secret which has allowed thousands of Christians through the centuries to endure trials courageously. They realized they weren't bearing them alone. They understood they were weak so that "Christ's power may rest upon me."[221] Far from being discouraged by their lack of courage, they were eventually glad that they experienced it, so that "Christ's power" would dwell in them. They were happy to conclude, along with the Apostle Paul, "When I am weak, then I am strong."[222]

This truth constitutes the heart of the Little Way which Thérèse of Lisieux felt called to teach the world. She held that the more we recognize our weakness, the happier the Lord is to carry us and lift us to the highest summits of holiness. A maxim of the foundress of the Carmelites in France, Madam Acarie, sums this up, "Jesus I can do no more; act for me."

JESUS IS HAPPY TO RECEIVE YOUR WEAKNESS

Marcel Van heard St. Thérèse say to him: "Why has Jesus required you to make known to your director the smallest things happening in you? It is so that you learn humility. Each time you act in this way, you are giving your will to Jesus. Jesus wants you to trust in your director just as you have trust in Him. That is why He must require you to confide to your

---

[221] 2 Cor 12:9.
[222] 2 Cor 12:10.

director all the little things about yourself. He wants you to make everything known to your director; and each time you do so, you let Him see your great weakness simultaneously.

"Nevertheless, Jesus is happy to receive your weaknesses more than He would be to accept your extraordinary mortifications. Why is this? Because, if you are weak, Jesus stays close to you continually and embraces you in His arms. Thus, every time you eat, you express your love for Jesus by means of your weakness...Marcel, thanks to your weaknesses, you can save a great number of souls. Jesus wants you to see all your weaknesses, so that people understand the mercy of their Father in heaven for the world."[223]

---

[223] Marcel Van, *Colloques*, (Paris: Editions St. Paul, 2001), 328–29. The Servant of God Marcel Van (1928–1959) was a Vietnamese Redemptorist brother who reported receiving locutions from St. Thérèse, the Blessed Virgin Mary, and Jesus. St. Thérèse taught him about the spiritual life and called him her "little brother."

7

Complexes
I have no self-confidence

*"I was really unbearable because of my extreme sensitivity;
if I happened to cause anyone I loved some little trouble,
even unwittingly, instead of forgetting about it and not
crying...I cried like a Magdalene and then when I began
to cheer up, I'd begin to cry again for having cried."*[224]

While humility is the fundamental virtue of a Christian life, we shouldn't envision it as a lack of self-confidence. This frequently infects the lives of certain good people; they are always imagining that they are worthless. Despite the compliments or encouragement they receive from their friends and relatives, they feel nothing but contempt for themselves. This lack of self-confidence prevents them from being happy, from appreciating the innocent pleasures life offers, and is entirely contradictory to the Lord's admiration for each of His children.

Does Thérèse have any advice for those who are living with this malady? Here it's not a question of analyzing all the possible causes

---

[224] A 44v.

for a lack of confidence or remedies for resolving them.[225] Rather, it's a matter of considering the way in which Thérèse was freed from them: her liberation seems to be an example of what could happen in the life of someone suffering from this kind of "complex."

Thérèse's complex

Thérèse actually suffered for a long time from an inferiority complex. It surfaced at the death of her mother—she was just four and a half years old at the time—and she was only freed from it ten years later, on Christmas Eve 1886.

During her early childhood, Thérèse had a "happy temperament" as she would later write, which helped to make life pleasant for her. However, after her mother's death she became "timid" and "extremely sensitive." A look was enough to make her burst into tears. Even with her Uncle Guérin she didn't feel at ease: she didn't like to be invited by herself on Sundays. She needed to have the atmosphere of the family "cocoon"; she required the gentle affection of her father and sisters. It's not that Thérèse was spoiled at Les Buissonnets; it wasn't at all a question of satisfying her whims. Rather, the family's "Benjamin" needed to feel that she was cherished by her family and that she was worthy of it.

Beginning with the death of Mrs. Martin, Thérèse's attachment to her father increased: he spent every afternoon with his "little queen" and Thérèse couldn't bear the thought of being separated from her "king." "I wasn't even able to think of Papa dying without trembling."[226] If her father died, she would die with him. She had a boundless admiration for him and her greatest joy was going to

---

[225] We discuss this question fully in our *Guide des difficulties de la vie quotidienne*.

[226] A 21r.

show him her homework in the Belvedere of Les Buissonnets. Having been orphaned, Thérèse was also very reliant on her sister Pauline, whom she chose as her second mother. She was at once her ideal, her confidante, and her spiritual guide. For instance, Thérèse's father couldn't take her out on a walk without Pauline's full approval. Thérèse agreed to leave only when Pauline seemed genuinely satisfied with her work.

Attached as she was to the warm atmosphere of the family home, Thérèse had great difficulty in adapting to life at school, which she entered at age eight and a half. In fact, she never adjusted completely, despite her academic success and the affection that surrounded her. "The five years I spent in school were the saddest in my life."[227] Faced with jealousies or teasing from her companions, Thérèse cried without saying a word.

Fortunately, each evening at Les Buissonnets she found again the affection which her overly sensitive heart needed. She leapt into her father's lap and told him about the good grades she had gotten that day and the kiss she received as a reward made her forget her troubles.[228]

Thérèse received another shock at age nine. She learned that her beloved Pauline would soon be leaving to enter Carmel. In her naivete she had imagined that her "little mother" would wait to enter with her! The wholly unexpected news created a deep wound in the child's heart. Separated from Pauline—Thérèse saw her again, it's

[227] A 22r. However, when her grades were not so good, Thérèse couldn't prevent herself from crying. When she was not at the top of her class, "Thérèse burst into tears and was impossible to console. The same thing happened for an average grade or if, in making some remark to her, the teacher raised her voice and seemed in any way dissatisfied, which happened quite rarely" (Mother Saint-Leon Loutrel, *La Petite Thérèse a l'abbaye*, Lisieux).
[228] A 22v.

true, every Thursday at the monastery—but she couldn't talk to her as she would have liked: she couldn't converse with her one on one, except in the last minutes of their parlor meeting, and she spent them crying openly.

The psychological trauma caused by this separation was the source of the malady that struck her in March 1883. This was her relatives' opinion and she also believed this later.[229] Her illness was actually a nervous attack provoked by her unconscious desire to recover her father's affection...he had had the unfortunate idea of departing for Paris during Easter week, with Marie and Léonie, leaving the two youngest girls in Lisieux! Thérèse fell sick "in order" to be pampered like a baby. Of course, this motive entirely escaped the child's awareness.

Her wonderful and miraculous healing of May 13, 1883 didn't deliver her from her psychological problems. Evidence of this is what occurred a year later at her first communion. Since she was the only orphan among her companions, she expected to be the one who would recite the act of consecration to the Blessed Virgin. When she heard that it would be recited by one of Fr. Domin's nieces (he was the chaplain of the boarding school), her disappointment was so great that they feared she would become sick again. Mrs. Guérin and Marie initiated a conversation with Mother St. Placid, and then with Fr. Domin, so that the recitation would be entrusted to Thérèse.

It's easy to diagnose in Thérèse's disposition the two characteristic signs of "the persistence of an archaic affective behavior": "a painful feeling of having nothing because one cannot have everything, and the even more painful feeling that every lack, every disappointment, appears to be a defrauding of a good to which one has a right."[230]

---

[229] PA 297; A 27r.
[230] Dr. Ch. H. Nodet, "Psychanalyse et spritualite," Supplement to *La Vie Spirituelle*, (February 1948): 406.

Moreover, Thérèse continued responding to separation from her family with health crises. In 1886, Thérèse went back to the abbey school by herself, since Céline had finished her studies. Obliged to return alone, she quickly became ill. So, at age 13 she left the school and continued her schooling through private lessons with Madam Papinau.

The attacks of scruples with which she struggled for a year and a half (May 1885 to October 1886), were another sign of the conflicts that continued to disturb her emotional life. Unable to see clearly into her conscience on her own, she had to hand over judgement to Marie, her older sister. (She obeyed her so well that her confessor never became aware of his penitent's scruples, by the way.) It was a heroic and beneficial obedience, but it only increased Thérèse's dependence on her godmother.

Still, Marie's entry into Carmel wasn't catastrophic for the adolescent girl. Having no one to confide in, she turned to heaven: she begged the four siblings who had died young to obtain peace and her prayer was granted. Freed from scruples, she passed into a new stage, winning her independence. From then on, it was no longer an older sister's judgement which constituted her conscience's law; she was capable of making judgements for herself.

All the same, she still wasn't indifferent to what others might think of her. She was still so sensitive about paternal or fraternal approval that the idea of having caused pain (she says "even involuntarily") to her father or Céline was unbearable to her. If something she did caused trouble, she cried "like a Madeleine." She couldn't endure the feeling that her family didn't find her behavior very pleasing. This is also why she cried if Céline didn't look "pleased and surprised" about services she had done for her. Thérèse recounts that her frequent crying displeased everyone, so much so that after she had cried, she once more wept about being unable to control herself.

Nonetheless, in the depth of her heart was the desire to be liberated from this oppression. This desire was finally granted a few days before her 14th birthday, on Christmas Eve.

The grace of Christmas 1886

Thérèse's first communion, at age eleven, hadn't ended her frequent crying. Certainly, she was united in it to the "divine power" but it was only two and a half years later that Jesus would make her "*strong and courageous.*" That was a *grace*, the divine answer to the prayer Thérèse had been making for a long time. She surely made this prayer again when receiving God "the strong and mighty one" during midnight Mass.

However, it was also a result *of a very powerful act of will* on the part of the adolescent Thérèse.[231] An act of the will which prompted the resolution of the emotional lag from which she had suffered for years. Let's briefly recall the incidents of this victory.

The family had returned from Mass. Going upstairs, Thérèse enjoyed the thought of the surprises she would find in the kitchen. Suddenly she overheard her father, who was in the process of setting out the gifts for the "Benjamin" saying, "At last, fortunately it's the last year!..." Tears sprang into the girl's eyes: her father seemed unhappy and she could not, as we know, bear such an idea. Usually much less was enough to make her burst into tears. However, at the top of the stairs, Thérèse said to herself, "It's true. Papa is right. I am no longer a

---

[231] Doubtless Jesus performed this miracle satisfied only with her "good will," she would write (A 45v). But this doesn't mean there wasn't a vigorous act of will on Thérèse's part. On her deathbed, Thérèse insisted on the necessity of not waiting for the grace "passively": "Today, I was thinking of my past life, about the courageous act I performed formerly at Christmas, and the praise directed to Judith came into my mind: 'You have acted with manly courage, and your heart has been strengthened.' Many souls say: 'I don't have the strength to accomplish this sacrifice.' Let them do, then, what I did: exert a great effort" (YN August 8, n. 3).

child. I am filled with all Jesus' strength which I just now received and I will demonstrate it to him." She forced back her tears and went quickly down the staircase, and began opening the gifts on the hearth as if her father had said nothing. In one moment, Jesus had changed her heart.

At first glance, on that Christmas Eve, this girl of fourteen was still a baby and allowed herself to be treated like one. Just imagine! She was delighted like a little kid about Christmas presents. But in fact, Jesus had just caused her to leave behind the "swaddling bands of childhood." Obviously, it was childish to still be finding her joy in such trifles. However, Thérèse would never again fall into such childishness, since she never again cried about anything not worthy of tears. Thérèse tells us that she found again that night "the strength of soul which she had lost at age four and half." She exercised "great mastery" over her actions henceforth.[232]

Nonetheless, we have to be careful: there is only an analogy between these two strengths of her soul. The one she found then was of entirely different character. It was the energy of a girl who had just gained her emotional autonomy. Henceforward, at Les Buissonnets, Thérèse was truly a queen: from then on she could control the first impulses of her emotions.

Likewise, it's remarkable that Thérèse reached her independence vis-à-vis her father at the moment when he demonstrated his intention to no longer treat her like a "baby." *She became a young lady at the very moment her father realized that he should no longer treat his youngest daughter as a little girl.* Through a forceful act of will, the youthful Thérèse clung unreservedly to her father's desire. A marvelous meeting of nature and grace! God's grace coincided wonderfully with the realization that had happened in Louis Martin's mind and fully confirmed his daughter's liberty.

---

[232] Discussed in chapter five of *The Story of a Soul*.

A grace of strength, the grace of Christmas Eve was also an out-pouring of the Spirit of love in Thérèse's heart: instead of living with-drawn in herself, in future she put herself at the service of others. She was no longer occupied with her feelings or with what others thought of her. She no longer had any desire except to give happiness to those around her and save sinners. This is how Thérèse ends the description of the Christmas grace in her manuscript: "I experienced a great desire to work for the conversion of sinners, a desire I hadn't felt so intensely before. I felt charity enter into my soul, and the need to forget myself and to please others; since then, I've been happy!"[233]

Undoubtedly, Thérèse remained very sensitive for her whole life, as demonstrated by the analysis of her handwriting.[234] Nonetheless it's true that beginning with Christmas 1886 Thérèse mastered her feel-ings and no longer lived in constant fear of causing her family distress.

The interplay of grace and freedom

How can the healing Thérèse received at Christmas 1886 help those suffering from an inferiority complex find freedom?

First of all, Thérèse's experience reminds us that to be healed, we must *desire* it and never be defeatist about the problem. For almost ten years, Thérèse made efforts to end her unbearable whining and she didn't hesitate to *beg* the Lord to deliver her from it. Those who lack confidence in themselves are invited to pound on the Lord's door to obtain the grace of healing.

Sooner or later, there has to be a point when we take advantage of the help offered in our difficulty and make a liberating *act of will*.

---

[233] A 45v.

[234] See the expert opinion of M. Trillat about Manuscript II, p. 83, in *Eph-emerides Carmeliticae* 9 (1958/1): 3–31, "The published Manuscripts and the 'Histoire d'une Ame.'"

That's what Thérèse did in completely accepting her father's desire, when he suddenly realized he should no longer baby his daughter. As an illustration: someone who has been deeply wounded by a word or scornful attitude from a family member, at some point has to realize she mustn't allow herself to be oppressed by that memory. Instead of spending the rest of her life ruminating on it, she has to bounce back in order *to live* her life to the full. However, it goes without saying that such attempts usually have to be made several times to escape definitively from stagnation.

There are also situations such as someone who suffers terribly from not achieving as highly as a sibling. When such a person has understood definitively that she can succeed in life perfectly well in a different way—by being fully herself, by accepting her limits, and by developing as fully as possible the talents she has received, both the small and the large—not simply knowing this, but then choosing to orient her life in this way, she is making the necessary act of will.

Usually, the elimination of a complex is achieved more fully if the wounded or jealous person is convinced they are someone precious in God's eyes. Still, it's known that this conviction isn't enough. The psyche of someone with a complex must receive a genuine grace of healing. Thérèse didn't hesitate to describe what she experienced on her return from midnight Mass as "a small miracle."

Effectively healed from her hang-up, Thérèse from then on quite valiantly battled all the difficulties she met in realizing her vocation. In May 1887, she wasn't afraid to tell her father about her intention to enter Carmel despite the risk of making him sad. In the following months, with a surprising strength of soul she began the process necessary to enter the monastery soon. And on April 9, 1888, she stepped though the cloister door without shedding a single tear. The next year, she bore with the same courage the thought that her father was ill. And when she heard it suggested by people around her that she was perhaps the involuntary cause of this illness (due to his grief because of her departure for the convent), she wasn't ruffled. She felt these "pin pricks" with sadness, but it was nothing like the time when she couldn't bear the idea of "even involuntarily" having caused someone pain. She no longer depended on the judgement of others: she had won complete independence.

Certainly, she still had to struggle; but never again did she let herself be dominated by her emotional sensitivity. During Mr. Martin's illness, when she couldn't console Céline who had recently visited her, she was at first quite pained but quickly realized that Jesus alone can comfort a soul.[235]

LOVE YOUR NEIGHBOR AS YOURSELF

God asks us to love ourselves, never to despise ourselves. This good love of self is an indispensable condition for happiness and for the love of neighbor.

This is a frequent theme in the works of Georges Bernanos. In the very last paragraph of *The Diary of a Country Priest*, Fr. D'Ambricourt concludes: "How easy it is to hate oneself! True grace is to forget. Yet if pride could die in us, the supreme grace would be to love oneself in all simplicity—as one would love any one of those who themselves have suffered and loved in Christ."[236]

At the beginning of the *Dialogues of the Carmelites* (the opera written by Poulenc based on Georges Bernanos' book), the old prioress warns the young postulant, the future Sr.

---

[235] See LT 55, 74, 81.
[236] Georges Bernanos, *The Diary of a Country Priest*, trans. Pamela Morris, (New York: Carrol and Graf, 1989), 296.

Blanche of the Agony of Christ, against the temptation to despise oneself: "The saints were not hardened against temptations; they did not rebel against themselves. Revolt is always something from the devil, and above all do not despise yourself! It is very difficult to despise oneself without offending God in us."[237]

So, like Thérèse, we mustn't hesitate to ask God for the healing of our sensitivity when our psyches have been affected by childhood wounds and setbacks in adult life. If the healing isn't accomplished in an instant in a quasi-miraculous fashion, it may be effected gradually over a series of years, with or without the help of therapy.

At any rate, for complete healing, we need to welcome the grace of sincerely forgiving the people who have hurt us in the past. Though it may happen that we still feel some effects of the trauma caused by such wounds, these don't prevent us from living in harmony with our neighbors. There are many saints who lived the Gospel to an especially heroic degree, even while affected to the end of their lives by timidity developed in childhood.

BECOME A PRIEST NONETHELESS

There are many priests who had to endure considerable humiliation before being ordained. Having lived through the Terror during his childhood, Jean-Marie Vianney was extremely behind in his studies. As a result of this delay, his

---

[237] Act 2, sc. 8.

memory was very poor and he had great difficulty in answering the theological questions he was asked in Latin—as was the custom—at the seminary in Lyon. "His first exam in 1813 demonstrated his incapacity. The seminary register gives the deplorable impression that he produced. The grade he was given classes him as *debilissimus* [very feeble]."

Thanks to the personal coaching given by Fr. Balley, parish priest of Écully, Jean-Marie was eventually deemed fit to be ordained. But in the first months of his priesthood, it was judged that he didn't know enough moral theology to hear confessions! The first person whose confession he heard was Fr. Balley![238]

Nearer to our own time, Bl. Marie-Joseph Cassant (1878-1903), a Trappist monk of the abbey of Our Lady of the Desert, experienced similar trials during his preparation for the priesthood. After having profited from the theology course taught by Fr. André, he was then entrusted to the tutelage of a young monk who dared to say to him on more than one occasion: "You are a complete dunce. It's useless for you to study, you will never learn more! Your ordination will dishonor the priesthood!"

Br. Marie-Joseph endured all these mortifications with serenity and was ordained a priest in 1902 in the abbey church of his monastery, one year before dying of tuberculosis. He was beatified by Pope John Paul II in October 2004.[239]

---

[238] René Fourrey, *Le Curé d'Ars Authentique*, (Paris: Fayard, 1964), 83–100.

[239] Br. Jean-Christophe, *Frère Marie-Joseph Cassant, L'instinct du Bonheur*, (Mesnil-St.-Loup: Le Livre Ouvert, 2005).

8

Fear of the Future
I worry about the future

*"I'm suffering only for an instant. It's because
we think of the past and the future that we become
discouraged and fall into despair."*[240]

Wise men and women of every age have frequently said that
people's unhappiness often comes mainly from the fact that
they don't live in the present moment. As the stoic philosopher Seneca
remarked, "The universal problem of mankind is less of doing evil
or failing to do something, but doing something other than what
they have to do."

In fact, we often waste time due to habitually letting our imaginations wander into the future or our memory into the past. On
the one hand, *we analyze the past*, and this produces feelings which
prevent us from being available to the riches of the present moment.
We move from vanity to sadness, when the memory of our past setbacks comes after that of our achievements—from regret to remorse
when longing for life's happy times gives way to the memory of our

---

[240] YN August 19, n. 10.

cowardly acts. Alternatively, *we become anxious about the future*: we fear meeting with new sufferings and insurmountable problems or we're so worried about finishing our work on time that we do it sloppily, only to regret later the mistakes caused by our haste.

The poet Paul Valery said, "What wearies us is not the work we are doing, but the work that remains to be done." It can even happen that a driver's fear of being late for a funeral can cause another one! How true is this maxim from Goethe: "You fear what will not happen; you weep about what you have not lost." And how many of us ought to ponder what an English humorist wrote on a sign over his mantel: "The greatest tragedies of my life never happened to me."

While there is a complete spirituality of the present moment in the Gospel, it doesn't eliminate the duty to prepare carefully for our future. Far from it, since, while Jesus didn't want us to worry about tomorrow, "Let the day's own trouble be sufficient for the day,"[241] He elsewhere told us not to act like the foolish virgins who couldn't see past the end of their noses.

The novelist Gilbert Cesbron offered an excellent image to show us *this twofold requirement* of the Gospel. He said, "We should arrange a system analogous to the zooming of a camera lens: capable of focusing in one moment on the plans farthest away just as on the closest. Similarly, we must learn to move from the future to the present, without losing one iota of clarity."[242]

This twofold requirement corresponds to two complementary aspects of the Gospel message. First, what is essential is already present and we can rejoice in it even now: Christ lives, He is with us, the Father loves us and is giving us His Spirit. Second, God's kingdom has not yet come in its fullness, and we have to work with all our might for

[241] Mt 6:34.
[242] Gilbert Cesbron, *Ce que je crois* (Paris: Grasset, 1970), 134.

its coming. The Christian life is a continual alternation between the joy of believing the Kingdom has already come and the joy of hoping that it will finally come through our persevering prayer and the impetus of our action—actions which must be foreseen and prepared.

Let's see how Thérèse peacefully fulfilled both of these complementary requirements. She lived every moment of her life intensely, gradually eliminating worries that arose in her mind, and conscientiously completing the tasks entrusted to her in the convent.

Living in God's now

This phrase, which Br. Roger of Taizé used to title one of his books, expresses quite well a vital feature of the Good News: we are asked to live and proclaim the gospel through the witness of a serenity which is as complete as possible amid our worries.

"A minute is a treasure"

If Thérèse didn't allow herself to become immersed in fruitless reminiscing or feverish worries, it was because she was convinced of the irreplaceable value of *every minute* God gave her to live. She received them like marvelous gifts that were not to be wasted, since they were all unique moments in which she could love the Lord with all her heart and work for the conversion of her brethren. She wanted to live them fully and fill them with great love.

She believed this especially because from childhood she had the intuition that she wouldn't remain long on earth. She wrote on July 18, 1897 to Fr. Maurice Bellière, "Never have I asked God to die young, this would have appeared to me as cowardliness; but He, from my childhood, saw fit to give me the intimate conviction that my course here below would be short."[243]

---

[243] LT 258. She had said several days earlier to Mother Agnes: "Ever since I was young, God gave me the feeling that I would die young" (YN July 13, n.13).

So, we shouldn't be surprised that, from early in life, she made many sacrifices each day to please Jesus ("practices" according to the language of the time). Later, when Mr. Martin was hospitalized in Caen, she encouraged Céline not to waste the privileged opportunities she had each day to offer many sacrifices for the salvation of souls. "Let us profit from our one moment of suffering!...Let us see only each moment!...A moment is a treasure...one act of love will make us know Jesus better...it will bring us closer to Him during the whole of eternity!"[244] "Céline, during the short moments that remain to us let us not lose our time...let us save souls..."[245] "Life is a treasure...each moment is an eternity, an eternity of joy in heaven... Let all the moments of our life be for Him alone."[246] "Perhaps the year about to begin will be the last!!!!!!...Ah! let us profit, let us profit from the shortest moments; let us act like misers, and let us be jealous of the littlest things for the Beloved!"[247] One month before Céline entered Carmel, Thérèse also wrote to her: "We have only the short moment of this life to give to God...and He is already preparing to say: 'Now, my turn...'"[248]

On the other hand, Thérèse never forgot that the Lord is master of time and that in His eyes "a thousand years are like a day" and thus He can prepare us in an instant to appear before Him. Thérèse experienced this herself on Christmas Eve 1886, when in one moment the

And she had written a month before in her last manuscript: "I never did ask God for the favor of dying young, but I have always hoped this would be His will for me" (C 8v). We can thus understand Thérèse's predilection for saints who died in the flower of their youth: the Holy Innocents, St. Cecilia, St. Agnes, St. Joan of Arc, Théophane Vénard, Tarcisus, Stanislaus Kostka, etc.

[244] LT 89.
[245] LT 94.
[246] LT 96.
[247] LT 101.
[248] LT 169.

Lord extricated her from her babyish whining and surrounded her with His divine strength. And wasn't Pranzini converted on August 31, 1887, at the last moment? Consequently, we should never give up hope on anyone: the worst sinners can be converted in a single day.

Indeed, the Lord is delighted to transform hearts opened to His merciful Love in a single moment: "Ah! since the happy day, it seems to me that Love penetrates and surrounds me, that at each moment this Merciful Love renews me, purifying my soul and leaving no trace of sin within it..."[249]

On April 25, 1897 Thérèse explained to Maurice Bellière why she wasn't worried about being still "a little and very imperfect soul," even as she faced death. "It is not because I am *prepared*. I feel that I shall never be prepared if the Lord does not see fit to transform me Himself. He can do so in one instant; after all the graces He has granted me, I still await this one from His infinite mercy."[250] Thérèse is reminding us, quite correctly, that a single second of genuine attention to God, of trust in Him, can repair entire years of indifference, pride, or cowardice. This is what happened with the man we call the Good Thief: the Lord converted him in a single moment.

In the same way, one second of attention between God and myself can produce communion, and create an entirely new understanding. When I enter into a real relationship with someone, when I truly become his neighbor, which is the real way to love, I form something unique and allow the Lord to be more present in the world: *ubi caritas, Deus ibi est* (where charity reigns, God is present).

In order to do this, we need to fight against *the mindset that prevents us from really living*. We have a great tendency to judge the value of a day by the number of activities completed, by how much

---

[249] A 84r.
[250] LT 224.

we've gotten done. In other words, we are tempted to judge a day as "successful" when we have been able to accumulate ideas, meetings, tasks, success or money. However, we have really used the day well when we are content to be available to events, attentive to God and others, even if we were unable to accomplish half of the work we envisioned.

For Christians, the "quality of life" we hear so frequently discussed mainly means peacefully loving each moment of our life as a unique instant in which the Father wants to bless us and in which we can make the world eternally more beautiful. Lacordaire said, "Each instant comes to us with an order from God." Similarly, we can say that each instant comes to us with a gift from God. It's our job not to let it slip away! It hardly matters if the wrapping of the gift is sometimes disconcerting, since "This slight momentary affliction is preparing for us an eternal weight of glory beyond all comparison."[251]

Consequently, we must extricate our hearts from the desire to have our work finished before we have even started it. The obsession with speed is ultimately the refusal of our state as creatures, a state subject to the law of maturation. We are not God. It takes us time—and often a lot of time—to do things. Furthermore, with a few exceptions, God Himself, without a miracle, usually takes quite a while to create His masterpieces. He prepared the coming of His Son among men for millions of years. And when He came among us, the Son was subject to the law of time: in Nazareth for thirty years, He learned His trade as man. So, why do we want to go faster than God? There is a proverb: "All haste comes from the devil."

Lacordaire wrote, "It's extraordinary what we can do with time, if we have the patience to wait."

---

[251] 2 Cor 4:17.

Hence we have to fight the frequent impression of "dead or wasted time," time that is uninteresting or useless. If we do this, we can profit from waiting at a red light, or in line, or for a phone call, to immerse ourselves in God again and allow ourselves to be overshadowed, as it were, with His Spirit. We need to learn how to use all of the empty minutes in life to join God in the inner room of our soul, saying to Him joyfully once again: "O You who are present in the depths of my heart, help me lose myself in You in the depths of my heart."

This is what Br. Lawrence of the Resurrection, the great Carmelite cook from the 17th century, called *the method of "spiritual plunges."* Taking this approach, the match of our life would become exciting and the "breaks" in play would no longer seem like wasted time. How can a single second of our life be "dead time" when the Father's will is to create and re-create us at every moment in order to gradually form our features for eternity?

With this attitude, our fraternal charity will become more selfless as well. Instead of being preoccupied with all the urgent tasks to be done and the future meetings we must plan, we would be entirely present to the person whom we are meeting now and who is waiting for our heart to open.

St. Teresa of Avila's bookmark, found
IN HER BREVIARY AFTER HER DEATH

Let nothing disturb you,
let nothing frighten you,
all things will pass away.
God never changes;
patience obtains all things,

whoever has God lacks nothing.
God alone suffices. Amen.

St. Thérèse had a copy of this prayer in her collection of images.

In one of her first poems, "Just for today," written on June 1, 1894,[252] Thérèse expressed her desire to live one day at a time.

1   My life is but an instant, a passing hour. My life is but a day that escapes and flies away. O my God! You know that to love you on earth I only have today!...

2   Oh, I love you, Jesus! My soul yearns for you. For just one day remain my sweet support. Come reign in my heart, give me your smile Just for today!

3   Lord, what does it matter if the future is gloomy? Oh, pray for tomorrow, oh no, I cannot!...keep my heart pure, cover me with your shadow Just for today.

4   If I think about tomorrow, I fear my fickleness, I feel sadness and worry rising up in my heart, but I'm willing, my God, to accept trial and suffering Just for today.

5   Divine Pilot! whose hand guides me, I'm soon to see you on the eternal shore. Guide my little boat over the stormy waves in peace Just for today.

6   Lord, let me hide in your Face, there I'll no longer hear the world's vain noise. Give me your love, keep me in your grace Just for today.

7   Near your divine Heart, I forget all passing things, I no longer dread the fears of the night. Jesus, give me a place in your Heart Just for today.

---

[252] PN 5, *Mon chant d'aujourdhui.*

8   Living Bread, Bread of Heaven, divine Eucharist, sacred Mystery! that Love has brought forth...Come live in my heart, Jesus, my white Host, Just for today.

9   Deign to unite me to you, Holy and sacred Vine, and my weak branch will give you its fruit, And I'll be able to offer you a cluster of golden grapes Lord, from today on.

10 I've just this fleeting day to form this cluster of love, whose seeds are souls. Oh! give me, Jesus, the fire of an Apostle Just for today.

11 O Immaculate Virgin! You are my Sweet Star Giving Jesus to me and uniting me to Him. O Mother! Let me rest under your veil Just for today.

12 My Holy Guardian Angel, cover me with your wing. With your fire light the road that I'm taking. Come direct my steps...help me, I call upon you Just for today.

13 Lord, I want to see you without veils, without clouds, But still exiled, far from you, I languish. May your lovable face not be hidden from me Just for today.

14 Soon I'll fly away to speak your praises When the day without sunset will dawn on my soul. Then I'll sing on the Angels' lyre The Eternal Today!...

Suffer one minute at a time

Additionally, it's especially noteworthy to observe how Thérèse lived this spirituality of the present moment in the last months of her life. Instead of being tormented by the thought that her suffering would surely be drawn out, she suffered *moment by moment*. She told Mother Agnes on June 14, 1897: "We can put up with very much from one moment to the next!"

She said in August, about her terrible sufferings: "I'm suffering only for an instant. It's because we think of the past and the future that we become discouraged and fall into despair."[253] And on August 23: "No, God gives me no premonition of an approaching death, but of much greater sufferings...But I don't torment myself, I don't want to think of anything but the present moment."[254] Her thought three days later was the same: "Ah! to suffer in my soul, yes, I can suffer much...But as to suffering of body, I'm like a little child, very little. I'm without any thought, I suffer from minute to minute."[255]

These reflections remind us of the answer that a boy suffering in the hospital one day made to the Curé of Ars. "Are you suffering a great deal, poor thing?" the Curé asked. "No, Father. I don't feel yesterday's pain today and tomorrow I will no longer feel my suffering from today."

What was in Thérèse's mind as she was offering her sufferings moment by moment like this? First, the conviction that *God was giving her, as needed, the graces of courage for her trial.* God did this in some way "drop by drop": at each instant He gave her the dose of patience needed. She was sure that, if the suffering increased, God would grant His grace in the same proportion. "God gives me courage in proportion to my sufferings. I feel at this moment I couldn't suffer any more, but I'm not afraid, since if they increase, He will increase my courage at the same time."[256] Eight days later, after having admitted to Mother Agnes that she had never had such a bad night, she added, "Oh! How good God will have to be so that I can bear all I'm suffering. Never would I believe I could suffer so much. And yet I believe I'm not at the end of my pains; but He will not abandon

253 YN August 19, n. 10.
254 YN August 23, n. 30.
255 YN August 26, n. 3.
256 YN August 15, n. 6.

me."[257] With this conviction she endured her agony on the night of September 29. Mother Marie de Gonzague asked her, "It's terrible, then, what you are suffering?" Thérèse answered, "No, Mother, not terrible, but much, much…just what I can bear."[258]

Since it was Jesus giving her the grace to bear her pains as needed, Thérèse never asked Him to increase them. She was content to receive what came to her. Evidence of this is a conversation related by Sr. Marie of the Eucharist in letter to her father from August 1897, "She told us yesterday, 'Fortunately, I have never asked for suffering, because if I had asked for it, I fear I would not have had the patience to bear it; whereas, coming to me from the pure will of God, He cannot refuse me the necessary patience and graces."[259]

Second, Thérèse was so certain of the value of each moment of suffering that she never grumbled at seeing her Calvary prolonged. She was never heard to complain: "When will I come to the end of these shooting pains and this sensation of suffocating?" What heartened her most on the days of greatest suffering was the thought that the Lord, like a thief, would come to find her, to collect her, in the manner of a vineyard keeper happy to pick a perfectly ripe grape.[260] However, most often, to avoid thinking the time too long, she thought, on the contrary, of how quickly her life had passed. In some way, God had caused her to skip steps, by consuming her in love so rapidly.[261]

How could she complain then that the time didn't pass quickly enough? Thérèse took her courtesy toward the Lord to this length.

---

[257] YN August 23, n. 1.
[258] YN September 29, n. 11.
[259] DE 758–59.
[260] YN July 25, n. 12.
[261] YN August 31, n. 9.

She didn't want to tell Him it was too much, "Lord, why are you making this night so long, so long, so long for me…?" If our time on earth is prolonged it's because it is valuable to ourselves and others. Therefore, there is no reason to argue about the quarter hours that the Lord is asking us to go on with the match.

Prepare for the future peacefully

God loves us more than the birds of the air…but He didn't give us prudence so that we would remain "bird-brained" all our lives. Lack of foresight isn't a Biblical beatitude. More than once the Bible praises the prudence of the man or woman who can organize household affairs.[262]

Abandonment to divine providence doesn't mean abandoning every project, every plan. The more responsibilities we accept, the more we have to plan long term projects. God not only asks us to develop our patience and trust, but also to make use of creative thinking and develop it, to find solutions to new problems that we and others face. While we are to pray as if everything depended on God, we must act as if everything depended on the creative power of our mind and the tenacity of our will.

Thérèse had no fear of using all the means at her disposal to advance what was important to her, to accomplish what she thought was God's will. In order to achieve her early entry into Carmel she didn't hesitate to visit her bishop or go to the hairdresser to have her hair done in a fashion that would make her look a little older. To help her novices better understand her "little way," she wrote a few modest poems, hoping the lessons would more easily be taken to heart. When she foresaw in the last months of her life, that the posthumous publication of her manuscripts would contribute to

---

[262] For example, Prov 31:10–31.

making her little way known, she gave very specific advice to Sr. Agnes about the way to publish these, and about what should be added or removed from the text.

Thérèse encouraged her novices to do their work without carelessness, to use the time prescribed for it conscientiously, making sure that they didn't yield to activism, but instead maintained freedom of heart. She said, "I remember reading, that when the Israelites were building the walls of Jerusalem, each laborer while working held a sword in one hand. That is a symbol of the interior attitude we should acquire in the matter of work: that at the point of the sword, we hold off all dissipation of soul in our external labors."[263]

In Thérèse's school, then, let's try to make our lives a true symphony… always bearing in mind that it will be an unfinished symphony because illness, the incomprehension of others, our own blunders, our sins, and finally our death, will prevent us from playing the notes as we planned. However, that doesn't matter! God asks us specifically to hope that He can transform the symphony of our life one day into an eternal alleluia. There will inevitably be false notes or sighs that sometimes last too long, or rests which aren't always respected in it—but it should be a symphony which we tried to play like a child under our Father's admiring gaze.

And let's play it, *non troppo presto*, but *moderato*—that is, without wanting to go faster than the heavenly orchestra conductor, who is directing the whole ensemble of players. He has put an original score into our hands…a score to decipher and play *con cuore*: "with all your heart."

[263] MSST 66.

POPE JOHN XXIII REGULARLY RENEWED HIS INTENTION TO LIVE FULLY IN THE PRESENT MOMENT

Today went better than yesterday, and tomorrow should go better than today, with God's grace and so forth. I must insist on a principle I have never sufficiently thought about: I must do everything, say every prayer, obey the Rule, as if I had nothing else to do, as if the Lord had put me in this world for the sole purpose of doing that thing well, as if my sanctification depended on that alone, without thinking of anything else.

This is a great principle which, if scrupulously applied, has the power to put distractions to flight, just as holy water makes the devil take to his heels; it is the principle of recollection, of the old saying *age quod agis*, "pay attention to what you are doing," and the practice of the presence of God. But to be effective, it must be observed from my very first actions every morning."

(At seminary in Rome, December 1902)

I shall attend to my tasks as they present themselves, calmly and composedly, with the greatest single-mindedness, as if I had been sent into the world to do just that, as if Jesus Himself had given me the order and were present watching me. As for other tasks, I will attend to them later on, in their turn, without any sign of haste or anxiety, without leaving anything unfinished, without brusqueness or negligence.

(Retreat in Rome, before Diaconal
ordination, December 1903)

One of my chief faults consists in not having learnt to make the right use of time still. I must find a way of doing much in a short time, and with this in mind I must be extremely careful not to waste a single moment on useless things, idle chatter, etc. Immediately after breakfast I will attend to the duties of my office, correspondence, etc. All the remaining time is for my lectures, which I shall prepare most conscientiously. I will read the newspapers at times when I have the least energy for other things, after dinner, on my walks, for example, or in any odd moments. Every day, last thing at night, I will read some good books which will be of use to my soul.[264]

(Retreat, October 1912)

[264] Pope John XXIII, *Journal of a Soul*, (London: A & C Black, 2000), 98, 146, 169.

Part 2

When I Consider Other People

9

Obsession with Being the Best
Pride isolates me

*"You know my weakness, Lord. Every morning I make
a resolution to practice humility and, in the evening, I
recognize that I have committed again many faults of
pride. At this I am tempted to become discouraged but
I know that discouragement is also pride. Therefore,
O my God, I want to base my hope in You alone."*[265]

As we saw in Chapter 7, it's a good thing to have self-confidence, to be free of a feeling of inferiority and the discouraging fear of being perpetually in the spotlight of others' scrutiny. But it's also terrible to be controlled by the demon of pride, to constantly want to prove to others that you are better, smarter, braver, stronger than they are. While at first someone might find a certain joy at the applause this yields, one ends up tiring of it. Sooner or later, a person who is proud realizes that all the praise doesn't satisfy his heart.

The people who have the most adulation in this world aren't necessarily the happiest. While they may not lack an audience, they often

---

[265] Pr 20.

lack true friends. By disdaining others from the height of their talents or success, they end up despised by those who began by applauding them. After having experienced the intoxication of success, they find themselves alone, terribly alone. And even if, without seeking to crush others, someone is simply content to admire themselves a lot, he or she eventually realizes that despite everything, they aren't so great after all, that they are much more sensitive and vainer than they had thought. And that hurts!

Can Thérèse help these proud people (which we all are more or less) to discover the secrets of true humility? For this is the way to understand the blessedness Jesus promised to the poor in spirit, to all those who, following Him, have become "meek and humble of heart." [266] St. Thérèse teaches that we can do this only after having received a grace that makes us realize that God alone is infinitely good and infinitely loveable and consequently, it's ridiculous to prefer our little ego to Him.

Only God is infinitely good

As Pascal recognized, only God is capable of filling the "infinite abyss" in our hearts.[267] God will never reproach us for having a mad desire to be loved. He is the one who placed that desire deep in our hearts. He did this precisely so that eventually we would turn to Him since He is the only One who can cherish us with an infinite love.

If Thérèse didn't seek to be noticed in her community, if she accepted being unjustly criticized so peacefully, it was because she was accustomed to valuing praise coming from heaven more highly. Her novice Marie of the Trinity once asked, "Why do you want so much to be ignored and counted for nothing. As for me, I find it very pleasant to be loved and recognized." Thérèse replied:

---

[266] Mt 11:29.
[267] Pascal, *Pensées*, fr. 1948.

I am very much of the same opinion. It is precisely because I thirst for love and glory that I despise those of earth, which are nothing but mirages and illusions. Only in heaven can I enjoy them truly and fully. There, for me to be satisfied, I need the love of every heart, and if there were even one missing, it would seem that I couldn't prevent myself from saying to Jesus, like Haman about Mordecai, 'Lord, as long as this one doesn't love me, my happiness will not be complete.'[268]

In the last month of her life, Thérèse was genuinely happy to hear it said that she wasn't a good nun. One day, entering the infirmary, Sr. St. Augustine, struck by the sick woman's radiant mien, asked her the reason for it. Thérèse answered her with candor:

I have felt a true joy and I will confide it to you. Just now I received a visit from a sister who told me, "You know how little you are appreciated here!...Recently, I heard a sister from the community say to another, 'I don't know why Thérèse of the Child Jesus is spoken about so much: she is doing nothing remarkable; we never see her practicing virtue; one can't even say that she is a good nun...'"

And Thérèse continued, "To hear it said on my deathbed that I am not a good religious—what a grace!"[269]

Yes, what a grace because this remark was an answer to one of Thérèse's profound desires, namely, to not be noticed, but also and especially because it supported her conviction of being only a very little soul in great need of the Lord's infinite mercy. Thérèse fostered the desire not to be noticed by meditation on the hidden life of Christ

[268] TLMT, 83.
[269] Circular of Sr. Thérèse of St. Augustine, 7.

and the blessed Virgin. She loved the *Discourse on the Life Hidden in God* by Bossuet and gave the book to her novices.[270] What she admired in the Virgin Mary was her simplicity and humility.

> You make me feel that it's not impossible
> To follow in your footsteps, O Queen of the elect.
> You made visible the narrow road to Heaven
> While always practicing the humblest virtues.
> Near you, Mary, I like to stay little.
> I see the vanity of greatness here below.[271]

In the same way, the image of the Holy Face continued to remind Thérèse that she should "live unknown on earth."[272] She ended the text of the novitiate's consecration to the Holy Face with this paragraph: "*O beloved Face of Jesus*, As we await the everlasting day when we will contemplate your infinite Glory, our one desire is to charm your Divine Eyes by hiding our faces too so that here on earth no one can recognize us...O Jesus! *Your Veiled Gaze is our Heaven!*..."[273] In addition, on August 4, 1897 she told Mother Agnes: "These words of Isaias: 'Who has believed our report?...There is no beauty in him, no comeliness, etc.,' have made the whole foundation of my devotion to the Holy Face, or, to express it better, the foundation of all my piety. I, too, have desired to be without beauty—alone in treading the winepress, unknown to everyone."[274]

When we have truly experienced the joy of being infinitely loved by the One whose love surpasses everything we can imagine, we no

---

[270] See MSST 68.
[271] PN 54, st 6.
[272] PN 20, st 2.
[273] Pr 12.
[274] YN August 5, n. 9.

longer seek the compliments and applause of those around us as eagerly as before.

God alone is infinitely loveable

Everything in God is wonderful, infinitely worthy of being loved. So, it's right and good to draw closer to Him wholeheartedly. St. Augustine put it so well at the beginning of his *Confessions*: "Thou hast made us for thyself Lord, and our hearts are restless till they rest in Thee." As long as we idolize ourselves—whether by idolizing our bodily health, our mental sharpness or the success of our endeavors—we will be unhappy, since we are making happiness depend on something that can never provide it. On the contrary, if we allow ourselves to be captivated by God's beauty, by the only one who is infinitely loveable, by the only one who deserves to be in the highest place, then we will find happiness.

This is what Thérèse did. Like the bride in the Song of Songs, she let herself be entranced by the incomparable beauty of her divine Bridegroom. She confirmed, "My beloved is entirely loveable"[275] and to her cousin Marie Guérin she wrote, "You must not forget that Jesus is All, so you must lose your little nothingness in His infinite All and think only of this uniquely lovable All..."[276]

Yes, when we let ourselves be captivated by the incredible Beauty of the adorable Face of Jesus, we are no longer tempted to think of ourselves as the most attractive. Like Thérèse, we are happy to repeat to Jesus: "O Divine Word! You are the Adored Eagle whom I love and who alone attracts me!"[277] Then we become so absorbed by Jesus' face and His smile that we stop considering the impression we

---

[275] LT 108.
[276] LT 109.
[277] B 5v.

are making on others…we are freed from the constant worry about being and appearing to be the best.

We shouldn't be surprised that we have a lot of trouble loving God this way. Having been born with the wound of original sin which affects all of us, we are always tempted to fall back into ourselves, making our little ego the primary focus of our life, relegating God to the rank of a means occasionally used for the success of our undertakings! *We are not naturally humble* as the Virgin Mary was from the first moment of her life. We are all born with a terrible propensity to glorify ourselves for the smallest achievement instead of immediately giving thanks to the one who made it possible to accomplish.

That's why Thérèse rejoiced at repeatedly discovering in herself new impulses of pride or imperfections which needed the Lord's healing. This renewed her humility in some way. In the weeks before her death she expressed in animated phrases what constituted "perfect joy" for her: "Oh, how happy I am to see myself imperfect and to have such need of God's mercy at the moment of my death!"[278] "I experience a very lively joy not only when I discover I'm imperfect, but especially when I feel I am. All this surpasses all praise, which only bores me."[279]

THE BEAUTY OF THE DIVINE HEART, FROM A LETTER OF ST. MARGARET MARY

The divine Heart is an abyss of riches into which the poor should cast their necessities; an abyss of joy into which we should cast all our sadness; an abyss of humiliation for our

---

278 YN July 29, n. 3.
279 YN August 2, n. 6.

pride; an abyss of mercy for the miserable and an abyss of love into which we should cast all our miseries.[280]

As a matter of fact, it is through recognizing our terrible inclination to pride that we eventually become humble. One day we realize the mistake we are making by considering ourselves the center of the universe, and we beg the Lord to be freed of that idolatry. We cry out to Him that we have a genuine need to be healed of our pride.

This is because, let's not forget, before being the result of our own efforts, humility is a grace. This is well-known. We prepare ourselves to receive it by reflecting on its benefits and meditating on the marvelous example of Jesus: though He was the Son of God, He lived in Nazareth for many years without revealing His identity to those close to Him. True humility is totally God's gift, as well as being the foundation of all other virtues. That's why Thérèse happily made use of the well-known prayer: "O Jesus, meek and humble of heart, make my heart like unto Thine."[281] Humility makes us participate in Jesus' humility. He is the Incarnate Word, who has a perfect awareness that He has nothing which was not given Him by His Father and that He can do nothing apart from Him.

ST. FRANCIS DE SALES: *REPROACH YOUR HEART COMPASSIONATELY*

Let us say that I had a great desire to avoid vanity and yet failed seriously, I wouldn't scold myself in this way: "Aren't

---

[280] Marguerite-Marie Alacoque, *Vie et Oeuvres de Ste Marguerite Marie*, letter 132 (Editions St. Paul: Paris, 1991), 464–65.

[281] Prs. 5 and 20.

you wretched and hateful to be carried away by vanity after so many resolutions? Die of shame and never again lift your eyes to heaven, you blind and shameless traitor to God," and so on.

I would rather reprove my heart reasonably and with compassion as follows: "Well, my poor heart here we are fallen again into that ditch which we had resolved so firmly to avoid. Let us get up once more and leave it forever, imploring God's mercy and trusting that he will help us to be more steadfast for the future. Let us return to the path of humility, have confidence and from now on let us be more on our guard; God will help us and we will do better." Then, I would make a firm and steady resolution not to fall again, asking the advice of my confessor as to the best means to this end.[282]

---

[282] St. Frances de Sales, *Introduction to the Devout Life*, trans. Michael Day, (Wheathampstead, Hertfordshire: Anthony Clarke, 1990), 116.

10

The Pain of Envy
Envy makes me sad

*"Just as a mother is proud of her children, so also, we
shall be proud of each other [in heaven], having not
the least bit of jealousy. With the virgins we shall be
virgins; with the doctors, doctors; with the martyrs,
martyrs, because all the saints are our relatives."*[283]

Even if I am truly comfortable with myself, sometimes I unexpectedly feel sad when I see that someone has succeeded better
than I have in some area in which, until then, I thought I was very
good. To be cured of this sadness I can first of all remind myself,
that in life there will always be those who are first and those who
are last, and that it would be very foolish to always wish to be in first
place. The world needs all sorts of people. As the composer Robert
Schumann put it, "If all the musicians wanted to be first violin, it
would be impossible to have an orchestra."

However, such ideas aren't sufficient to cure the pains of envy. To
rejoice fully in the rose's beauty, the violet must be certain of being

[283] YN July 13, n. 12.

quite beautiful itself. Once again, let's be Thérèse's pupils so we can rid our hearts of the poison of envy. To be freed of it, we know quite well that it's not enough simply to repeat with conviction, "You shouldn't be envious." It's also not enough to repeat to the Lord, "My God, make me love my brethren enough that I can recognize their superiority joyfully." We need something more. And as a matter of fact, this wasn't the way that St. Thérèse helped her novices overcome this problem.

She had observed that our temptations to envy can take two forms, depending on the kind of goods we are tempted to envy in others. Sometimes these are natural gifts; sometimes supernatural charisms the Lord has granted others but not us. Envy happens frequently in this situation, especially when it's a question of the fervor of charity. Thérèse employed different Gospel principles depending on which kind of envy had to be conquered.

Others' successes take nothing away from me

The first source of envy: others have supernatural gifts and charisms we don't have. For example, Thérèse remarks, if other sisters receive more abundant lights in prayer, you may be tempted to interpret this inequality as a sign that the Lord loves you less; then you become sad about it. What an error! There are two reasons for this.

First, *the essential worth of a human being* isn't based on the number of talents the Lord has entrusted to him, but on how he makes these fruitful, and ultimately, through the *quality of his love. The quality of a person's love is something only God knows.* "Jesus willed to create great souls comparable to lilies and roses, but He has created smaller ones and these must be content to be daisies or violets destined to give joy to God's glance when He looks down at His feet. Perfection consists in doing His will, in being what He wills us to be."[284]

[284] A 2v.

If we can be certain of pleasing God by quietly accomplishing His will, why should we seek to shine? Why envy those whose lives have more sparkle? In her last manuscript, Thérèse frequently returned to the primacy of charity, without which the most extraordinary charismatic gifts are nothing. As St. Paul declared, "If I speak in the tongues of men and of angels, but have not love, I am a noisy gong or a clanging cymbal."[285] Thérèse commented:

I do not hold in contempt beautiful thoughts which nourish the soul and unite it with God; but for a long time, I have understood that we must not depend on them and even make perfection consist in receiving many spiritual lights. The most beautiful thoughts are nothing without good works. It is true that others can draw profit from them if they humble themselves and show their gratitude to God for permitting them to share in the banquet of a soul whom He is pleased to enrich with His graces. But if this soul takes delight in her beautiful thoughts and says the prayer of the Pharisee, she is like a person dying of hunger at a well-filled table where all his guests are enjoying abundant food and at times cast a look of envy upon the person possessing so many good things. Ah! how true it is that God alone knows human hearts and that creatures are terribly narrow in their thoughts! When they see a soul more enlightened than others, immediately they conclude that Jesus loves them less than this soul, and that they cannot be called to the same perfection.[286]

In short, supernatural insights aren't a foolproof measure of holiness. *Like all riches, they are also a danger*, since the soul who receives them

---

[285] 1 Cor 13:1.
[286] C 19v.

risks becoming smug about them and falling into pride. This is the first principle the Carmelite invoked for teaching, both herself and her novices, how to fight the temptation to envy others because of natural qualities or supernatural lights.

The second reason is as entirely Pauline as the first. It is for the *benefit of the Mystical Body as a whole that the Lord gives charisms* to its various members. "Just as in nature all the seasons are arranged in such a way as to make the humblest daisy bloom on a set day, in the same way, everything works out for the good of each soul."[287] Thérèse frequently returned to this truth. God grants certain souls lights that others don't receive directly, for the benefit of others; such souls are instruments which the Lord uses for doing good to others. "If a piece of canvas painted on by an artist could think and speak, it certainly would not complain at being constantly touched and retouched by the brush, and would not envy the lot of that instrument, for it would realize it was not to the brush but to the artist using it that it owed the beauty with which it was clothed."[288]

In 1893, the year she began teaching the novices, Thérèse explained this idea to Céline. If her letters were helping her, it was because Jesus is free to make use of any means to accomplish His work in souls: "Creatures are all at His service." She continued:

In fact, I really feel that often He gives me some lights, not for myself but for His little exiled dove, His dear spouse. This is really true. I find an example of it in nature itself. Here is a beautiful peach, pink and so sweet that all confectioners could not imagine a taste so sweet. Tell me, Céline, is it for the peach that God has created this pretty pink color, so

---

[287] A 3r.
[288] C 20r.

velvety and so pleasing to see and to touch? Is it for the peach that He has given so much sugar?...No, but for us and not for it. What belongs to it and what forms the essence of its life is its stone; we can take away all its beauty without taking from it its being. Thus, Jesus is pleased to shower His gifts on some of His creatures, but very often this is in order to attract other hearts to Himself.[289]

So, Thérèse realized that she shouldn't become proud about certain traits the Lord had bestowed on her: she had received them only so she could fulfil her duties to the novices. "I understand that it is not for my sake but for that of others that I must walk this road that appears so dangerous. In fact, if I were to pass in the eyes of the community for a religious filled with faults, incapable, without understanding or judgment, it would be impossible for you, Mother, to have me help you. This is why God has cast a veil over all my interior and exterior faults."[290]

Thérèse came back to this idea in her conversations with Céline later, when her sister had the notion that Thérèse's position as novice mistress was a sign of greater love on the Lord's part. "I am only truly what the Good God thinks of me. With regard to loving me more because He is giving me charge of souls and to be His interpreter for a little group of novices, I find it rather to be the opposite. He is making me *their servant*. It is *for you* that God has placed in me the charms of exterior virtue; it's not for me."[291]

These were the two principles specified by Thérèse for conquering the first kind of envy, the one which has the gleam of supernatural or natural goods in others as its cause.

---

[289] LT 147.
[290] C 26v.
[291] MSST 114.

The holiness of others belongs to everyone

All the same, can we resist the "holy envy" we feel when we witness the heroic charity of some of our brethren? We are then faced with a real treasure: something of genuine value. How can we not envy such a good?

St. Aelred of Rievaulx:
The unity of the mystical body

Let no one consider as his own the charism he has received from God. Let no one envy the charism his brother has received! Instead, let him reflect that what is his is the good of all his brothers. Let him not doubt that the good of his brother is his. God acts in this way that each one may have need of others, and that what one person does not possess, he has in his brother, and that this way humility may be preserved, charity increased, and unity manifested! Let the weak one say: I am strong! For the strong brother suffers through his weakness, just as the weak one is strong through the strength of his brother![292]

This second form of envy is found frequently in souls enamored with the idea of perfection. They have such a great desire to advance in love of the Lord that they become irritated at seeing themselves "surpassed" by others. Then they get discouraged and imagine that God isn't pleased with them; conversely, they may seek to reassure themselves cheaply by attributing what they initially admired in others to self-love or hypocrisy. (We all know people who cannot praise

[292] Excerpt from sermon 7.

somebody else without following it up immediately with malicious criticism. For example: "My neighbor is self-sacrificing in every trial… but he puts himself forward a bit." Nine times out of ten, envy is the origin of such comments.)

Envy always brings sadness in tow, causing discouragement about self or contempt for others. Many souls, even generous ones, lack joy and enthusiasm in their spiritual lives because, dominated by the demon of envy, they are grieved to see in others a certain holiness they lack. What would Thérèse propose for overcoming this second kind of envy?

First, we should mention that, in combatting envy due to the perfection of others' actions, Thérèse never used the principle that we don't know the deep intention animating a person's acts. To conquer the temptation to condemn others she said, "What appears to me as a fault can very easily be an act of virtue…"[293] Against the temptation to envy others she could have invoked a similar idea: "What seems to me to be a heroic act might very easily have been an act of pride, because of the intention. Didn't St. Paul say the same thing: that even if one handed over one's body to be burned, without charity it was nothing? As a matter of fact, Thérèse *never used this approach.* She was right. It would be against charity to regard others with an unfavorable prejudice.

All the same, Thérèse took seriously the fact of inequality among souls. Ever since childhood, she had been pondering this mystery. She was still quite young when she wondered "about why God does not give equal glory to all the elect." She was afraid that everyone wouldn't be happy.[294] Placing a large glass and a thimble side by side and filling them up, Pauline explained to her little sister that each of

---

[293] C 13r.
[294] A 19r–v.

the elect would have the glory he or she could hold and, in this way, the last would have nothing to envy in the first place.

Thérèse pondered this mystery again at the end of her first manuscript. Since God decided to give to each soul a certain amount of holiness and glory, we must accept this inequality. We must accept that God has preferences. Let's be content to be daisies or violets in Jesus' garden, if that is our vocation, and not envy the lot of the lilies or roses. We could say this is the "aesthetic" solution applied to the problem of inequality among souls: it takes all kinds to make a world. This is as true in the spiritual world as it is in the material world. "I understood that if all flowers wanted to be roses, nature would lose her springtime beauty, and the fields would no longer be decked out with little wild flowers...He willed to create great souls comparable to Lilies and roses, but He has created smaller ones."[295]

However, this solution isn't the only one Thérèse offers. This solution still views souls as juxtaposed to each other and that is alien to the charity of the communion of saints, which allows each soul to participate in the treasures of the entire Mystical Body. According to Thérèse, this blessing is the key weapon we must wield in order to conquer once and for all the temptation to envy our neighbor because of the excellence of his or her charity. Again, it's in a response Thérèse gave to Sr. Genevieve that she expressed her thought most clearly. The novice once more told her younger sister about her temptations to envy: "What I envy in you are your works. I would like to do some good, make beautiful things which make God loved!"[296]

Thérèse answered first with the principle mentioned above, namely that the accomplishment of spiritual works was not evidence of a greater love. Then she elevated the discussion. Supposing that such

[295] A 2v.
[296] MSST 53.

works were inspired by an authentic charity and therefore had a supernatural value in the Lord's eyes, we ought to offer them to Him, and so share in their merits. This is the mystery of the communion of saints and, she said, *our lack of ability should never make us sad. Instead, we should focus only on love.* Then Thérèse quoted Tauler, the spiritual author in whom she found the most perfect expression of this facet of the dogma of the communion of the saints: "If I love the good which is in my neighbor more than he loves it himself, then that good is more mine than his. If I love all the favors God granted St. Paul, all that belongs to me by the same right by which it belongs to him. Through the communion of the saints, I can be rich with every good in heaven and on earth, in the angels, the saints, and all those who love God."[297]

Thérèse returned to this subject frequently in her conversations with Sr. Genevieve, because she couldn't help but lament her lack of generosity when she compared herself to her younger sister.

You are so delicate with God and I wish to be the same, however, I am not!...Perhaps my desire for it will make up for what I lack?..."Exactly," Thérèse answered. "Especially if you accept the humiliation. If you even rejoice in it, perhaps this would be even more pleasing to Jesus than if you had never lacked delicacy/sensitivity. Say: 'My God, I thank you for not having had a single delicate feeling and I rejoice to see it in others...You fill me with joy, Lord, in all that you do.'"[298]

A magnificent commentary on St. Paul's description of charity! "Charity rejoices in the truth."[299] Life is transformed when we truly grasp this! Instead of wasting time envying good works done by

---

[297] MSST 143.
[298] MSST 50.
[299] 1 Cor 13: 6.

others, instead of looking for their weak points, we should on the contrary, find joy in discovering all the good accomplished around us; we should regard these as goods belonging to everyone in God's "family" and offer them to Him.

In point of fact, this is what we do at Mass. We not only offer to the Father Jesus Christ's infinite merits, but through Him, with Him, and in Him, the merits of all the saints in heaven…and here on earth. By taking them in our hands like this in order to offer them to Him, these merits in some way become ours. The more we rejoice in all the good accomplished by our brethren, the more we share in their merits.

Thérèse understood this completely. In her Act of Offering to Merciful Love (June 1895) she wrote:

Since You loved me so much as to give me your only Son as my Savior and my Spouse, the infinite treasures of his merits are mine. I offer them to you with gladness, begging you to look on me only through the Face of Jesus and in his Heart burning with Love. I offer you, too, all the merits of the Saints (in Heaven and on earth), their acts of Love, and those of the Holy Angels. Finally, I offer you, O Blessed Trinity! the Love and merits of the Blessed Virgin, my dear Mother.[300]

AUGUSTINE OF HIPPO: *TAKE JOY IN EVERY GOOD WORK*

St. Augustine frequently exhorted his faithful to rejoice in all the good works accomplished by other Christians.

"Everywhere that a good work is done, it belongs to us as well, if we can rejoice in it." And the members of the mystical

---

[300] Pr 6.

body of Christ are so united to each other that what the one cannot achieve by himself, in some way he accomplishes through the other. The Bishop of Hippo explains this, for example, in a letter to the widow Proba, and to the widows and virgins living in community with her. "By fasting, by vigils, and all mortification of the body, prayer is greatly helped. Let each one do what she can; what one cannot herself do, she does by another who can do it, if she loves in another what personal inability alone hinders her from doing.[301]

The possibility of sharing in the merits of others shouldn't make us slip into quietism. We have to do everything in our power to love the Lord and make Him loved. Thérèse was careful to insist on this with Sr. Genevieve: "You will do as much good as I, and even more... However," she continued, "when we have the exhausting sense that we are doing nothing important compared with everything others are doing, we can and we should offer to the Lord all their good works. With this very action we are participating in their merits."

This is what Thérèse did. When she was in choir, she offered her sisters' prayers to God: "I then feel the fervor of my sisters supplements mine."[302] When she received holy communion, she offered Jesus the love and merits of the Blessed Virgin, the angels, and saints.[303] She repeated this in her last poem:

The treasures of a mother belong to her child,
And I am your child, O my dearest Mother.
Aren't your virtues and your love mine too?

[301] St. Augustine, *Sermon 35*; *Letter to Proba*, 130.
[302] C 25r.
[303] A 79v–80r.

So, when the white Host comes into my heart,
Jesus, your Sweet Lamb, thinks he is resting in you!...[304]

In the last months of her life Thérèse frequently expressed her hope of sharing in the merits of her spiritual brothers and sisters. For instance, there is the noteworthy passage in which she says to Maurice Bellière that she trusts she will share in the palm of martyrdom through him. "Since the Lord seems to will to grant me only the martyrdom of love, I hope He will permit me, by means of you, to gather the other palm we are striving after."[305] The same idea appears in the letter of the following month to Fr. Roulland: "In consideration of your merits, I hope God will grant me the favor of sharing in your glory, just as on earth the sister of a conqueror, were she deprived of the gifts of nature, shares in the honors bestowed on her brother in spite of her own poverty."[306]

While it is the supreme antidote to envy, the assurance of sharing in the saints' merits also promotes the genuine recognition of others' value. We perceive the good qualities and merits of our brothers and sisters more easily when we consider them a "common good." And when we see them, we are entirely happy about them.

Accordingly, Thérèse is clearly teaching also that you must love yourself in order to serenely accept others' worth and successes. We can't conquer temptations to envy by expecting to admire others more than self. God doesn't ask us to humiliate ourselves before others, imagining that in comparison with them we are nothing or almost nothing. On the contrary, He asks us to remember the aspects of the Good News which allow us to believe, whatever the circumstances of our lives may be, that we are also stars of the first magnitude, pleasing in His eyes.

[304] Pn 54, st 5.
[305] LT 224.
[306] LT 226.

11

Annoyance
Others irritate me

"Certainly, we don't have any enemies in Carmel,
but there are feelings. One feels drawn to a
certain sister whereas with another one may
make a long detour to avoid meeting her."[307]

Everything we have discussed up until now is quite right and important, you will certainly say, but how can we remain joyful when we are dreadfully annoyed by the behavior of someone around us? Does Thérèse have something to tell us about the way to handle temptations to impatience? These so often poison our relationships with others and prevent us from living with them peacefully.

Absolutely! Thérèse pinpointed the way to react in temptations that come when we are in the midst of an emotional storm, ready to explode when faced with some senseless or unjust act, and also the approach when we have begun to calm down and can examine the situation with a cool head.

---

[307] C 15v.

Use the right approach

In assisting her novices Thérèse ended up coming to the realization that we shouldn't expect to apply a certain type of treatment, a "cold therapy," too soon. As long as someone was dealing with emotional turmoil as such, "heat therapy" should be used.

Sr. Genevieve recalled:

At the beginning of her life as Novice Mistress, our dear little Sister used to strive to put an end to our interior conflicts either by reasoning with us or by trying to convince us in our little difficulties in the novitiate that our companions were not at fault. She soon realized that this method only served to open up long useless discussions, with no profit whatsoever to our souls, so she adopted another means. Instead of trying to close the issue by denying that there was any cause for complaint, she would urge us rather to face reality. Let me illustrate the point by an example.

If one of the novices had failed in her appointed duty and had, as a result, inconvenienced the rest of us in the novitiate, I might go to Thérèse at the end of the week with a complaint like this: "Here it is Saturday and, evidently, Sister X has not given a thought to her weekly assignment. This annoys me for you know how conscientious I am whenever this duty falls to me in the novitiate!"

Thérèse would then seem to become interested. Without minimizing the frustrating side of the situation (and apparently with no desire to make me ashamed of myself for complaining) she would invite me to examine the details at closer range. "Suppose," the Saint would say, "that your companion is as blameworthy as you believe her to be..." and so on.[308]

---

[308] MSST 18.

Initially, Thérèse encouraged the novices to master any temptation to impatience right away by an immediate and vigorous condemnation of its cause: "Why get upset? It's foolish. There is no reason to let myself get into such a state!" In other words, when Thérèse hadn't yet perfected her pedagogy, she thought that sometimes people could overcome a temptation to impatience by a simple "rational argument." As her job continued, she eventually understood that "a very little soul" shouldn't always try to rise above things by reasoning. Instead, a little soul should be content to *go under* the problem. Thérèse recommended this as the only method, the "heat therapy," whose marvelous effectiveness she had tested.

To make her idea clear, Thérèse reminded Sr. Genevieve of something that happened in their childhood. One day the adults couldn't enter the prefecture of Alençon because there was a horse blocking the entry. One of their friends, aged seven, suggested to them that they should go between the horse's legs. Thérèse concluded:

> That is the advantage of staying small. There are no obstacles
> for little ones; they can slip in unnoticed everywhere. Great
> souls can rise above their trials. They can surmount human
> obstacles, either by reasoning things out or through the
> practice of virtue. But in our case, because we are so little, we
> must never attempt to use such means. Let us, rather, always
> pass under our difficulties. In other words, let us not reason
> too much about our human affairs; we should not consider
> them at very close range.[309]

In other words, instead of wanting to act like a "great soul" capable of instantly controlling the first impulse of emotions, a "very little soul" should humbly recognize that she still lacks this "magnanimity"

---

[309] MSST 37.

and willingly endure the double sacrifice of being wounded by others and not being pleased with herself. "My God, I admit to being upset again by the hurtful behavior of others. Doubtless I am attaching too much importance to this, but for the moment I am offering you the sacrifice for which it provided the occasion."

Sr. Genevieve continues:

It would not be long until I should find myself rejoicing that I had been imposed on, and would even begin to desire that all the Sisters should utterly disregard me and show me no consideration at any time. Neither would the promptings of divine grace cease at that point, for I would soon feel springing up within me very generous desires to be scolded and to bear alone the blame whenever my companions neglected any duty—or even to be reproached for some careless piece of work in which I had had no part whatsoever.

It was by such methods that Thérèse would have me soon established in an attitude of mind that was close to perfection. *Then* (note the importance of this word), this victory assured (that is, when the hot treatment was done, she would proceed to relate in detail the countless acts of hidden virtue which the novice in question had often practiced. A warm admiration would then replace my critical thoughts and I was ready to believe that all the Sisters were far more virtuous than I.[310]

In short, Thérèse had realized that at times when we are feeling impatient, we should first place ourselves in an attitude of complete availability before God and His human instruments, too.

[310] MSST 18.

In order to be prepared for the moment of trial, Thérèse added, we must "soften our heart beforehand."[311] Namely, we should prepare in advance, during prayer, for encounters we are obliged to have with others; we should expect emotional outbursts in advance.

Put on the right glasses

"Everything is grace." Thérèse's faith in the wondrous mystery of Providence allowed her to bear with admirable patience the annoyances and frustrations which inevitably happen in the life of every community. When she was irritated by unkind comments or by the strange behavior of one of her sisters, Thérèse saw her as a *chisel* God was using to give her an opportunity to offer Him a fresh sacrifice and thus, to save sinners. In this way, she completely adopted St. John of the Cross's idea on this topic. In the *Precautions*, the summary of the principles for religious perfection, he states:

> The first precaution is to understand that you have come to the monastery so that all may fashion and try you. Thus, to free yourself from the imperfections and disturbances that can be engendered by the mannerisms or attitudes of the religious and draw profit from every occurrence, you should think that all in the community are artisans—as indeed they are—present there in order to prove you; that some will fashion you with words, others by deeds, and others with thoughts against you; and that in all this you must be submissive as is the statue to the craftsman who molds it, to the artist who paints it, and to the gilder who embellishes it. If you fail to observe this precaution, you will not know how to overcome your sensuality and feelings, nor will you get along

[311] MSST 109.

well in the community with the religious or attain holy peace or free yourself from many stumbling blocks and evils.[312]

The language here is similar to what Thérèse used. To remain patient when we are still smarting from a wound received, we must not assume the role of a "justice of the peace," attempting to evaluate the guilt of the person who inflicted it. No one is the judge of his own case.[313] At such times, we should see that person simply as an *instrument of providence, whose presence God is permitting* on our journey to give us the opportunity to offer Him a new sacrifice.

Indeed, Thérèse was deeply convinced that "everything works together for the good of those who love God."[314] If God was allowing the presence of bothersome people in her life, she should profit by this, by offering the Lord another smile, even if she wanted to lose her temper. The Lord would receive that smile with joy and He would use it for the conversion of sinners. The lucidity of Thérèse's faith explains the perfection of her patience. Here are some examples to help us learn how to follow in her footsteps.

Consider Thérèse: "Pinpricks"

In Thérèse's day, there was a clear distinction in the community between "choir nuns" and "converse sisters." Dispensed from participating in the majority of the Office, the converse sisters undertook all the heavy work in the monastery. This division of labor sometimes caused strain. The converse sisters, who kept the novices' white veil for their

---

[312] St. John of the Cross, *Collected Works*, rev. ed., trans. Kieran Kavanaugh, OCD and Ottilio Rodriguez, OCD (Washington, DC: ICS Publications, 1991), 724. See also TLMT 27. This work was written for the Carmelites of Beas and later spread to the other Carmels.
[313] See MSST 82.
[314] Rm 8:28.

whole life—hence the name of "white veils"—sometimes reminded others sharply of the immense value of their labor. This happened especially when they had the impression of being treated as second class nuns at community recreation, or of not having the same right to speak as the others. They sometimes also took revenge by means of sour comments addressed to a choir sister. From the time of her entrance into Carmel, Thérèse had been forced to endure these more than once. Two converse sisters had targeted her.

Having entered the convent a few months before Thérèse, on December 23, 1887, Sr. Martha of Jesus sometimes spoke unkindly to her postulant companion. All things considered these remarks were nothing more than an expression of a certain envy. Out of politeness Thérèse often sat next to her in recreation; she endured her unpleasant teasing silently.

However, it was another older converse sister, Sr. St. Vincent de Paul, who particularly tried Thérèse's patience by making her feel she was just a *petite bourgeoise* incapable of performing as well as she could. Raised by the Sisters of St. Vincent de Paul, this orphaned girl had learned as a young child both sewing and all sorts of manual labor. Thérèse bore all the verbal barbs this nun aimed at her without a word, because she kept her focus on Jesus' hand; He was permitting those "pinpricks." In her unwavering faith, she went so far as to grasp that it was Jesus Himself who was pricking his "little ball" through this intermediary. In a letter to Sr. Agnes in January 1889, during her retreat in preparation for receiving the habit, she wrote:

> Ask Jesus to make me generous during my retreat. He is riddling me with pinpricks; the poor little ball is exhausted... Nothing near Jesus. Aridity!...Sleep! But at least there is silence!...Silence does good to the soul...But creatures! oh!

creatures!...The little ball shudders from them!...Understand
Jesus' little toy!...When it is the sweet Friend who punctures
His ball Himself, suffering is only sweetness, His hand is
so gentle!...But creatures!...Those who surround me are very
good, but there is something, I don't know what, that repels
me!...I cannot give you any explanation. Understand your
little soul. I am, however, very happy, happy to suffer what
Jesus wants me to suffer. If He doesn't directly puncture
His little ball, it is really He who directs the hand that
punctures it![315]

Uncle Guérin's decision

In September 1890, Thérèse was hoping that her father, whose health
had been improving, could come to give her his blessing on the day
she took the veil. This seemed possible but, at the last moment, her
uncle Guérin deemed that the ceremony would be too emotional for
his brother-in-law, and opposed his attendance. Thérèse was deeply
affected by this; she wept a great deal and this was all the more surprising given that on the day of her profession, three weeks beforehand,
she hadn't appeared saddened by her father's absence.

Still, the circumstances weren't the same. There had been no
question of Mr. Martin coming to the Carmel for his daughter's
profession, whereas Thérèse had been expecting his coming for her
reception of the veil. On September 23 she felt "disappointment."
Furthermore, on the day she made her vows it was her father's illness
which prevented his coming. Now, it was due to her uncle's decision.
It's much easier to recognize God's will in an illness than in someone's
choice. However, the young nun of seventeen immediately spotted
the Lord's hand in the trial: "It is Jesus alone who is conducting

this affair, it is He, and I recognized His touch of love...but it's not a human hand that has done this, it's Jesus. It is His veiled look that has fallen upon us!..."[316]

So, amid her tears Thérèse saw behind her uncle's "human prudence" her Lord's "divine hand." This prudence, which she regarded as overdone, was, in the end, only a "docile instrument" in the divine artist's hands. He chooses to form souls in this way to make them more beautiful and more fruitful.

As we can see from this last example, the faith that helps us conquer temptations to anger and impatience doesn't prevent our emotions from being stirred up. A bout of tears or an inner feeling of irritation are entirely compatible with a total victory over the temptation to yield to resentment against the person who caused our annoyance. Far from being imperfections in the moral sense, such emotional reactions are weaknesses, about which the apostle Paul "boasted."[317] According to Thérèse, they are also the occasion for experiencing our spiritual poverty and placing ourselves absolutely in Jesus' hands; He is, following the vivid words of Psalm 46, "our refuge, our shield, our fortress in the time of danger."

Accordingly, at the instant we feel the first movement of irritation rising in our souls, the only thing the Lord asks of us is to take refuge in Him, just as we are, that is, with all our emotions, and say to Him with childlike simplicity, "Lord, you see how weak I still am! Here I am again, totally upset because of someone's comment to me, or because of someone's attitude toward me. However, I don't want to see in these anything but your loving hand which, by this means, is giving me the occasion to offer you a new sacrifice. I offer it to you gladly, Lord, for the benefit of the whole Church."

[316] LT 120; see also A 75v.
[317] Cor 12:10.

Fr. Pichon's ploy

This availability with respect to God and His instruments must not deteriorate into passive resignation in the face of events. St. Thérèse knew this. It's clear from her reaction to a stratagem by Fr. Pichon, her own spiritual director. Fr. Pichon had proposed that Céline join him as a missionary in Canada when Louis Martin died. Since there were already three Martin girls in the Lisieux Carmel, and the constitutions stipulated that there should be no more than two sisters of the same family admitted to the community, he thought Céline wouldn't be able to benefit from another "bending of the rules" to join her sisters in Carmel, as Thérèse had. Céline should come to Canada, then! She could found a kind of secular institute there (before the term existed). However, he wrote to her, in order to avoid spoiling the plan she shouldn't say a word about it to her Carmelite sisters.

After Mr. Martin's death (July 29, 1894), Céline had to reveal Fr. Pichon's project to her sisters. They were unable to hide their astonishment. Thérèse wrote to her sister: "I am heavy at heart!..." And said she would do everything in her power to see that her sister didn't leave for Canada: her place was in the Carmel of Lisieux.

However, again Thérèse saw this trial as coming from God's hand also and she also asked her sister to view it in the same way: "But I thank God for this trial which He Himself has willed, I am sure...If you were to hear Sister Marie of the Sacred Heart, I assure you she would astound you!...She does not hesitate to say that her beloved Father is mistaken...But he was only the docile instrument of Jesus, so little Thérèse is not vexed with him!..."[318] And this was certainly the reason she didn't get angry with her spiritual father. She didn't examine the motives which might have inspired him; she saw him only as "Jesus' docile instrument." The lucidity of her faith

---

[318] LT 168.

once again explains the perfection of her patience. Along with the Lord making use of Mr. Guérin's prudence, in 1890, to purify her filial affection and attach her more firmly to her Father in heaven, He now was using Fr. Pichon's maneuver to purify her fraternal affection for Céline.

St. John Vianney: Crosses are always from God

We must not look at where the cross comes from; crosses are always from God. Whether it's a father, a mother, a spouse, a brother, the priest or the assistant pastor, it's always God who is giving us the means to demonstrate our love to Him.[319]

Let's be students of Thérèse

Thérèse could encourage her novices to practice patience: she practiced what she preached. And the novices were amazed at the joy with which their young Mistress accepted the humiliations they caused her: "With a simplicity which delights me, they tell me all the struggles I give them, what displeases them in me; finally, they are under no restraint any more than if they were talking about another person, for they know they give me pleasure when acting in this way."[320] In order to spur her novices to be patient, Thérèse reiterated to them the same truth constantly: regard those who are wounding you as *God's instruments*. Allow yourself to be humiliated! It's God Himself who is forming you. For example, she told Sr. Genevieve: "Whenever you

[319] John Vianney, *Le curé d'Ars: sermons et catechisms*, manuscript compilation of Faure de la Bastie, Parish Archives of Ars, 151.
[320] C 27r.

are annoyed with a nun, the best way to regain your peace is to pray for her and beg God to reward her for making you suffer."[321]

The use of this tactic is especially helpful when we are unjustly accused and want to clear ourselves from guilt immediately and definitively! At such a time, it would be useless to attempt to seek the attenuating circumstances excusing a rash judgement. The simplest thing to do is to accept this new occasion for sacrifice in silence and with a smile. In other words, instead of immediately asking us to demonstrate our forbearance toward the person who has offended us, Thérèse invites us first to make an act of abandonment into the Lord's hands. He never ceases to surround us with His love, even if at times, that love uses our neighbor to crucify us.

Someone might object: "But, in offering ourselves like this to the action of God's chisel, don't we fall into a pathetic *passivity*? In this way don't we become the plaything of the evil one?" To be sure, our patience must be accompanied by a courageous attitude and a brave fighting spirit when faced with human wickedness and injustice. Without this battle, our patience wouldn't be truly Christian, conformed to Jesus Christ's, but passive submission before evil. Before letting Himself be led to Calvary, Jesus contended with the sin of mankind. He condemned it to the point of dying from it. Following His example, a Christian has to be a fighter, a warrior. He must fight against evil in every form, in himself and in others.

St. Thérèse did this. We know the perseverance with which, during her short life, she performed the duty of fraternal correction, with regard to her novices and even senior nuns. She wasn't afraid to do battle. There was even one situation in which she publicly took a stand against Mother Marie de Gonzague. This happened when Mother Marie, in charge of the novitiate at the time, wanted

---

[321] MSST 109.

to postpone improperly Sr. Genevieve's profession so that she could receive her vows herself, until when she would be prioress again—as she expected! In the course of a conversation on the subject Sr. Aimée de Jesus remarked that the novice mistress did actually have the right to test Sr. Genevieve. Thérèse intervened firmly, knowing full well that her comment would be repeated "in high places." She said: "There are some kinds of tests which should not be given."[322] The patience with which Thérèse accepted "pinpricks" or humiliations didn't prevent her from being firm when it was necessary.

In addition, we should observe how evangelical patience proves helpful in the fight against evil, since, in order to obtain a change in others' conduct "honey is more effective than vinegar." Thérèse knew this: she never made a remark to others that was inspired by self-love, because she was aware that it would do no good. What we say only bears fruit on the condition that the words aren't inspired by resentment. Gentleness isn't only pleasing to God, it is an extremely effective weapon in our battle against evil, a sure means of bringing more love into the world.

We can conclude, then, that the Gospel doesn't operate in us like an opiate that produces sleepiness, by soothing the irritations we experience so frequently when we come into contact with our neighbor. Instead, it grants the certainty that God only allows their presence in our lives to give us the occasion to offer Him a fresh sacrifice—a sacrifice whose fruitfulness infinitely surpasses everything we can imagine. This certainty will produce in the depth of our souls a peace and serenity similar to that of the saints, a serenity which often glowed on their faces.

[322] PO, Sr. Aimée de Jésus, 573.

12

Inconvenient Interruptions
Other people make me waste time

"I don't know if I have been able to write ten lines without being disturbed; this should not make me laugh nor amuse me; however, for the love of God and my Sisters (so charitable toward me) I take care to appear happy and especially to be so."[323]

As long as we prefer giving time to activities we have planned in advance and which we like, we will find it painful to let ourselves be disturbed by people who come unexpectedly, upsetting our schedule by asking us to do something or listen to something which doesn't seem completely necessary. Even if we welcome them with a smile, out of courtesy, we often fret and fume inwardly at being forced to waste time we'd choose to devote to something else. In short, we interrupt our work, reading, or conversations, without any enthusiasm to respond to the call directed to us in these situations.

Thérèse faced this problem frequently. When she was busy working—Carmelites aren't always in the chapel, but they always have

---

[323] C 17v.

work to do—people came unexpectedly to ask for a favor.[324] And because she often said yes with a genuine smile, she had many requests. Let's try to discover the secret of the joy with which Thérèse made herself available to her sisters, so that we can give our time *willingly* and happily in our turn.

Thérèse's availability

Raised in a family which always employed a maid, in childhood Thérèse was accustomed to being cared for, especially since she was the youngest and her older sisters enjoyed serving her. Referring to her 13th year, she wrote: "Being the youngest in the family, I wasn't accustomed to doing things for myself. Céline tidied up the room in which we slept, and I myself didn't do any housework whatsoever."[325] Today many girls perform more household tasks than Thérèse did at age thirteen. However, this was typical in the bourgeois milieu of her day. Conversely, there were many other occasions to show her courtesy: for example, she devoted herself to entertaining Marie Guérin, who frequently suffered from migraines. In October 1886, freed from scrupulosity, Thérèse opened up to others. She set to work helping out at home. In addition, Marie's departure for Carmel required her to take a larger share of the domestic duties. By freeing

---

[324] Thérèse had read in her *Manual for Spiritual Direction* that a Carmelite must always be ready to render services to whoever asked: "The remainder of the time, from the end of Compline until Matins, one has the freedom to use as one wishes, according to each one's needs and devotions. If one has not said one's rosary, this would be a good time to say it. However, in this period, as in any other, if someone wants something particular of you, you should give it to them. Always prefer charity and renunciation of self to every personal devotion; a soul which desires perfection must not be possessive about anything, not even a single minute" (p. 73).

[325] A 44v.

her from herself, the grace of Christmas 1886 allowed her to give herself to others; she felt the need to forget herself so that she could make others happy.[326]

However, it was in the convent that her readiness to serve was fully demonstrated. From the beginning of her postulancy, what surprised the community was not her recollection and piety, but her willingness to serve. She tried to render every possible service. As a novice, she volunteered to lead Sr. St. Pierre to the refectory (an infirm nun who wasn't easy to satisfy), and succeeded in getting her to be friendly through her genuine smile. This didn't stop her from later admitting that this service had cost her a great deal.[327]

At the beginning of 1890 she learned she had to wait several months before sending her request for profession to the superior of the Carmel. At first, she was perturbed by the delay imposed on her. Then she understood that she should benefit by it to prepare for her vows more thoroughly. "I applied myself to practicing little virtues, not having the capability of practicing the great. For instance, I loved to fold up the mantles forgotten by the Sisters, and to render them all sorts of little services."[328]

Through her deepening understanding of the requirements of the Gospel commandment of brotherly love, Thérèse realized what the full extent of her availability to others should be. Above all, she *understood that she must not have a possessive attitude about time.* Her free time belonged to her sisters as much as to herself. Consequently, she had to consider the possibility of being disturbed as normal. This is *the source of her fully sincere smile;* it lit up her face when someone came to ask for another favor out of the blue.

---

[326] A 45v.
[327] C 29r.
[328] A 74v.

Thérèse commented that it was easier to offer her services of her own accord than to agree to grant them to those who don't ask very politely.

> Here is what Jesus teaches me also: "Give to EVERYONE who asks of you, and from HIM WHO TAKES AWAY your goods, ask no return." Giving to all those who ask is less sweet than offering oneself by the movement of one's own heart; again, when they ask for something politely, it doesn't cost so much to give, but if, unfortunately, they don't use very delicate words, the soul is immediately up in arms if she is not well founded in charity.[329]

Thérèse also observed that when we agree to perform a service it's very tempting to make the person asking feel that we are doing them a big favor by granting their request. She described this in a funny passage. The person then finds "a thousand reasons to refuse what is asked of her, and it is only after having convinced the asker of her tactlessness that she will finally give what is asked, and then only as a favor; or else she will render a light service which could have been done in one-twentieth of the time that was spent in setting forth her imaginary rights."[330]

St. Thérèse had many opportunities to demonstrate her readiness to serve. Almost all of her poems were written to please her sisters: she dedicated all of her leisure time to this.[331] She agreed to make her personal retreat at the same time as Sr. Martha, her older companion in the novitiate, so that the latter could spend an hour with her each day.[332]

[329] C 15v-16r.
[330] C 15 v–16r.
[331] See MSST 78.
[332] PA 177.

At the beginning of 1896, when she was relieved of her duties at the turn and painting to go back to the sacristy, she arranged to go there through the passage where her original task was happening so that the nun there could ask for any favor. This was a true "refinement" of availability.[333] Mother Agnes stated: "It was her habit never to appear in a hurry so that the sisters would be entirely free to ask for her services and so that she would always have the opportunity to follow Our Lord's advice, about which she wrote in her manuscript: 'Do not avoid anyone who wants to borrow from you.'"[334] In brief, Thérèse was expecting to be disturbed all the time.

She gave this advice to Sr. Genevieve:

> It looks as though you are going into solitude (they had a monthly day of recollection) for your own gratification, and to give an extra little present to self. It should be the other way around. I take my day of retreat each month in a spirit of fidelity to grace and in order to give more to God...If, for example, I have a fair amount of writing planned for that day, I am careful to keep my heart detached, and I reason along these lines: "I am putting such an hour aside for this task, but in anticipation, I offer up that hour to you, my God. It will probably be punctured by many unforeseen interruptions and disturbances which usually come my way, so even now I enter heart and soul into your plan for me...and if it should turn out that I am left at peace, I shall thank you, my God, for such an unexpected favor." In this way, nothing surprises me and I am always happy.[335]

[333] MSST 81.
[334] PA 173–174.
[335] MSST 81.

It was by pondering the Gospels that Thérèse succeeded in adopting an attitude of total availability toward her sisters at the end of her life. For instance, here is the conclusion she drew from Jesus' words, "If anyone would sue you and take your coat, let him have your cloak as well."[336]

> To give up one's cloak is, it seems to me, renouncing one's ultimate rights; it is considering oneself as the servant and the slave of others. When one has left his cloak, it is much easier to walk, to run, and Jesus adds: "And whoever forces you to go one mile, go two more with him." Thus, it is not enough to give to everyone who asks; I must even anticipate their desires, appear to be very much obliged and honored to render service.[337]

"Consider yourself the servant, the slave of others." This was the advice Thérèse one day gave to Sr. Genevieve to encourage her to respond right away to the requests of sick sisters, which could be unpredictable. "Whenever your bell is rung or when you are called to perform some disagreeable task for the sick, you should consider yourself a *little slave* whom everybody has the right to order about. A little slave, you see, because one who is a slave never thinks she has any right to complain."[338] A slave considers all the services requested of him as completely normal. *It's not enough, then, merely to appear happy to be disturbed, it must be genuine, from the heart.*

---

[336] Mt 5:40.
[337] C 16v–17r.
[338] MSST 84.

ST. VINCENT DE PAUL:
DO WHATEVER CHARITY REQUIRES

It is our duty to prefer the service of the poor to everything else and to offer such service as quickly as possible. If a needy person requires medicine or other help during prayer time, do whatever has to be done with peace of mind. Offer the deed to God as your prayer. Do not become upset or feel guilty because you interrupted your prayer to serve the poor. God is not neglected if you leave him for such service. One of God's works is merely interrupted so that another can be carried out. So, when you leave prayer to serve some poor person, remember that this very service is performed for God. Charity is certainly greater than any rule. Moreover, all rules must lead to charity. Since she is a noble mistress, we must do whatever she commands.

With renewed devotion, then, we must serve the poor, especially outcasts and beggars. They have been given to us as our masters and patrons, and we are unworthy to render them our small services.[339]

Two weeks before her death, Thérèse told her sister she had achieved such an attitude of availability that she no longer had to make much effort not to feel annoyed when someone knocked at her cell door. "I have done this all my religious life, but at the beginning, *my house* was not *fully at peace*."[340]

---

[339] St Vincent de Paul, *Conversation with the Daughters of Charity*, in *Office of Readings for the Divine Office*, English translation by ICEL, (Boston: St. Paul Editions, 1983), September 27.

[340] MSST 236, referring to St. John of the Cross, Canticles 1 & 2.

Thérèse had practiced this in the preceding month, on her sick-bed. She was preparing her last manuscript and the good sisters of the community, intending to please her, continually came for little chats with her.[341] This was when she said to Mother Agnes, "I am writing about fraternal charity, but one must practice it! Oh Mother, on earth fraternal charity is everything! We love God to the extent that we practice it."[342]

Availability for others and managing time

To benefit from Thérèse's example, we should first keep in mind that we shouldn't waste time—those precious minutes God grants us each day as a magnificent gift. So, the duty of being available for others should not make us forget the equally important duty of using our time well. We shouldn't waste it in vain curiosity, worldly chatter, and *a fortiori* not in gossip. St. Thérèse was serious about devoting herself to her work while avoiding all idle conversation. She also knew that sometimes we have to refuse doing a favor when asked if the duties of our state in life require us to be elsewhere. However, we should explain this with the greatest kindness. She says, "There is such a delightful way of refusing what cannot be given that the refusal gives as much pleasure as the gift itself."[343]

A great disciple of Thérèse, Marthe Robin did this with great courtesy, when she received guests at the farm of Chateauneuf-de-Galaure. Visitors came from quite a distance to meet her. When welcoming three priests from my diocese, she understood immediately that they didn't need counsel from her and that she shouldn't keep them long. She simply said to them with conviction, "You are priests! Oh, then

---

[341] C 17v.
[342] PA, 194.
[343] C 18r.

be men of faith, men of prayer, men of the Church! Thank you for having come to see me." They never forgot this advice, and it was a very thoughtful way of taking leave of them. This is what the saints do: in order to grant time to people truly in need, they are often obliged to shorten their meetings with others…whom they like just as much!

All the same, to succeed in practicing the availability for others Thérèse attained at the end of her life, we first have to be convinced that a day well spent isn't necessarily one when we were able to do all the tasks we promised ourselves we'd finish. Instead, it's a day when we have succeeded in answering "Here I am" to all the Lord's calls, wherever they came from. A day's success isn't measured by the number of problems we were able to solve, the number of people we contacted, the number of messages we sent, but by *the love with which we did these tasks,* whether they were planned beforehand or imposed at the last minute, and so caused complications in our agenda. In truth, what counts is love.[344]

Thérèse reminded Sr. Genevieve of this two weeks before her death, having had the joy of responding immediately to someone's request for a favor: "Oh, if you only knew!…" she said. "At the moment of death, you will find this before you…This is a more glorious act than if by some skillful measures you had obtained the good will of the government for religious communities, and for ours in particular, and all France hailed you as a second Judith!"[345]

In other words, what often prevents us from being available to others is exactly the same fault as that which prevents us from being faithful to our prayer times: we want to fill our lives with many accomplishments,

[344] 1 Cor 13:1–13.
[345] MSST 132.

forgetting that it's essential to fulfill them with great love. Yes, we have used the minutes of our day perfectly when we put a lot of love into them.

The Cistercian Abbot De Rancé[346] told his monks in the 17th century: we must regularly practice the art of being "disoccupied." That is, while being conscientiously busy with what we must do, we should continually detach ourselves enough from it so that we don't turn the work of our hands into an idol—a reproach frequently in the mouths of Old Testament prophets.[347] Fr. Teilhard de Chardin said quite rightly that with regard to our work we should have a "passionate indifference."[348] And Thérèse told her sister that she ought to be disinterested about her work "in order to use the time prescribed for it with detachment of heart."[349]

Embracing the correct detachment vis-à-vis our work makes it possible for us to stop fretting and fuming when someone unexpectedly asks for a favor which costs us. And, if we remember that it is Jesus Himself that we are going to serve, that it is Him we are pleasing, we can switch our task with genuine joy and put on servant's garb as we would put on party clothes.

---

[346] Having spent his youth badly, Arnaud Jean Le Bouthillier de Rancé (1626–1700) converted and reformed the abbey of La Trappe, of which he was the abbot. The Cistercian abbeys that adopted this reform were called "Trappes," the monks "Trappists," and the nuns "Trappistines."

[347] See Is 2:8, Jer 44:8.

[348] At the very beginning of his *Spiritual Exercises*, St. Ignatius of Loyola asks his retreatants to place themselves in a *holy indifference* with respect to all created goods. God alone must be the object of our search. Without denying the value of this indifference, Teilhard de Chardin observes correctly that we likewise have the right and the duty to be passionate about the work God has asked us to accomplish on earth.

[349] MSST 65.

TO PLEASE THE LORD WE DON'T HAVE TO FINISH MANY TASKS

One day Jesus said to Br. Marcel Van: "Marcel, when you are working, you don't have to get a lot of work done; it's enough to do a few things, as your sister Thérèse advised you before: *'Even if in the course of a whole day you only managed to clean a single chair, you shouldn't be upset by it.'* It's not the quantity of work that pleases Me; Thérèse already told you that and you have forgotten it. I am reminding you: your duty is to love and work. To work out of love for Me."[350]

---

[350] Marcel Van, *Colloques* (Paris: Editions St. Paul, 2001), 117.

13

Hardness of Heart
I don't love enough

*"Yes, I feel it, when I am charitable, it is
Jesus alone who is acting in me."*[351]

At age eighteen people sing, "It's wonderful to love!" but twenty years later people often say that it's hard to love. And when you are a saint and coming to the end of your life, you recognize in all humility that you still have a lot of progress to make before you can say truly that you love your neighbor as you should. This is hard!

Accept that we need to improve

Thérèse had this experience at the end of her short life. Despite the exceptional generosity with which she had chosen to refuse God nothing, starting in childhood, she realized during her last months that she still didn't love her sisters in the way the Lord wished. The community situation at that time required Thérèse to open her eyes to the progress she still needed to make to love all her sisters genuinely. On March 21, 1896 Marie de Gonzague again became prioress

[351] C 12v.

of the Lisieux Carmel. Instead of giving the responsibility for the novices to Mother Agnes, Thérèse's sister, whom she had just "beat" in the election, she kept the official post and asked Thérèse to act as novice mistress. Thérèse was then busy with the novices much more than under Mother Agnes' priorate. Several times per week she gave them lessons on Carmelite spirituality and met with them regularly to discuss their spiritual lives. She assumed this important responsibility tactfully in order to avoid injuring the Prioress' feelings.

She was also asked to continue sacristy work under her former novice mistress, and continue painting. Since no one wanted to take over her work in the laundry and be subjected to the moods of Sr. Marie de St. Joseph, Thérèse willingly agreed to do it. She knew quite well what she would have to endure. However, what she didn't know was the fantastic progress the Lord would grant her via that relationship. Through the fourteen months she spent with her in the laundry, Thérèse grasped the requirements of fraternal charity in a new way. Further, when Mother Marie de Gonzague asked her, on Mother Agnes' suggestion, to return to writing about her life, Thérèse told her sister, "I am going to talk about fraternal charity. Oh! I must, because I have received such great lights on that subject; I don't want to keep them to myself. I assure you that charity is not understood on earth and nonetheless, it is the principal virtue."[352]

Meditation on the Gospel

It was by reading the Gospel that Thérèse discovered little by little the demands of fraternal charity, as explained in the Sermon on the Mount. First, Thérèse was struck by *the importance* Jesus gave to the second commandment. He says that it is *like* the first. If it's like it, she thought, it's because we should put as much zeal into loving our

---

[352] PA 173, Mother Agnes.

neighbor as into loving God. All the efforts we make to serve Him are as pleasing to God as the acts of love and adoration we address directly to Him.

Thanks to meditating on the Gospel, Thérèse also discovered *all the essential elements of authentic fraternal charity*. Like Jesus' love, it must be full of mercy for the poor sinners God places in our path. "It's necessary for love to lower itself": we mustn't hesitate to join our brethren in their misery, not for the sake of staying there, but to lift them up and help them grow.

We shouldn't hesitate to show our love to them. Thérèse wrote, "I understood above all that charity must not remain hidden in the bottom of the heart. Jesus has said: 'No one lights a lamp and puts it under a bushel basket, but upon the lampstand, so as to give light to ALL in the house.' It seems to me that this lamp represents charity which must enlighten and rejoice not only those who are dearest to us but 'ALL who are in the house' without distinction."[353] Thus, it's not enough to love others. They must feel loved, feel themselves surrounded by our fraternal affection, and rejoice in it.

We know how intently Thérèse endeavored to spread joy at the community recreations. She tried to brighten dull faces by transmitting her contagious gaiety. She specifically sat beside Sister Teresa of St. Augustine so that she wouldn't guess her strong antipathy for her. She succeeded so well in this that, for more than thirty years, the nun imagined she had been Thérèse's favorite. It was only a few weeks before her death in 1929 that she realized the heroic acts of patience she had caused the saint to make. (Thérèse had been canonized for four years).

St. Thérèse was so aware that charity "must not remain hidden in the depth of the heart" that at the end of her life she expressed her

---

[353] C12r.

fraternal charity with a tenderness and spontaneity she definitely wouldn't have allowed herself at the start of religious life. Her love had developed such purity that she no longer feared to love her sisters in a way that was "too natural." As an illustration, here is a personal memory from Marie of the Trinity.

> The news of the health of our saintly invalid was increasingly sad and I was suffering great grief. One afternoon, I went into the garden and there I saw her in her little wheelchair, under the chestnut trees. She was alone and signaled that I should come over to her. I told her, "No. We will be seen and I do not have permission to speak to you." I went into the hermitage of the Holy Face near where she was, and began to cry, with my head in my hands. Raising my head, I saw with surprise that she was seated on the trunk of a tree, next to me. She said to me, "No one has forbidden me to come to you; even if it kills me, I want to console you." She wiped away my tears and put my head on her heart. I begged her to return to her chair for I saw that she was trembling with fever. "Yes, but not until you smile at me." I obeyed immediately, fearing that she would come to harm, and helped her back into her chair.[354]

Thérèse's heart was so fixed on God that she no longer feared showing all her affection to those she loved. More than ever, she felt that the love she inspired in her sisters' hearts went straight to God. She explained this one day to Sr. Marie of the Trinity, who feared she might love her novice mistress too much. On the back of an image that Thérèse gave her for her reception of the veil (May 1896), she wrote this thought from St. John of the Cross: "When the love we

---

[354] Circular, 15–16. See TLMT, 36–37.

have for a person is completely spiritual and founded on God alone, as it increases, love of God increases also in our soul; then as often as the heart remembers its neighbor, the more it also remembers God and desires Him, with these two loves growing again and again."[355]

By the same token, it's in the light of this third discovery that we should read all the testimonies about the saint's *cheerfulness* during her last illness. Her good cheer was the expression of her love for God and her perfect resignation to the divine will, but it was *also the manifestation of her desire to console* her friends, saddened by her sufferings and the prospect of separation.

Despite this, we should remember that Thérèse had to insist on much self-sacrifice before she was able to manifest her love with such freedom. It would be contrary to her ideas to encourage anyone to show their affection without any reserve at the first opportunity. Thérèse wrote the following in capital letters:

Love is nourished only by sacrifices, and the more a soul refuses natural satisfactions, the stronger and more disinterested becomes her tenderness...How happy I am now for having deprived myself from the very beginning of my religious life! I already enjoy the reward promised to those who fight courageously. I no longer feel the necessity of refusing all human consolations, for my soul is strengthened by Him whom I wanted to love uniquely. I can see with joy that in loving Him the heart expands and can give to those who are dear to it incomparably more tenderness than if it had concentrated upon one egotistical and unfruitful love.[356]

[355] St. John of the Cross, *Maxims et Avis Spirituels* (Paris: H. Oudin, 1895), vol. 1, 409. See also LT 188.
[356] C 21r–22v; see also A 62r, 70v, C 9r.

St. Benedict Joseph Labré: *Real Love*

True love of God requires three hearts in one: the first must be completely on fire with love for God; the second must be completely flesh for one's neighbor; the third must be completely bronze for oneself.

Ask Jesus to come and love in me

Finally, it was especially in reading the Gospel of John that Thérèse grasped the novelty of what Jesus asked of his disciples on the night of the Last Supper. He commanded them to love one another *as* He loves them. Thérèse affirmed[357]: "But this is impossible! Impossible, unless the will of Jesus is precisely to come to love in us all whom He commands us to love. Yes, I feel it, when I am charitable, it is Jesus

---

[357] In her manuscript, Thérèse quotes the verse from John following the translation in her *Christian's Manual*. However, it wasn't the commentaries of the translator that showed her the path. In fact, here's the way he commented in the notes on the phrase "new commandment": "This commandment is from all time; but Jesus Christ renews it here, and at the same time He commands them to observe it in a special way." Hence, this note orients the reader's mind toward seeing in the commandment of Holy Thursday only a reminder of the commandment relating to love of neighbor—a precept that the Lord has given us "on every page of his Gospel." For the author of the notes in the *Manual*, the "new commandment" isn't very new. Commenting on a verse from the first Epistle of John, he wrote: "This commandment is not new because it is imprinted in the depth of our nature and it is inscribed in the Mosaic law. [...] Though this precept was almost effaced due to men's wickedness, it was renewed and perfected by Jesus Christ and for all these reasons it can be called a *new* commandment, as Jesus Christ himself called it." Therefore, the commentaries Thérèse had available didn't prepare her for observing the novelty of the Gospel command in relation to the Levitical commandment.

alone who is acting in me. The more I am united to Him, the more I love all my sisters."[358]

So, when we feel with Ignatius of Loyola that we are "terribly poor in love," we shouldn't be surprised. We should consider again that without Jesus we can do nothing.[359] It is He "who works in you to will and to act"[360]; it is He who makes the Spirit of Love come into our hearts. Without Him we would be absolutely unable to have authentic charity for our brethren.

It's clear that there is a connection between the institution of the holy Eucharist and the promulgation of the new commandment. If Jesus waited until the evening of the Last Supper to ask His disciples to love each other *as* He loved them, it's because He wanted to show us that we can't begin to follow this command except by allowing a new heart to be grafted onto our own. And this is what happens every time we receive Jesus Christ's Body and Blood in holy communion.

From a Letter of St John Bosco to his confreres: Gentle and humble of heart

First of all, if we wish to appear concerned about the true happiness of our foster children and if we would move them to fulfil their duties, you must never forget that you are taking the place of the parents of these beloved young people. I have always labored lovingly for them, and carried out my priestly duties with zeal. And the whole Salesian society has done this with me.

[358] C 12v.
[359] Jn 15:5.
[360] Phil 2:13.

My sons, in my long experience very often I had to be convinced of this great truth. It is easier to become angry than to restrain oneself, and to threaten a boy than to persuade him. Yes, indeed, it is more fitting to be persistent in punishing our own impatience and pride than to correct the boys. We must be firm but kind, and be patient with them.

I give you as a model the charity of Paul which he showed to his new converts. They often reduced him to tears and entreaties when he found them lacking docility and even opposing his loving efforts.

See that no one finds you motivated by impetuosity or willfulness. It is difficult to keep calm when administering punishment, but this must be done if we are to keep ourselves from showing off our authority or spilling out our anger.

Let us regard those boys over whom we have some authority as our own sons. Let us place ourselves in their service. Let us be ashamed to assume an attitude of superiority. Let us not rule over them except for the purpose of serving them better.

This was the method that Jesus used with the apostles. He put up with their ignorance and roughness and even their infidelity. He treated sinners with a kindness and affection that caused some to be shocked, others to be scandalized, and still others to hope for God's mercy. And so, he bade us to be gentle and humble of heart.

They are our sons, and so in correcting their mistakes we must lay aside all anger and restrain it so firmly that it is extinguished entirely. There must be no hostility in our minds, no contempt in our eyes, no insult on our lips. We must use mercy for the present and have hope for the future, as is fitting for true fathers who are eager for real correction and improvement.

In serious matters it is better to beg God humbly than to send forth a flood of words that will only offend the listeners and have no effect on those who are guilty.[361]

To escape our egotism and experience the joy of loving our neighbor more—loving him in deed and in truth—let's remember that we please the Lord every time we serve others and give them joy. Let's also ask Him with *trustful, persevering, and confident prayer* to fill our hearts with His Spirit so that we can love our brethren as He loves us—with a heart entirely aflame with love. For indeed, "there is more joy in giving than in receiving."[362]

---

[361] *Office of Readings*, 1327–28.
[362] Acts 20:35.

14

Resentment
My judgements are too critical

*"Once I had a little experience which
showed me that we must never judge."*[363]

Frequently, we are forced to admit that we have very severe judge-ments about some of our brethren. "He is incompetent, an ego-tist, a fake, a trickster, a blackguard." We are unhappy about this, since we realize that such harshness is in complete contradiction to Jesus' formal command: "Judge not, that you be not judged."[364] Once more, let's ask Thérèse, as her students, to show us the secret of regarding people mercifully, rather than yielding to bitter feelings about others as we can be tempted to do.

Our view of other people can and must be *clear.* The Lord doesn't ask us to look at the world through rose-colored glasses. The media never stops telling us about terrible crimes committed by others and we are sometimes the witnesses or victims of injustice. Such things provoke feelings of anger.

363 C 13r.
364 Mt 7:1.

As we saw, Thérèse didn't hesitate to denounce publicly at one point the prioress' unacceptable attitude toward Sr. Genevieve (her sister Céline), and she was faithful about speaking the truth to the novices under her guidance. Likewise, she dedicated many pages of her last manuscript to explaining how she performed this duty of fraternal correction. This responsibility cost her a great deal but she applied herself to it strictly, always careful not to act under the influence of bad temper. She would have gladly confirmed the well-known proverb: "A truth which is not charitable always comes from a charity which is not true."

By allowing the Holy Spirit to sweeten and soften her heart, Thérèse found the means to maintain "charitable thoughts" for all her sisters.[365] When she wanted to show how her union with Jesus had deepened her charity, the first example that came to her mind was an instance of favorable judgement about one of her sisters.[366]

As a realist Thérèse understood that if she *must not* judge others it was because she *could not* judge them truly, since God alone sees hearts and minds. For this reason, we cannot know our neighbor's true worth, his real value; it's known by God alone. In Thérèse's school let's learn what we have to do to avoid having our minds plagued by false ideas about others.

We saw earlier in chapter 11 that Thérèse learned to distinguish *two forms of treatment for the temptation to impatience.* As long as we are intensely frustrated about someone's behavior or statements, we shouldn't try to form a favorable judgement about him. It's sufficient—and it's already plenty—to consider him or her as an instrument of providence whose presence God is permitting to give us the opportunity to offer Him a fresh sacrifice.

[365] C 13v.
[366] A 12v.

This is what we called the "heat therapy." It should be used at the beginning of this kind of temptation, when emotions are cut to the quick, for instance, by an unkind remark from someone close to us. *Once the tempest abates,* Thérèse observes, it's possible to consider the event in a more composed fashion and view the person in a different way, namely, the Lord's way. Such "cold therapy" shouldn't be attempted right at the beginning of the problem. It's only later that we can reflect on the various causes which led that person who so irritated us to act or speak as they did. This consideration would have been useless—even impossible—a few days or hours earlier.

Reflection made with a cool head quite often shows that we have been wrong in too quickly criticizing an act as injustice or spite when the real motives for it escaped us. Let's take Thérèse as our guide for enumerating the various unknown factors at work when we think we can judge our neighbor's conduct. By recognizing our ignorance about these we can definitively conquer our bitter feelings, and move from resentment to pardon.

Have a favorable predisposition

We are usually ignorant of the motives for other people's actions. "What appears to me as a fault can very easily be an act of virtue because of [a person's] intention."[367] Thérèse had the painful experience of this one day herself. During one fairly dull recreation the cellarer came to ask for help. Specifically, she wanted a sister to come along as a "third" to lead a worker to the place he would be laboring, so that the nun wouldn't be completely alone with the craftsman (according to the custom of the day, she needed to be accompanied by another nun, who was thus acting as "third"). When asked to do this, Thérèse took off her apron very slowly on purpose to allow someone else to

---

[367] C 13r.

have the pleasure of volunteering for this and so leave the atmosphere of the rather dreary recreation. One of the nuns immediately interpreted Thérèse's slowness as a sign of a lack of willingness to serve. This episode happened in December 1896.

Yes, it can happen that an action done with the best intentions may be misinterpreted by those around us. Schooled by this experience, Thérèse explains that from then on she was quick to attribute good intentions to any nun in the community who appeared to be failing in regard to the Carmelite Rule.

Assume others are making an effort

It's true that others' intentions often seem clear to us and that they aren't always good! In this case, how can we avoid giving in to bitterness and harsh judgements? Thérèse proposes that we assume the existence of other motives, unknown to us, in those we meet every day. For instance, our neighbor's hidden effort to eradicate this or that bad habit. Instead of letting ourselves be absorbed by someone's ongoing failures, we can and we should think about their victories, perhaps gained by resisting temptations of the same kind previously. Who can know the merits they certainly gained in hidden battles against themselves—who, but God alone?

Of course, living in a monastery where everyone is constantly together and the occupants end up understanding each other well, it would be difficult to say when seeing another nun falling into faults which are habitual: "It's a passing weakness." At least perhaps one could make the following reflection: "Who knows if the efforts she has made to correct herself have not been more pleasing to the Lord than certain acts of virtue done by some others publicly?"[368] Thérèse made use of this line of thinking to inwardly excuse one sister. "I tell

---

[368] C 12v.

myself that even if I did see her fall once, she could easily have won a great number of victories which she is hiding through humility."[369]

Search for good qualities

On the other hand, we don't normally pay enough attention to the genuinely good qualities of those around us. We should try to find in others qualities we don't typically perceive and which give them real merit in God's eyes. Thérèse observed to one of her novices that we often let our judgement become obscured by our neighbors' superficial imperfections, their character flaws; in fact, simply by the traits that conflict with our own. We end up forgetting what's essential: the qualities deep within their hearts. One day she told Sr. Genevieve this parable as they were walking in the garden:

> Those pears aren't a bit attractive at present, are they? In the fall, however, when they are stewed and served to us in the refectory, we shall find them to our taste, and it will be hard to connect them with the fruit which we are looking at now. That is a good reminder of the truth that on the Last Day, when we shall all be delivered from our faults and imperfections, those Sisters, whose natural qualities may now be displeasing to us, might appear to us as great saints. And we shall perhaps gaze on them open-mouthed in wonder.[370]

So it was that Thérèse overlooked the grim appearance of Sr. Thérèse of St. Augustine in order to admire God's work in her. Instead of stopping at the exterior of this unpleasant nun, she looked into the inner sanctuary of her soul to admire its beauty and generosity. "Each

---

[369] C 12v–13r.
[370] MSST 83.

time I met her I prayed to God for her, offering Him all her virtues and merits. I felt this was pleasing to Jesus, for there is no artist who doesn't love to receive praise for his works, and Jesus, the Artist of souls, is happy when we don't stop at the exterior, but, penetrating into the inner sanctuary where He chooses to dwell, we admire its beauty."[371]

Thérèse adopted the same attitude when another nun's defects surfaced in her mind: "When especially the devil tries to place before the eyes of my soul the faults of such and such a Sister who is less attractive to me, I hasten to search out her virtues, her good intentions."[372]

We should pay close attention to the last part of that sentence. Thérèse hurried to find the other person's virtues. Faced with all the defects of others, her approach wasn't merely abstention: "I reserve judgement, I refrain from judging because I don't know the whole story." It wasn't even a simple favorable prejudice: there must be good in the other's action. Instead, Thérèse *searched* for her sisters' good qualities and loved them for those qualities.

Do we need to add that this way of behaving isn't contrary either to the spirit or letter of the Lord's precept: "Judge not, that you be not judged. For with the judgment you pronounce you will be judged, and the measure you give will be the measure you get."[373] While the first part of this obliges *us not to condemn others*, so that we are not condemned by the Lord, the second part invites us to *judge favorably* so that we will be judged with mercy also.

---

[371] C 14r.

[372] C 12v. In French the phrase is *good desires*, i.e., *desires to do the right thing*, which, united with an awareness of one's personal weakness, is very pleasing to the Lord; it is "this dog of good will" that the devils can't endure. (See MSST 24 and Chapter 5.)

[373] Mt 7:1–2.

Plead extenuating circumstances

Thérèse recommends, too, that in each case we think about the extenuating circumstances which often excuse our neighbors' defects. She invites us not to forget all the graces we have received and stick to the following line of reasoning: if that person had received half the graces of light and strength I have, what would they have become? Surely, much better than I am! If we had lived in the family milieu in which they were raised for their entire youth, or if we had inherited their temperament—would we be better than they are?

When Céline entered the Carmelite convent, Thérèse taught her that illness or moral suffering can weaken a person so much that the smallest good action might be heroic and basically redeem other actions which seem to others to be negligence.

> Thérèse frequently urged us to practice great charity in judging others, for, as she used to point out to us, that which seems to be a fault in another is often an act of heroism in the sight of God. The unfinished task of a nun who may be over-tired or suffering interiorly, she told us, often brings more glory to God than a duty meticulously completed by another nun robust of soul and body. In other words, it is effort and not success that counts most with God. We should judge our neighbor favorably in every circumstance, therefore, and make it become a habit of our lives to overlook his faults.[374]

Thérèse added that the faults of those around us may also be due to a lack of understanding or a mistake in judgement. The Saint concluded: "And if, in a given case, we cannot ascribe a charitable motive, we can always have recourse to an interpretation like this: Although Sister

---

[374] MSST 81.

X is obviously at fault, evidently she is not conscious of it. If I, on the other hand, have clearer light in the present case, all the more reason why I should use much care in judging her mercifully and myself more severely for my inclination to blame her."[375]

If Thérèse endured so patiently the rude comments of certain nuns in the monastery, it wasn't only because she considered them as occasions for sacrifice. She sincerely excused the sources of the "pinpricks." For example, she realized that the nervous condition of Sr. Marie de St. Joseph explained her unpleasant moods. Far from judging her harshly, Thérèse unequivocally pitied her. "Ah, if you knew how you must pardon her; how worthy she is of pity. It is not her fault if she is not very nice. She is like a poor clock which must be wound every quarter of an hour."[376]

ST. FRANCIS OF ASSISI ON DETRACTION

"All the brothers, both those in authority and subjects, will take care never to become upset or irritated because of the sin or bad example of others: for the devil seeks to corrupt many brothers through the sin of one."

St. Francis here notes that in judging one of their own severely, the members of a community risk falling into a graver sin than that of the person they are condemning. The sinner in a community is in some way like a small fish Satan is using as bait to catch the large fish in the community. Francis was very strict about the sin of detraction.

---

[375] MSST 82.
[376] PO 247, Sr. Marie du Sacre Coeur.

Hope against hope

Ultimately, we are ignorant about what God will make of our brethren, and we hope that in His mercy He will cause them to attain holiness. This is the fundamental reason which finally prevents us from ever condemning anyone.

Here, we come to Thérèse's most profound response to her neighbor's faults. If she didn't condemn sinners, it wasn't so much because she considered their past to find extenuating circumstances, it was especially because she was thinking about God's Heart: *He is always ready to pardon* His children's faults and misdeeds. *Her mercy was a participation in God's merciful justice* which takes into account our weakness and smallest efforts when judging us.[377] It was also, and primarily, a participation in the divine longanimity which doesn't tire of waiting for a sinner's conversion and is never annoyed by its slowness.

Thérèse knew that in God's eyes a single day is as a thousand years and therefore He can prepare souls to appear before Him in an instant.[378] She didn't forget that on Christmas Eve 1886 Jesus had done "in an instant" in her soul the work she herself was unable to achieve in ten years. No human being is finished on earth. Therefore, without being blind to someone's repeated faults, we should endure them patiently by pondering, in joy and hope, what God can do with them in the future.

---

[377] "What a sweet joy it is to think that God is *just*, i.e., that He takes into account our weakness, that He is perfectly aware of our fragile nature" (A 83v). "I expect as much from God's justice as from His mercy. It is because He is just that 'He is compassionate and filled with gentleness, slow to punish, and abundant in mercy, for He knows our frailty, He remembers we are only dust'" (LT 226). Recognizing our neighbors' hidden merits or extenuating circumstances is simply justice. This "recognition" is an act of justice inspired by charity.

[378] See Prayer 6.

Thérèse also thought frequently about the Lord's patience with her. She loved Psalm 102, and this isn't surprising if we think of it as a hymn to divine mercy. She quoted it more than once and she especially liked verse 8: "The Lord is merciful and gracious, slow to anger and abounding in steadfast love." In the Bible this phrase "slow to anger" indicates God's patience. Certainly, Thérèse wasn't a great sinner; the Lord didn't have to wait a long time for her conversion, as He waited for the deathbed conversion of the unfortunate Pranzini. Thérèse could even say that she had refused God nothing, from the age of three. However, there was a period of her life in which she specially experienced God's patience towards her. In 1889, in the months after her reception of the habit, the young novice perceived that she had practiced the virtue of poverty imperfectly until then. "During my postulancy, I was content to have nice things for my use and to have everything necessary for me at my disposal. 'My Director' bore this patiently." Immediately afterward, Thérèse states the reason for this leniency: "He doesn't like pointing everything out at once to souls. He generally gives His light little by little."[379]

So, Thérèse didn't condemn her sisters, despite their defects, because she recognized God could do in a single moment in a person something they were unable to achieve by their own efforts for many years. Instead of condemning sinners, Thérèse simply desired and hoped for the Lord's mercy for them. "Charity hopes all things" says St. Paul. Thérèse never gave up hope: she never thought a sinner had sinned "too much" to deserve the grace of conversion in spite of everything. She recognized that "all things are possible with God."

---

[379] A 74r. Thérèse doesn't state here the deeper reason that God doesn't normally give His light to souls except gradually, namely, that God respects the *temporal* reality of human nature which He created and which must die progressively, over time.

Let's recall with what trust Thérèse expected the conversion of Pranzini and later, at the end of her life, the conversion of Fr. Hyacinthe Loyson, which she didn't live to see.[380] She awaited the progress of her novices with the same trust. Far from making a distinction between candidates who were "viable" and those who were not, Thérèse looked after all the novices with equal solicitude. She left worries about success to God,[381] knowing He could work marvels in souls in an instant, and so the young novice mistress was never discouraged or annoyed at the "slowness" of their progress.

As a matter of fact, Thérèse's novices were far from benefitting rapidly from her teaching and example. Sr. Martha never succeeded in completely correcting her contradictory spirit[382]; Sr. Marie-Marguerite of the Blessed Sacrament didn't have complete confidence in her novice mistress. She admitted after Thérèse's death, "I fled from her gaze for fear of being found out." It was only after Thérèse's passing that she changed: "Previously I wasn't in a state to benefit from her advice, but at the time of her entry into heaven, I surrendered care of my soul to her and how she has transformed me! It's incredible, I am entirely peaceful and trusting! I don't recognize myself!"[383]

---

[380] As a result of his unwillingness to accept the definition of the pope's infallibility proclaimed by Vatican I, this Carmelite priest left the church. After having received in January 1911 a copy of *Story of a Soul*, Fr. Loyson thanked the Lisieux Carmel for the gift. He said he was "truly touched" by what he had read in that book. "I must add," he continued, "that I am far from being convinced." In another letter addressed to Sr. Genevieve, from July 21, 1911, he wrote, "From what I understand, your pious and heroic sister is far from being a stranger to me, and, without approving of everything in her, I admire her and am grateful to her." He died in Paris in February 1912, while kissing his crucifix, saying "My sweet Jesus!" (CG II, 642).

[381] "Our lot is to work; the victory is for Jesus." MSST 17.

[382] Death circular, p. 2.

[383] Circular, p. 3.

Poverty and charity

There was an intimate connection between hope and charity in Thérèse's heart. Her trust in God allowed her to love all her novices without distinction and her charity made her desire and hope they would receive the Lord's graces in abundance. In addition, Thérèse's increasingly profound awareness of her spiritual poverty helped her develop heartfelt mercy for others. She was so convinced of being weak herself that she could not judge others with a feeling of superiority. For instance, she didn't forget the attraction worldly charms exercised on her during her visit to Alençon. How could she throw stones at people who were taken in by these, since she had only escaped the danger through a special grace from the Lord? We can see here how much *the experience of spiritual poverty can advance charity*. To the extent that we feel little and humble before God, we are moved to forbearance for others. In this light we should read the passage given above where Thérèse says she sincerely rejoiced in her imperfections and even in her falls: this was because they promoted in her soul both distrust of herself and mercy for others. She told Sr. Genevieve: "God frequently allows us to experience in ourselves the same weaknesses which we deplore in others, such as absent-mindedness, involuntary negligence, an attitude of boredom or weariness. When we see that we ourselves have fallen into those faults we are then more prompt to excuse them in others."[384]

To thwart the temptation to judge our neighbor unfavorably and avoid grudges toward others when they have more or less deeply wounded us, following Thérèse, we must go beyond appearances. We should ponder what is now invisible in the other person, but will be apparent

[384] MSST 82.

later, and which we may already glimpse: our brothers' deep intentions in their actions; their secret efforts already accomplished; their good qualities; the circumstances in their lives which excuse certain actions; the holiness God can grant them later.

In brief, to obey the gospel command not to judge, we should follow the Apostle's dictate: "charity covers all things."[385] It isn't a question of being blind to others' faults, but instead of stopping at these, we should consider a person's desire for what is good and the circumstances in his life which explain his faults. Above all, we should ponder God's infinite mercy which is ever ready to transform someone from top to bottom.

MARIE NOËL: GOD WILL REPAY YOU A HUNDREDFOLD

Marie Noël, lay Catholic and a Nobel Prize winning poet, describes the marvelous gift God granted her when she gave up using her wit to target those around her unkindly:

> At age eighteen, I sold my mind to God the way others sell their soul to the devil. At that point, I was awkward, ugly, puny, ashamed like the ugly duckling, but I had a bright mind. It was lively, quick, acute; it would sting and wound unmercifully.

---

[385] This is the meaning of the verb that St. Paul uses in 1 Cor 13:7: *stégei*. Charity covers, hides, others' faults.
The normal translation "charity excuses all things" does not impart, it seems to us, the richness of the inspired text. In fact, the primary reason we are forbidden to judge our neighbor unfavorably isn't the existence of "excuses," of extenuating circumstances in someone's life or character whom we might be tempted to condemn; it is the existence of an infinite mercy and transformative power in God's heart.

As soon as some poor ridiculous person ventured into my vision, I caught him in the air and fixed him with a witty remark as one fixes an insect to a board with a pin. This amused me a great deal and made my companions laugh. But my family considered me "catty" and my brother called me a "viper." It would have been better to say mosquito or wasp.

One fine day, I believed them and I saw myself as I was, with my nasty sting. Could a Christian abide himself like that?

Remorse.

I reflected on it one morning with our Lord in the little chapel of the Virgin, in St. Peter's church.

Renounce my mind? Without it, what was left to me? I had neither beauty nor charm, nothing pleasing. Sacrifice it? I couldn't bring myself to do it. It would cost me too much. It would cost me everything.

In my conscience, God waited with an air of reproach. Then an idea came to me—perhaps He inspired it—to surrender my mind to him for some compensation.

I sold it to him. It cost! Without fixing a price. God is rich. God is just. I expected He would pay well. Once the deal was concluded—I am honest in business matters—I never dared to use the item I had sold.

At first, I appeared constrained, self-conscious like someone seized by a sudden illness. Words would come to my lips faster than my will; I clamped my mouth shut; I choked them back. It wasn't always easy.

But habit helped me more and more. And I became gradually the sweet little old woman—invisible, unknown, to whom no one pays attention, neither at home, nor out and about; no more attention than you'd give to a used match.

Twenty years passed. Success came…remarkable, unexpected. Payment? Compensation? Who knows what God gave me in exchange for my malice?

Not love. Not happiness.

The gift of Poetry? But that I had from childhood.

I think instead that it's a gift of a new way of looking, of perceiving, right away, rather than what is ridiculous, what is good and beautiful in people, even in those who don't have these. As a result, I love them so much, even the ridiculous, foolish and mediocre ones, that I can once more play with my malice simply for my own entertainment, without doing anyone harm.[386]

---

[386] Marie Noël (Marie Rouget), *Notes Intimes*, (Paris: Stock, 1959), 83–84.

15

Blunders

My mistakes grieve me

"Whenever I involuntarily caused anyone any
trouble, I would beg God to repair it, and then I
no longer tormented myself with the matter."[387]

Occasionally I forget to make a call as I promised a friend and
I know he will surely be disappointed. I imagine his disappointment...perhaps he will even be angry with me: "How could
you forget to call me? It shows that you don't really think much
of me! In the end, you don't like me as much as you said you did."
Who hasn't endured this kind of forgetfulness? How can we be
joyful in such a situation? How can we avoid feeling terrible about
having involuntarily caused pain to someone we truly care about?
St. Thérèse has an answer for us.

Thérèse's absentmindedness

While there were no telephones in the monastery of Thérèse's time,
the postal system was very efficient; there was even mail delivery on

[387] YN July 13, n. 9.

Sunday. One October Thérèse forgot to send a letter for her sister's name day with her greetings for the feast of St. Céline. When she realized her oversight, she sent Céline a note to ask her pardon: "If you knew the grief I have experienced when I think that I let the 21st pass without sending wishes for the name day of my Céline!...Will Céline have doubted the heart of her Thérèse?...Nevertheless, for a long time I have loved this feast, but the life in Carmel is so eremitical that your poor little solitary never realized the date...Céline, my forgetfulness really affected me."

Still, Thérèse didn't lose her peace. Truly convinced that Jesus was directing the course of events, she immediately acknowledged Jesus' hand in this omission, just as she had acknowledged Jesus' hand a few months earlier in her father's mental illness. She continued to do this when she wrote to her sister: "If you knew how I see the pain I endured today as wanted by Jesus, since He is pleased to sow in this way little pains in our life." How amazing Thérèse's faith was! Instead of being weighed down by her mistake, she immediately considered the double pain caused by it, hers and her sister's, as *providentially* willed by Jesus.[388]

Jesus allows great trials in our lives—Mr. Martin's dementia and admittance to the asylum in Caen is a good example—but He wishes to add little sorrows as well. This is so that we have the occasion to offer Him new smiles, since these are just as pleasing to Him as those we offer Him in the most difficult trials. Now, as we

---

[388] On July 16, 1897 Thérèse sent a note to Sr. Martha, her former novitiate companion, to repair another oversight: "Dear little Sister, I remember just now that I did not celebrate your birthday. Ah, believe me, it is an oversight that is breaking my heart. I was getting such a great joy over it. I wanted to offer you the prayer on humility; I am not entirely finished copying it, but soon you will have it. Your little twin, who would be unable to sleep if she were not to send you this note" (LT 256).

know very well, we sometimes have trouble forgiving ourselves for our mistakes: they humiliate us so much, they bring home to us the fact of our stupidity, and the limits of our brains! However, when we accept them, when we don't make a big deal of them, they intensify our humility and renew our trust.

If we ask the Lord to repair our deficiencies He does it in a divine way, namely, with an infinite generosity! So, we have the right and the duty to hope that in maintaining our smile in such situations, we will obtain for those whom our mistakes have disappointed or injured many more graces than they would have received by our correct actions.

Thérèse showed this confidence when she realized she had forgotten to tell her sister something during a parlor visit. She explained it to Mother Agnes a few days after she had gone to the infirmary permanently. "When Sister Geneviève used to come to visit me, I wasn't able to say all I wanted to say in a half hour. Then, during the week, whenever I had a thought or else was sorry for having forgotten to tell her something, I would ask God to let her know and understand what I was thinking about, and in the next visit she'd speak to me exactly about the thing I had asked God to let her know." Thérèse continued:

> At the beginning, when she was really suffering and I was unable to console her, I would leave the visit with a heavy heart, but I soon understood it wasn't I who could console anyone; and then I was no longer troubled when she left very sad. I begged God to supply for my weakness, and I felt He answered me. I would see this in the following visit. Since that time, whenever I involuntarily caused anyone any trouble, I would beg God to repair it, and then I no longer tormented myself with the matter.[389]

---

[389] YN July 13, n. 9.

In this passage we must stress the evolution in Thérèse's understanding. "In the beginning" she said, her "heart was heavy" when she left. Much later she understood why she shouldn't fret about these mistakes.

In the same spirit, a few evenings before, she told Mother Agnes the following: "You go to too much trouble over things that aren't worth any trouble." Then she added with a smile: "When you've done something like this, what is even worse is that you fear the consequences too much..."[390]

God makes use of our mistakes

Ultimately, the unconditional faith of the saints in the amazing mystery of Providence allows them to remain perpetually joyful despite enormous mistakes they may have made. They realize that human error is part of our earthly condition, and that they shouldn't blame God—or themselves, since they are not infallible!

It's true that sometimes it's hard to forgive mistakes the way we forgive sins. Thus, it's a question, in both the one and the other case, of acknowledging that we aren't divine: our freedom is fragile and our minds are limited. Instead of exclaiming with Paul Valéry, "I am sick of being a creature!" we should cry out with all the angels and saints that God alone is holy. And we should rejoice in this! As Thérèse wrote to Sr. Marie de St. Joseph in July 1897: "It does so much good to recognize that He alone is perfect."[391]

This is what I tried to do when I heard, in a message left on my answering machine, that a large group of Catholics had been expecting me the previous night for a talk I was supposed to give. I had been sure that this talk was to happen two days later: that was

[390] YN July 11, nn. 6 and 7.
[391] LT 250.

the date I had written in my calendar. I told myself that God had arranged it in order to give those people, very disappointed by my absence, what I was supposed to have brought them. Further, I am certain that these graces were all the greater because my surrender to God's will was greater.

It goes without saying that such peaceful acceptance of our mistakes should never slide into passive toleration. We must do everything we can to avoid subjecting others to the deplorable effects of our blunders and oversights. If we have an unfortunate tendency to get distracted, we should resolve to check our planners regularly! And we must have the habit of writing down all our meetings there and writing them on the correct page!

Mistakes aren't sins

However, it's also important to resolve frequently not to let ourselves get upset by the foolish mistakes we make. By not giving them too much importance, we specifically affirm the immeasurable difference between error and sin, even venial sin. There is an infinite distance between these two types of evils. Only sin, disobedience to God's commands, is something grave, something serious.

In a magnificent passage, John Henry Newman, the well-known Anglican convert, who after a long search joined the Catholic Church, expressed his enthusiasm for this discovery in Church teaching. It was a claim he had found nowhere else, namely, the immeasurable distance separating a physical evil from a moral evil. A mere venial sin is infinitely graver than an earthquake.

This is what we should try to keep in mind when, for instance, through an involuntary error we have a car accident! When we are usually very attentive about observing what is happening on the road, but we didn't notice the muddy patch in which our car skidded before colliding into another vehicle!

While giving the statement for the accident, we should force ourselves to repeat with St. Thérèse: "Everything is grace!" Despite all the inconveniences coming from the accident, we remain the Father's beloved children. We can even benefit from this misfortune which has disrupted our peace—and that of others—to live fully the Lord's commandment communicated through St. Paul: "In all circumstances give thanks!"[392]

JOHN HENRY NEWMAN:
NATURAL CATASTROPHES ARE LESS SERIOUS THAN SIN

This is a truth that reason could discover on its own, but it is so counteracted by human rebellion against the Creator that it is good for it to be taught by the Church as an essential truth. An additional reason for Newman, for grasping why it is fitting that God instituted on earth an infallible authority charged with reminding people of such natural truths.

A power, possessed of infallibility in religious teaching, is happily adapted to be a working instrument, in the course of human affairs, for smiting hard and throwing back the immense energy of the aggressive, capricious, untrustworthy intellect...

And first, the initial doctrine of the infallible teacher must be an emphatic protest against the existing state of mankind. Man had rebelled against his Maker. It was this that caused the divine interposition: and to proclaim it must be the first act of the divinely-accredited messenger. The Church must denounce rebellion

[392] 1 Thess 5:18.

as of all possible evils the greatest. She must have no terms with it; if she would be true to her Master, she must ban and anathematize it. This is the meaning of a statement of mine which has furnished matter for one of those special accusations to which I am at present replying: I have, however, no fault at all to confess in regard to it; I have nothing to withdraw, and in consequence I here deliberately repeat it. I said, "The Catholic Church holds it better for the sun and moon to drop from heaven, for the earth to fail, and for all the many millions on it to die of starvation in extremest agony, as far as temporal affliction goes, than that one soul, I will not say, should be lost, but should commit one single venial sin, should tell one willful untruth, or should steal one poor farthing without excuse."[393]

In this chapter we have presented objective truths once again, drawn from Scripture, which allow the saints to remain joyful in every situation. Instead of grieving when mistakes happen, the saints are obliged to think and repeat: "This is not serious! Everything is grace."

MADELEINE DELBREL: NOTHING HAPPENS BY CHANCE

A person cannot believe in both chance and providence. We believe in Providence. We live as if we believed in chance.

[393] John Henry Newman, *Apologia Pro Vita Sua*, (London, Longmans Green & Co, 1890), 246-247.

From this spring the inconsistences of our life, its unhealthy agitations, and its unhealthy passivity.

We put up with what we haven't chosen...these are our zeros: the zero of a required task, of obligatory companions, nameless customers, professional visits. Zero! Zero! Zero! To other situations, other meetings, other duties, we attribute the numbers 2, 5, 7 of the divine will. We concentrate the best of our efforts there, as if our life began there.

Nevertheless, each morning we receive our whole day from God's hands. God gives us a day that He prepared for us. In it there is nothing "not enough" or "too much," nothing indifferent, nothing useless. He has just asked us to live a masterpiece of a day. However, we look at it like a page in a planner, labeled with a number and a month. We treat it lightly, like a piece of paper...If we could look into the world and see how from the beginning this day was developed and composed, we would understand the weight of a single human day.

And if we had a little faith, we would want to kneel before our Christian day.

There is no such thing as chance, it's only our will that is random, and doesn't ever want difficulties and it skimps, and bargains, and botches things. There is trouble to be borne well just as there are tasks to be done well. When we get up in the morning, we have our problems to bear, just as we have our work to do. And the details of that work are willed by God, just as the details of the problem are also willed by God.

We can bear our troubles well just as we can do our work well. We can easily check and verify the holes in our work. We will only know after death the irreparable breaches caused in the edifice of grace by the holes in our difficulties...

When we are waiting for a train which doesn't arrive on a cold platform, in addition to this integration with God's will, through our troubles, we become dispensers of God's grace.

You will say all these are just small nuisances. Nevertheless, we recognize an artist just as much in his way of playing a children's song as in the most challenging concerto.[394]

---

[394] Madeleine Delbrel, *La joie de croire*, (Paris: Ed du Seuil, 1958), 139, 141–42.

16

The World's Woes
Suffering in the world prevents me from being happy

*"Our Lord enjoyed all the delights of the Trinity when He
was in the garden of Olives, and still His agony was none the
less cruel. It's a mystery, but I assure you that I understand
something about it by what I'm experiencing myself."*[395]

Many Christians ask themselves in their generosity if they have
the right to be happy when there are so many miseries just
beyond their door: the woes of the unemployed and homeless, the
suffering of the sick, traffic accidents, divided communities, and
distress of every kind. There are also the many woes the news never
stops reminding us about: suffering caused by war, violence, social
injustice, natural disasters and so on. It goes without saying that
serious struggle against this misery is at the heart of every authentic
Christian life. But do we have to give up living joyfully, as the Apostle
Paul specifically asks us to do? "Rejoice in the Lord always; again I
will say, Rejoice."[396]

[395] YN July 6, n. 4.
[396] Phil 4:4.

To correctly understand the right—and the duty—of Catholics to remain joyful when faced with the world's many woes, we should keep in mind, with Thérèse and all the saints, that here on earth we must live one of the paradoxes which God knows: in God infinite joy exists along with infinite compassion for all suffering in the world. This mysterious co-existence of joy and compassion happens in a similar way in the hearts of the saints.

God's paradox

As diligent readers of the Bible, Catholics have always understood that suffering and joy mysteriously co-existed in Jesus' human soul and in some way, also in God's heart, though in God this suffering doesn't exist in the same way as in human beings. This is because the terrible sufferings which a person may endure and that the Son of God Himself experienced in his human nature—cannot destroy the indescribable blessedness of the divine nature.

Clearly, it's important first of all to distinguish the way in which Jesus experienced suffering and joy throughout his earthly life and the way He experiences them now, in the glory of His Father.

Suffering and joy in Jesus

Every week Thérèse prayed the Way of the Cross and was deeply moved by the sufferings Jesus endured in His passion. When *The Dolorous Passion of our Lord Jesus Christ* (according to the visions of Anne Catherine Emmerich) was read in the refectory (during Thérèse's third Lent in Carmel), she could not eat.

Thérèse also understood the spirituality of the Sacred Heart enough to know that Jesus suffered more than anyone during his earthly life. It was fitting that St. Margaret Mary received the task of representing the Heart of Jesus crowned with thorns and surmounted by a cross. His whole life was profoundly marked by his vision of humanity's sins. However, she also knew that in the midst of His greatest torments Jesus rejoiced in the deepest part of His soul knowing that He was the beloved Son and seeing all the love the Father had for Him. Thérèse was happy to find in her *Imitation of Christ* this thought from Fr. Lamennais: "Our Lord enjoyed all the delights of the Trinity when He was in the garden of Olives, and still His agony was none the less cruel." And she added, "It's a mystery, but I assure you that I understand something about it by what I'm experiencing myself."[397]

One text that John Paul II quotes in the letter *Novo Millennio Ineunte* says that the saints' serenity while going through a spiritual "dark night" is explained by the fact that they are aware also of participating through it "in Jesus' experience on the cross, a mixture of beatitude and sorrow."[398]

Suffering and joy in the Resurrected Christ

Thérèse rejoiced in the thought that after having suffered a great deal "under Pontius Pilate" Jesus was henceforth infinitely happy; having entered forever into His Father's glory, He can suffer no more. When she was suffering terribly because of her intestines, she said to Céline, who had just held a crucifix out to her, that she preferred crucifixes which represented Jesus as already dead. "That is because then I think He is no longer suffering."[399]

In the mornings, she liked to put her crucifix on her pillow, saying to Jesus, "My Jesus, you have worked enough, during the thirty-three years of your life on this poor earth! Now, rest…it is my turn to fight and suffer."[400]

---

[397] YN July 6, n. 4.
[398] *Novo millenio ineunte*, n. 27.
[399] YN August 19, n. 3.
[400] This is the context for Thérèse's comment (probably in the winter of 1896–97): "Before I entered Carmel, when I woke up in the morning, I used

All the saints experienced joy at the thought of their Beloved's happiness. Charles de Foucauld often said that one of the greatest causes for his happiness was the thought that Jesus now was happy forever. That is why, as we saw earlier, he especially loved the feast of the Ascension, since it celebrates Christ's definitive entry into glory.

It's true that Christ continues to suffer in the members of His mystical body, since it is He who is hungry, cold, and naked in the person of all the world's unfortunates.[401] In this sense we can say with Pascal, "Jesus will be in agony until the end of the world. He cannot rest during that time."[402] Yet this is an agony which in no way diminishes His infinite happiness.[403]

Joy and compassion in God's Heart

What we can say about the Risen Christ is also true about the Holy Trinity in some way. While being infinitely happy, the Father

---

to think about what the day could possibly have in store for me, happy or troublesome; and if I foresaw only troubles, I got up depressed. Now it is the opposite. I think only of the pains and sufferings that await me, and I get up so much more joyful and full of courage when I think of the opportunities that I will have to prove my love to Jesus and earn a living for my children, since I am a mother of souls. After that, I kiss my crucifix, I put it gently at my place on the pillow when I am getting dressed, and I say to Him, 'My Jesus, you have worked and wept long enough during the thirty-three years of your life on this poor earth! Today, you rest…It is my turn to fight and to suffer!'" (TLMT, 104).

[401] Mt 25:40.

[402] See Chapter 1.

[403] The French mystic Marthe Robin said, speaking about what she suffered each week in experiencing again in her body and soul the Savior's Passion, "One has the impression that Jesus suffers in you, outside of time, outside of space, but Jesus in his glory." Jean Guitton, *Portrait de Marthe Robin*, (Paris: Grasset, 1985), 197.

and the Holy Spirit were not insensible to the suffering endured on earth by the beloved Son in His humanity or to His cry from the cross, "My God, My God why have you forsaken Me?" The Blessed Trinity is not without compassion for the sufferings men and women have experienced through the ages, as pilgrims on earth and who are being prepared in this fashion to enter into Their boundless joy. This is why the Fathers of the Church didn't hesitate to speak of a certain suffering in God. For example, Origen said, "The Father himself too, the God of the universe, who is 'long-suffering and very merciful' and one who pities—does he not suffer in some way?"[404]

Indeed, Catholics bear in mind that, with respect to the mystery of God, we must affirm simultaneously that God is infinitely happy and infinitely compassionate. St. Bernard of Clairvaux states:

> While God is impassible, He is not thus stripped of compassion since nothing is more proper to Him than to have pity and to pardon. That is why the blessed inhabitants of heaven participate in God's compassion for mankind: delivered from suffering, they have compassion for ours. Their sensitivity is not diminished, it is transfigured; by being clothed with God, they have not been despoiled of affection for us. Freed from weakness, they are not without pity. For charity never fails."[405]

---

[404] Origen of Alexandria, *Exegetical Works on Ezekiel*, trans. Roger Pearse, *Hom.* VI.6 (Ipswich: Chieftain Publishing, 2014), 193. The Church's dogmatic teaching has always maintained that, strictly speaking, God is impassible (that is, incapable of suffering) because He is unchangeably perfect, and that this is the basis of His power to save us from our sins and suffering. The Son of God truly suffered but according to His human nature, not His divine nature. The qualification Origen offers is to be understood metaphorically.—Translator
[405] St. Bernard, Sermon 26 on the Canticle of Canticles.

The saints' paradox

Having pondered at length this coexistence of joy and compassion in God, Thérèse tried to live out the twofold requirement of joyfulness and mercy. Illuminated by Christ's example, Thérèse knew she had the right, and the duty, to remain peaceful deep in her heart whatever the trials her brethren—far or near—were going through. She wasn't indifferent towards others' misfortunes and didn't hesitate to use every means in her power to relieve them. One illustration of this: at the end of January 1895, during the evening recreation, Céline learned that instead of being named Sr. Marie of the Holy Face as had been intended, she was to take the name of the monastery's foundress, who had died in 1891, and thus would be called, Sr. Genevieve of St. Teresa. Thérèse immediately divined her sister's pain and wanted to console her. This is what she did: it was not an exhortation to offer this sacrifice lovingly, but a gesture filled with fraternal delicacy. At the end of recreation, she wrote in pencil on a scrap of paper: "Sr. Genevieve of St. Teresa. It was little Thérèse who wrote it first." Then she passed the note to her sister.

Thérèse never took her neighbors' trials lightly, yet she only truly pitied those who didn't understand their redemptive value. The tranquil strength with which the members of the Martin family accepted their sufferings filled her with joy. Thus, during Mr. Martin's illness, we don't hear of Thérèse pitying her father; she didn't pity Céline: "I am going to surprise you, dear little sister, by telling you that I am far from pitying you, but, you see, I think your lot is worthy of envy. Jesus has designs of an indescribable love for you."[406] Later on, Thérèse didn't pity Mother Agnes, who was elected prioress, for all the annoyances she endured because of the jealousy and moodiness of Mother Marie de Gonzague. After a rough scene between the

---

[406] LT 82.

latter and Mother Agnes, Thérèse confided: "I rejoice: the more I see our Mother suffer, the happier I am. If you understood the good it does her soul!"[407]

Another instance from Thérèse: one day someone complained to her about Sr. Marie-Philomena of Jesus, about the excessive fatigue she "put on" during the community tasks. She replied, "Don't complain. She is much more fortunate than you. The saints who suffer never make me feel pity: united to the good God, they have the power to bear their sufferings and even find them sweet. But those who are not saints—oh, that's different. I pity them."[408]

Such were Thérèse's sentiments: she only pitied souls who didn't know how to profit from their sufferings. In her three manuscripts she only uses the word pity a single time and it was to say: "Oh, how I pity souls who are lost!"[409] *Yes, she truly only pitied those souls who were lost.*

Joy never prevents the saints from being marvelously attentive to the sufferings of others, offering them compassion and doing everything they can to relieve their afflictions. They didn't wait for analysis—quite correct—of contemporary psychologists to realize that we are all the more able to listen and help others when we aren't crushed by our own problems. Mother Teresa of Calcutta said more than once: "Don't go and care for the dying today. With the way you are, you can't do anything for them!"

---

[407] PO 479.

[408] Andre Noche, "La Response des textes des archives," in *La Petite Sainte Thérèse de Maxence van der Meersch devant la critique et devant les textes*, (Paris: Editions St.-Paul, 1950), 310.

[409] A 40r.

St. Teresa of Avila: *Peaceful compassion for souls who are offering up their sufferings*

In the case of spiritual affection…although the weakness of our nature may at first allow us to feel something of all this, our reason soon begins to reflect whether our friend's trials are not good for her, and to wonder if they are making her richer in virtue and how she is bearing them, and then we shall ask God to give her patience so that they may win her merit. If we see that she is being patient, we feel no distress— indeed, we are gladdened and consoled. If all the merit and gain which suffering is capable of producing could be made over to her, we should still prefer suffering her trial ourselves to seeing her suffer it, but we are not worried or disquieted.[410]

Francis of Assisi stated: "Your misery is the Lord's concern; others are waiting for your joy." That said, it's true that compassion—that stirring of emotion we experience at the sight of others' sufferings—is, just as with joy, a beautiful fruit of the Spirit in our hearts. This is what the Good Samaritan experienced when faced with the wounded man who was half dead on the side of the road. It is what Henry Durant felt when faced with the soldiers who returned terribly wounded from the battle of Solferino (1859)—a compassion without which the Red Cross would never have existed. And if Raoul Fallereau hadn't been moved by seeing how lepers were abandoned in leper houses in Africa when he visited, his international campaign against leprosy would never have come about.

---

[410] St. Teresa of Avila, *The Way of Perfection*, trans. and ed. E. Allison Peers (Garden City: Image, 1964), 38.

Holy Scripture frequently urges us to be compassionate. "Be kind and compassionate to one another."[411] And it condemns the attitude of those who close their heart to the sorrows of their brethren. At the same time, the genuine saints of the Church's history never hesitated to let themselves be overwhelmed by the joy of the risen Christ.

St. Francis de Sales: I am like a bird which sings in the midst of a forest of thorns.

St. Philip Neri: Grim faces are not fit for the joyful house of paradise.

Seraphim of Sarov: Acquire peace and thousands around you will find their salvation.

St. Teresa of Calcutta: Never let sorrow overcome you to the extent that you forget the joy of the risen Christ.

THE HUMOR OF THE SAINTS

In her study, *Les saints du Moyen Age*, the historian Regine Pernoud highlighted countless stories about their pervasive smiles. Here are two examples.

When her brother, St. Benedict, refused to prolong their yearly meeting, St. Scholastica addressed herself to God. Then there burst forth a wonderful storm which kept her recalcitrant brother with her. She said: "You wouldn't listen to me, but God did!"

---

[411] Cf. Eph 4:32, Ps 37:21, Heb 10:34; 1 Peter 3:8.

On the feast of St. Yves in France this well-known song is sung: "A lawyer and not a thief! You can hardly believe it."

Let's also recall Thomas More, the author of *Utopia*, full of wit. When someone was surprised at the small size of his two successive wives, he answered, "One should choose the lesser of two evils." As Chancellor to Henry VIII, he dared to contest his religious positions and was condemned to death.

As the stairway up to the scaffold wasn't stable, he asked for assistance. "Pray, Sir, see me safe up; and as to my coming down, let me shift for myself." Then to the executioner who was embarrassed, he made this recommendation: "Pick up thy Spirits, man, and be not afraid to do thine office; my neck is very short, take heed therefore thou strike not awry for having thine honesty." Laying his head upon the block, he bid the Executioner wait till he had put his beard aside, lest it should complicate things. "It need not be cut, for it has committed no treason."

Taking up a joke from St. Cyprian, bishop of Carthage, St. Thomas had right before this asked someone to give a coin (in fact, a golden angel) to his executioner since the porter who takes you directly to paradise deserves a tip!

And here are some witty remarks from recent popes:

The first one to laugh at his corpulence, John XXIII told Edouard Herriot who also didn't lack *embonpoint*: "We are from the same *arrondisment*." To a diplomat who asked him how many people worked in the Vatican, he answered: "Oh, not more than half!"

Seemingly more serious, Paul VI also sometimes had his witty repartees. When someone once asked him to bless a golden rosary, he said "That's excellent. The blessing will stick to it better."

Finally let's remember John Paul I's smile and all the humor of Pope John Paul II. To a Jesuit not gifted with languages who was attempting to speak Polish, Pope John Paul II replied smiling, "I see, Father, that you speak Polish as well as I speak Korean."

Part 3

When I Consider God

17

Dry Prayer
It's hard for me to pray

*"Jesus takes away His tangible presence from them [his
faithful sheep] in order to give His consolations to sinners.
If He does lead them to Tabor, it is for a few moments..."*[412]

When Catholics are asked about their prayer life, they generally answer that they frequently send out a cry to God amid
their activities. A cry of distress: "Lord, help!" Or a song of gratitude:
"Thank you, my God." Sometimes even a canticle of praise. Gazing
at a magnificent sunset, we spontaneously murmur, "It's so beautiful, my God."

However, many Catholics complain that they haven't yet managed
to dedicate a long period to God in the heart-to-heart of silent prayer
each day (sometimes called mental prayer). They realize the practice
of daily prayer would profoundly change their life, but they don't
have the heart to set about it. Or rather, they haven't yet received the
grace of light which would make them understand once and for all

---

[412] LT 142.

what Thérèse understood very early on, namely, that regular prayer is both a right and a duty, and the source of countless blessings.

In this chapter on prayer, we focus on three points: I have the right to pray. I should do it to please God. God will reward me a hundredfold for the time I consecrate to Him.

I have the right to pray

Overwhelmed by the staggering number of miseries in the world needing to be relieved, many Christians ask themselves if prayer is time stolen from others. Strictly speaking, we can pray, but only for the time needed to recharge the batteries of our spiritual engine. They think prayer has to be like the ultra-rapid stops used by automobile racers: as soon as the oil tanks are filled and the air is changed, they rush back onto the track. Isn't this what the Lord expects of us? We should dedicate as much time as possible to serving our brothers. "Truly, I say to you, as you did it to one of the least of these my brethren, you did it to me."[413] Doesn't Jesus teach us that the second commandment is like the first? Shouldn't we conclude that the only way to love God is to love our neighbor?

This interpretation is especially convincing because it seems to be the one given by St. John in his first epistle. One actually has the impression that the apostle summarizes the whole Christian life there in two verbs: *believe* in God's love for us and *love* our brethren as God loves them. Shouldn't we conclude that in the scheme of the New Testament, God is not asking humanity to love Him, to spend time praying, but simply to believe in His love and dedicate all their heart and all their strength to loving their brethren?

The partial truth this reading of the New Testament offers is obvious. Love for others is indeed the touchstone of our love for

[413] Mt 25:40.

God.[414] We know that at the end of his life, the apostle John never stopped reminding his flock of the importance of the new commandment announced by Jesus during the Last Supper.

Moreover, it's true that we ought to learn to pray in our different daily circumstances and even in the hubbub of public transportation. "Your cloister is the street," St. Vincent de Paul told the first Daughters of Charity. How true this is! But such prayer, in the middle of the human sphere, isn't possible—and St. Vincent de Paul and Mother Teresa wouldn't contradict me—unless at other times of the day, we are recollected in the silence of a church or our own room. All the saints did this. This is required even to think! We don't believe we are wiser than the saints!

By elevating the Levitical precept: "You shall love your neighbor as yourself"[415] to the dignity of the second commandment, "like unto the first," Jesus didn't overturn the primacy of the first commandment. *A fortiori*, He didn't suppress it! Hence, we all have the right to build into our day genuine heart-to-heart talks with God, because we all have the duty to love Him with all our heart, to seek and find in Him our essential joy, and especially to enjoy His love. The whole of Church tradition declares that prayer is not time stolen from others, that we have the right to sit at the Lord's feet, just as Mary took time to do at Bethany.[416] God doesn't want us to love Him with all *our strength* only during the hours of our professional or apostolic work. Indeed, we must love Him also and especially with all *our heart* in the intimacy and freedom of a loving encounter.

In her childhood Thérèse received the grace of prayer, and against the odds she persevered in the conviction that she had the right to

---

[414] 1 Jn 4:20.
[415] Lev 19:18.
[416] Lk 10:42.

it. When her father brought her along on fishing trips, she drew apart a bit and prayed seated on the grass. "My soul was absorbed in real prayer."[417] On holidays she enjoyed playing "hermits" with her cousin Marie Guérin. She invented this game and it shows her early attraction for the contemplative life.[418]

When she remained alone at Les Buissonnets rather than going to her uncle Guérin's house, she withdrew to a corner of her bedroom, which she closed off with the bed curtains—and there she "thought"! "I understand now that I was doing mental prayer without knowing it and that God was already instructing me in secret...At this time in my life nobody had ever taught me how to make mental prayer, and yet I had a great desire to do it. Marie, finding me pious enough, allowed me to make only my vocal prayers."[419]

A converse sister at her Benedictine boarding school gave Thérèse her first "class" on prayer. One day she was bold enough to ask Sr. Henriette to help her bury a dead bird. Feeling she could trust her, she then asked her suddenly, "Sister, how does a nun pray?" The kind sister explained that she could talk with God just as she did with her father she when she got home from school. "About everything that happens, your joys and your sorrows." After discussing this with Pauline during a parlor visit, Thérèse adopted this method, saying, "I believe it's not difficult to pray."[420] On the contrary, she was confirmed in the idea that she had already been praying when, in the morning before getting out of bed, she meditated by herself.[421]

When she was fourteen, Thérèse spent hours with Céline at their second-floor window in the room called the Belvedere, because of

[417] A 14v.
[418] A 23r.
[419] A 33v.
[420] *La Petite Thérèse a la Abbaye*, 43.
[421] A 31r.

its lovely view over the town. "It seems to me the outpourings of our souls were similar to those of St. Monica with her son when, at the port of Ostia, they were lost in ecstasy at the sight of the Creator's marvels! It appears we were receiving graces like those granted to the great saints."[422] These prayers produced fruits of conversion since the practice of virtue "became sweet and natural to us," Thérèse states.

In Carmel Thérèse was always very faithful about doing her two hours of daily prayer in the choir of their chapel. She never missed it and couldn't bear the thought of reducing it.

In August 1894 the Guérin family, reinforced by some priests, tried to deter Céline from entering Carmel. Thérèse reminded her sister about the Lord's very clear statements in Bethany. "The most fervent Christians, priests, find that we are exaggerated, that we should serve with Martha instead of consecrating to Jesus the vessels of our lives, with the ointments enclosed within them."...But what does it matter? "We are not idlers, squanderers either. Jesus defended us."[423]

Truly, Thérèse never doubted that she had the right to consecrate hours in prayer to the Lord. Jesus had declared this right when He said that we were created to love God with all our heart, and He forcefully reminded His disciples of this at Bethany.

I should pray in order to please God

Unfortunately, we often naturally find more joy in doing our work than in our prayer times. Frequently Martha's activity attracts us more than Mary's apparent inactivity at the Lord's feet. Let's be frank about this. Essentially, what prevents us from praying is that frequently we are bored by it. What we are passionate about is "getting things done."

[422] A 48r.
[423] LT 169.

We have a tendency to think that a really successful day is one allowing us to check off many tasks, a day where we have gotten ahead in our work. On the other hand, time consecrated to prayer commonly seems like time lost.

In other words, the great obstacle to the regular practice of prayer is a notorious idolatry of our own works. The prophets of Israel denounced this emphatically in the past: "Their land is filled with idols; they bow down to the work of their hands, to what their own fingers have made."[424] We deserve this reproach when we give *more importance to our own work than to the Lord's work in us.*

God doesn't reprove us for not accomplishing many things in a day: this often happens to us if we have the good fortune to have a job. However, God asks us not to fall into activism, that is, into the erroneous mentality of measuring someone by the number of his activities rather than evaluating him as the Judge does: by the quality of his love. What counts in God's eyes is what can't be measured—the fervor and purity of our acts of love.

Prayer is precisely the time when, instead of using our hands to work, we join them together; we still them to make time to listen to God telling us about His love and allowing Him to act. At the end of a half an hour of prayer it isn't our work which has progressed, but God's. We have given Him the joy of shaping us with His hands for a time.

What does it matter if we are bored during our prayers? *God isn't bored.* When we finally realize that we are pleasing God by being there, alone with Him, in the heart-to-heart that is prayer, we will become faithful to it. We don't pray for the sake of experiencing pleasant emotions at the level of feelings, or to hit upon excellent ideas likely to enhance an upcoming catechism class—we go to prayer for Him, out of love!

---

[424] Is 2:8.

That's what Thérèse did. In the first month of her postulancy she experienced great aridity in prayer. "Dryness was my daily bread."[425] Not having had enough sleep at night, she frequently fell asleep during the morning prayer time. (This lasted about seven years, she said in 1895). Yet she wasn't bothered about it. "I remember that little children are as pleasing to their parents when they are asleep as well as when they are wide awake; I remember, too, that when they perform operations, doctors put their patients to sleep. Finally, I remember that: 'The Lord knows our weakness, that He is mindful that we are but dust and ashes.'"[426]

Thérèse experienced dryness in prayer especially during her retreats in preparation for receiving the habit, and for her profession. "Nothing near Jesus. Aridity!...Sleep!"[427] "Today more than yesterday, if that were possible, I was deprived of all consolation. I thank Jesus, who finds this good for my soul…"[428]

Four days before her profession on September 4, 1890, she wrote: "My soul is always in the subterranean passage, but it is very happy, yes, happy to have no consolation whatsoever, for I find that then its love is not like the love of earthly fiancées who are always looking at the hands of their fiancés to see if they have brought them any gifts, or else at their faces to catch there a smile of love which delights them…"[429]

St. Thérèse really wasn't disappointed about not receiving consolations when she prayed, since she was seeking primarily to "console Jesus for the ingratitude of the wicked" and "to see him smile / When

---

425 A 73v.

426 A 75v–76r.

427 LT 74.

428 LT 76.

429 LT 115. See also Letters 132, 142, 143.

my heart is exiled..."[430] This is why she wrote to her godmother at the opening of her letter from September 1896, "Do not believe I am swimming in consolations; oh, no, my consolation is to have none on earth."[431]

Marthe Robin: Prayer and Eucharistic communion

It costs more to pray than to receive communion. Communion is an exterior act which is in itself a pleasure, a consolation, a joy for the soul...Prayer which is a secret conversation between God and the soul, and especially in the beginning, on the contrary, is an assignment and a struggle...It requires a lot of effort. Moreover, sacramental communion can be impossible for a long period because of various infirmities that God sends his creature to test it and this privation, when it doesn't depend on us, doesn't prevent holiness. Prayer is always possible, if only for a few minutes.

Communion doesn't always presuppose virtue: one may receive communion and be guilty of the Body and Blood of the Lord; daily prayer doesn't mean one is virtuous, *however it is proof that one is working seriously to become so.*

Someone said: one can find Christians who receive communion daily and are in a state of mortal sin; Christians who give alms generously and who are in state of mortal sin; Christians who mortify themselves in all sorts of ways and are in a state of mortal sin; *but one never finds a soul who prays every day and who remains in sin.*

---

[430] The first phrase is from the *Act of Offering* and the second PN 45, st 5.
[431] B 1r.

Reading these lines, my spiritual Father didn't misunderstand my intentions and didn't see in this a decline in desire and eagerness for holy communion. I only wanted to describe the error of certain souls, who are anxious about a communion they couldn't make and who don't care enough about the prayer they could have made and which they have voluntarily shortened or missed, who insistently and importunely ask to make up for it but who never go to the trouble of making up for a prayer, as they could easily do.

Oh! We who know the gift of God and who understand his designs concerning us, let us oblige ourselves never voluntarily to miss prayer, make up for it if we must, and never shorten it or leave it.[432]

God gives me back a hundredfold for the time I give Him

We can't emphasize enough, as mentioned above, the character of prayer as a free gift. We make the time for it in order to respond to the Lord's invitation to please Him. But we must also point out the benefit found in every authentic encounter with our Creator: the transformation occurring in the soul's depths during this interlude.

The oratory where we go for a heart-to-heart conversation with the Lord is also a laboratory. We can also view it as an operating table on which the Lord, like a cardiac surgeon, is giving us a new heart. During prayer, we hand our soul over to the divine Potter to be fashioned in His image, to become what He wants to make of us: a unique masterpiece in the crown of His children. Normally we

---

[432] Raymond Peyret, *Prends ma vie Seigneur: La longue messe de Marthe Robin*, (Paris: Desclée de Brouwer, 1985), 85.

don't experience the transformation God is producing in us when we pray, but the more we have the courage to "waste time" for Him, the more we perceive that all areas of our life are benefitting from it over the long term. Below is a list of some of the blessed results in our life coming from faithful prayer.

The development of deep peace in the core of our hearts. The fact of spending significant periods meeting with God habituates us to not living at the surface of our psyches, tossed about by circumstances, happy when events correspond to our hopes and discouraged when the opposite occurs. God makes us experience the peace He grants to those who choose to rest in Him. It's a peace in the soul's core—completely compatible with life's inevitable disappointments.

A different way of working. Instead of hurrying along "greedily" to my work, with the desire to move faster, I act more calmly, under God's gaze. I act with the joy of knowing that God is quite close to me, and also in me, helping me do it. I work better! More efficiently!

A different way of viewing others. Freed from the mania for efficiency, I let myself more easily be interrupted by others when I am working. And at the same time, I learn to welcome them as a matter of course, to listen to them, and to love them wholeheartedly. Our hearts are enlarged through being opened to God's action.

Similarly, we could show that the habit of regular prayer gives us a different way of reacting to trials, remembering failures, developing plans, viewing life and death.

It's easy to find in Thérèse's life innumerable benefits from her regular habit of prayer. By opening her soul to God's action in prayer, she received from Him the remarkable serenity she maintained during trials. This serenity was the fruit of the Holy Spirit in her,[433] but

---

[433] See Gal 5:22.

also the application of her desire to take very seriously the reasons for remaining joyful she found in Scripture.

"Ah! if I were able to convey to you the peace Jesus placed in my soul at the height of my tears," she wrote to Céline on September 23, 1890. At this time, she was very disappointed that her father hadn't been allowed to come the day after her reception of the veil.[434] Three years later, July 16, 1893, she wrote, "Jesus teaches me to do *all* through love, to refuse Him nothing, to be content when He gives me a chance of proving to Him that I love Him. But this is done in peace, in abandonment, it is Jesus who is doing everything in me, and I am doing nothing."[435] The following month, after reminding Céline of certain passages from the *Imitation of Christ*, she wrote: "How these words give peace to the soul, my Céline."[436] It's clear that it was through meditation on Scripture or her beloved *Imitation* that Thérèse received the grace to remain at peace. Yes, she says, addressing the Lord, "I feel that your words are truth, for they give peace, joy to my little heart."[437]

Additionally, through spending many hours in the monastery chapel, the good Carmelite Thérèse learned not to make her work an idol. She taught this detachment to Céline, who was always wanting to have a day "spent well." She told her:

> You have not come to Carmel merely to turn out a mountain of work or even, strictly speaking, to become an indefatigable worker. Are you unduly concerned at the present moment as to what is happening in other Carmelite Monasteries, and whether the nuns there are busy or not? Does their work

434 LT 120.
435 LT 142.
436 LT 145.
437 LT 190.

interfere with your prayer and meditation? Well, in the same way you should become detached from your daily occupations, conscientiously devoting to them the time prescribed but with perfect freedom of heart.[438]

As for how she viewed others we have shown sufficiently in earlier chapters that it was profoundly altered by pondering the Last Supper discourse. She returned to this reflection more than once in prayer. She also wrote in her last manuscript: "Meditating upon these words of Jesus,[439] I understood how imperfect was my love for my sisters."[440] Unquestionably, we see her reading these texts closely in order to put them into practice in her life.

Even if we don't have the strictly contemplative vocation Thérèse had, we are all called to keep the Lord's command, addressed to every Christian through the Apostle's pen: "Rejoice always, pray constantly, give thanks in all circumstances; for this is the will of God in Christ Jesus for you."[441] To pray without ceasing and live our whole life in thanksgiving, it's crucial that our calendar contains significant periods for intimate conversation with the Lord, times dedicated exclusively to this. As Madeleine Delbrel rightly observed:

> The prayer that is first asked of us is a sacrifice. It is a group of times whose only purpose is to be offered to God. This dimension of prayer is essential for us, since it's the call in our daily life, the putting into action of the belonging to God

---

[438] MSST 65.
[439] Jn 15:13.
[440] C 12r.
[441] 1 Thess 5:16–18.

we claim to have chosen. Seen from this vantage, to pray is to choose God.

It is also loving others without pretense, since God would have no need of our sacrifices, of *the* sacrifice that, during prayer, we must become, if there were no need for redemption: we are not innocent, we are the redeemed, whose actual redemption is always still to be accomplished.

She also said, "Every love has actions which are proper to it: the simplest demand time. A mother doesn't tuck her child into bed while she peels potatoes."[442]

[442] *La joie de Croire*, 202–4. Madeleine appreciated St. Thérèse very much. She wrote: "Maybe Thérèse of Lisieux, patroness of all the Missions, was intended to live at the beginning of this age, when time is reduced to the minimum, actions cut down to the minimum, a life of heroism indiscernible to the eyes of those who saw her, and her mission reduced to a few square kilometers, in order to teach us that a certain kind of effectiveness is beyond time's measurement; that the visibility of actions doesn't always encompass their every facet; that the far-flung missions would be joined by missions inside of humanity, deep down, where the human spirit questions the world and oscillates between the mystery of God who wants man to be small and poor and the mystery of the world which wants him to be great and powerful." Madeleine Delbrêl, *Ville Marxiste, terre de mission* (Paris: Editions du Cerf, 1970), 178.

18

Constant Distractions
I have lots of distractions when I pray

"It is especially the Gospels that sustain me
during my hours of prayer, for in them I find
what is necessary for my poor little soul.
I am constantly discovering in them new lights,
hidden and mysterious meanings."[443]

Here is another source of sorrow when I try to pray: my mind is besieged by so many distractions that it seems it would be better for me to do something else. When this happens I think I would be more pleasing to God if I was doing something useful rather than dejectedly fighting against thoughts which aren't necessarily bad, but distract from my conversation with God. As a matter of fact, this is one of the reasons why many faithful Christians give up or shorten their daily prayer: they think that such a disrupted prayer doesn't do them much good and can hardly be pleasing to God.

Did Thérèse ever have the same problem? If so, what advice can she give us?

[443] A 83v.

Inevitable distractions

It sometimes happens during our prayer that ideas or incidents surface that to some extent dominate our minds so that it's nearly impossible to think of anything else during that time. In her last manuscript, Thérèse describes the way she responded to her neighbor's habit, during the community prayer hour, of distracting herself by running her fingernail over her teeth. Thérèse recounts the story wittily.

> For a long time at evening meditation, I was placed in front of a Sister who had a strange habit and I think many lights because she rarely used a book during meditation. This is what I noticed: as soon as this Sister arrived, she began making a strange little noise which resembled the noise one would make when rubbing two shells, one against the other. I was the only one to notice it because I had extremely sensitive hearing (too much so at times). Mother, it would be impossible for me to tell you how much this little noise wearied me. I had a great desire to turn my head and stare at the culprit who was quite certainly unaware of her "click." This would be the only way of enlightening her. However, in the bottom of my heart I felt it was much better to suffer this out of love for God and not to cause the Sister any pain. I remained calm, therefore, and tried to unite myself to God and to forget the little noise. Everything was useless. I felt the perspiration inundate me, and I was obliged simply to make a prayer of suffering; however, while suffering, I searched for a way of doing it without annoyance and with peace and joy, at least in the interior of my soul. I tried to love the little noise which was so displeasing; instead of trying not to hear it (impossible), I paid close attention so as to hear it well, as though it were a delightful concert, and

my prayer (which was not the Prayer of Quiet) was spent in offering this concert to Jesus.[444]

What realism! After having tried for a while not to pay attention to the unwanted noise made by her neighbor, Thérèse took the route of just listening and offering it to the Lord, as if it were a "delightful concert." *Whenever we go to prayer to please the Lord, the condition of soul we feel during that hour hardly matters.* To please God, it's better to smile than grumble! But sometimes it's only "in the soul's depth" that we experience joy and peace.

A few pages earlier, Thérèse tells us her method for dealing with distractions. "Sometimes when my mind is in such a great aridity that it is impossible to draw forth one single thought to unite me with God, I very slowly recite an 'Our Father' and then the angelic salutation; then these prayers give me great delight; they nourish my soul much more than if I had recited them quickly a hundred times."[445] In fact, this method has been normally used to fight dryness or distractions.[446] A person should recite a prayer he knows by heart, or sing a song he likes, and remember that this vocal prayer pleases the Lord just as much as the highest mystical ascents: then peace returns.

Acting on the advice that Sr. Henriette had given her in her childhood, at other times Thérèse was content to let her heart speak to God of her joys, her needs, and her love, knowing He was present. "For me, prayer is an aspiration of the heart, it is a simple glance

---

[444] C 30 r–v.

[445] C 25 v.

[446] When publishing the manuscripts, Mother Agnes kindly modified the text so that Sr. Marie of Jesus wouldn't guess "the prayer of suffering" she had occasioned in one of her neighbors for so long. *The Story of a Soul* only mentions a nun who "didn't stop fidgeting or making noise with her rosary or some such thing."

directed to heaven, it is a cry of gratitude and love in the midst of trial as well as joy; finally, it is something great, supernatural, which expands my soul and unites me to Jesus."[447]

Sometimes Thérèse would simply pray for the person about whom she happened to be thinking since she knew that "for a Carmelite to remember, and especially to love, is to pray."[448] It even happened that with the Prioress' permission, Thérèse wrote to Céline during the evening prayer time. "Our dear Mother is allowing me to come make my prayer with you…"[449]

Lastly, we can be satisfied with repeating to the Lord that we love Him very much and want to love Him more. Isn't this what the apostle Peter did beside the lake with Jesus, the Lord who had just filled his nets with fish?[450] That's what Thérèse did many times as she specifically told Céline on July 18, 1893.

> I have experienced it; when I am feeling nothing, when I am INCAPABLE of praying…then is the moment for seeking opportunities, nothings, which please Jesus more than mastery of the world…I want at least to tell Him frequently that I love Him; this is not difficult, and *it keeps the fire going*. Even though this fire of love would seem to me to have gone out, I would like to throw something on it, and Jesus could then relight it.[451]

Distractions we can avoid

Distractions that occur during our prayer can also have an entirely different source. They can come from a lack of nourishment: we have neglected spiritual reading for too long, and as a result, we come to

---

[447] C 25 r–v.
[448] LT 131.
[449] LT 122.
[450] Jn 21:15.
[451] LT 143.

prayer with our heads empty. It's well known that reading Scripture and spiritual authors is absolutely necessary for the regular practice of prayer. The Curé of Ars had more than four hundred books in his library and did spiritual reading twice a day. Monks are required to rise early every day in order to do their celebrated *lectio divina* even though most of them don't have any teaching ministry.

Catholics don't attempt to produce a mental void so that they can then hear God speaking to them. They begin by reading the word of God, re-reading it, and being saturated with it. The books of the Bible are their Lord's "expressions of love"; they are to be meditated on and savored at length. These gradually replace the memories and preoccupations which spontaneously arise in their minds from their activities in the world. More precisely—since a Catholic isn't seeking to escape the world during prayer—Bible verses, gospel parables, and reflections of the saints gradually become embedded in the memory and end by nourishing prayer and illuminating a Catholic's whole life. Worries are always present, but they are, so to speak, surrounded by God's infinite tenderness, revealed on each page of the Bible.

We can see from this fact alone the immense distance separating the methods for mental emptiness taught in various places from the royal road of Christian prayer in which silence is not an indispensable preliminary but instead a natural consequence of peacefully listening to God's Word.

BLESSED NICHOLAS BARRÉ: *PREPARE FOR PRAYER*

Going to prayer without having prepared some topic, putting oneself in an attitude of emptiness with regard to everything and expecting God to fill it, is something risky. Few people succeed through this method, although some force themselves to proceed with it, thinking it to be the most perfect and excellent. The surest way is to follow the advice of the sage: before prayer prepare your soul and do not be like one of those who tempt the Lord.[452]

It's obvious that the Holy Spirit plays a key role in our assimilation of God's Word. The Lord didn't send us the Holy Spirit to communicate messages He didn't have time to deliver during His earthly life among us, but rather to make us *better understand*, and above all, *savor the realities of the Good News* He came to proclaim to us.

It's recognized that Thérèse was well nourished by the Word of God. Even though the Carmelites of her time weren't allowed to keep a complete Bible in their cells, it's incredible the deep understanding Thérèse had of it. (A large volume was required to compile the sage commentary she offered on many verses.[453])

In 1892 she removed from her *Christian's Manual* the text of the four Gospels and rebound them so she could carry them with her all the time: a pocket gospel before the time! She opened this little book quite frequently during her prayer time, as she wrote at the end of her first manuscript.[454] We know through Sr. Marie of the Trinity's testimony that Thérèse might have slept during her morning prayer time if she hadn't had the possibility of "pecking" at her Gospel.[455]

---

[452] Blessed Nicholas Barré, *Complete Works* (Paris: Cerf, 1994), 333. This priest, a friar of the Order of Minims, was beatified in March 1990 by John Paul II. See Sir 18:23.

[453] Thérèse de Lisieux, *La Bible avec Thérèse de Lisieux* (Paris: Cerf, 1979).

[454] A 83r.

[455] Testimony given to Fr. Phillipe of the Trinity in 1940 (TLMT, 143–44), in which Thérèse herself admitted that she often slept during her prayer hour (A 75v).

However, she was bothered by the differences between translations. One day she said to Sr. Genevieve, "If I had been a priest, I would have studied Greek and Hebrew in order to understand the divine word of God as He deigned to express it in our human language."[456]

Thérèse read Scripture with a child's heart, as someone seeking to discover the "character" of her God[457]—or as a bride careful to hear her bridegroom's loving confidences. Also significant is that her preferred book of the Old Testament was the Song of Songs. She quoted it as frequently as the book of the Psalms and would have liked to write a commentary on it if she had had the chance.[458]

Reading the long letter Thérèse sent to Céline on July 7, 1894, we can see how she used certain passages of the Song of Songs—and St. John of the Cross's commentary on it from his *Spiritual Canticle*—to get through times of aridity in prayer better. Following the great tradition of *lectio divina*, she continually passed from one passage of Scripture to another during her meditation.

MADELEINE DELBREL, GOD'S WORD AND AMATEURISHNESS

Amateurishness is our greatest risk with respect to God's Word, because when we maintain a certain contact with it we have a 'secure conscience.'

In a life which ought to be born and reborn from this Word, finding there its stability and strength, receiving from it each day, not only examples but a direct course, the parable of the Sower should be a continual warning.

---

[456] MSST 69.
[457] PO 275.
[458] See TLMT 66.

To be an "amateur" in relation to God's Word is especially to take or leave it; to leave it out of our minds, rather far from us, "on the way," so that its light doesn't influence our days, our attitudes, our actions. We take a little dip in the Gospel, then we let its light be or evaporate on us or on the bath towel.

To be an "amateur" is also, with regard to God's Word, to take it or leave it in the sense of "leaving it alone." We shouldn't confuse an inner inspiration, a taste that the Holy Spirit gives us for a certain train of thoughts, feelings, things to do, with God's will, or with desires that surface in us because of intellectual research into a text for some study; or even with the desire to justify some passing inclination or a mere tendency of our laziness, with passages picked at random. You read what your eyes fall on or what comes to hand as a lifesaver and close the Bible or Gospel with the feeling of duty done.

To be an "amateur" is also to "believe for a time." We go in answer to a call of the Lord, for example, and then give ourselves the right to forget it, as if what is asked of us is always an occasional invitation.

To be an "amateur" is finally and perhaps especially to read God's Word like a *conversation* about it, even with Him, instead of a *conversion*—a conversion in which we are told all that the Lord is saying.

Some natural comparisons can help us to understand how we are "amateurs."

We claim to love the Lord and it's true that we do love Him. But let's ponder how those in love act when a separation forces them to write. Let's think about the central place the mail holds for them during the day. See them seize their letters and carry them like a treasure. See them find—as if by a miracle—the time to reply with floods of writing.

The Gospel is News, good news, and new each day.

Let's think about others and ourselves, when waiting for news, seeking to find out something, turning and returning to the things we don't understand.

Let's consider ourselves waiting for news from those we love when we are worried, waiting for news about the development of an international conflict, waiting for news about the causes of a disaster, waiting for news on the questions which affect us most in the Council…or the results of a matter close to our hearts.

When we have pondered the attitude of others or ourselves like this…when it's a question in the human realm of love, action, knowledge, we will see better, we will recognize clearly what our attitude toward God's Word is.

I don't think we will be proud of ourselves…that wouldn't be a good anyway.[459]

CHARLES DE FOUCAULD: *DON'T SKIMP ON GOOD BOOKS*

Charles de Foucauld encouraged his sister to obtain good books for her children.

Yes, my dear, I am praying, I am praying more and more for you, don't worry! Above all, don't be anxious!…Yes, be simple, yes, avoid all useless expense… Move further and further away, in your way of being and living, from all that has the feel of the world, of

---

[459] Madeleine Delbrel, *La joie de croire*, (Paris: Ed. du Seuil, 1958), 226–28.

vanity, of pride…follies that only serve to diminish your future glory in heaven, by prolonging purgatory, and that burden us with having given an unhealthy example to others, that show solidarity with a way of acting that natural reason condemns, and Christianity even more…

Don't take away anything, anything, anything that can contribute to the good moral and intellectual education of your children, nor anything else that can be useful in your own spiritual progress; no skimping on good books. If souls consecrated to God, monks who are thinking of perfection from morning to night, to the end of their lives, feel the need to read and reread the works of the masters of the spiritual life, the lives of the saints, their forbears, how much more do you have need of it when you live in the world, amid so many distracting occupations.[460]

[460] Charles de Foucauld, *Lettres à sa soeur Marie de Blic*, ed. and annotated Ph. Thiriez (Paris: Livre Ouvert, 2005), 87–88.

19

Fruitless Communions
My communions seem ineffective

"I am not always faithful, but I never get discouraged; I abandon myself into the arms of Jesus. The little drop of dew goes deeper into the calyx of the flower of the fields, and there it finds again all it has lost and even much more."[461]

There are many Catholics who don't know how to benefit from their regular communions at the Masses in which they participate. They receive communion devoutly, often quite fervently, but admit that these frequent encounters with the Lord don't transform their lives. As soon as they are immersed in the routine of their daily activities, they forget having received the Lord's living body, that very morning, into their hands and heart. St. Thérèse's way of receiving communion can definitely help us over time to become better communicants as well.

Jesus looks at me and smiles at me

Let's consider her prayer before the Blessed Sacrament, for example, in a poem composed in June 1896 for the feast of Corpus Christi,

---

[461] LT 143.

specifically for Sr. St. Vincent de Paul,[462] who liked to spend many hours in adoration before the tabernacle. This poem shows us Thérèse preparing in prayer for her next Mass and next communion.

My own heaven

To bear the exile of this valley of tears
  I need the glance of my Divine Savior.
This glance full of love has revealed its charms to me.
It has made me sense the happiness of Heaven.
My Jesus smiles at me when I sigh to Him.
Then I no longer feel my trial of faith.
My God's Glance, his ravishing Smile,
That is Heaven for me!...[463]

From the moment Thérèse arrived in the chapel she thought about Jesus *regarding* her, gazing at her. The word is repeated several times in this stanza and the penultimate one also speaks of His *regard*. She had previously honored it in her poem of February 1895, *Living on Love*:

Just one glance [*regard*] of yours makes my beatitude.
I live on Love!...[464]

---

[462] This was the nun who gave St. Thérèse the nickname "the big nanny goat" because she found her too slow at the community's manual labor. And it was she who, one day in 1897, made the comment: "What will one say about Sister Thérèse of the Child Jesus after her death? She is a nice little nun, but she hasn't done anything!" Just a few hours after St. Thérèse's death, Sr. St. Vincent de Paul would change her opinion. Laying her head against the feet of the deceased, she asked her pardon for her offenses and begged her to obtain healing for her cerebral anemia. And she was cured in an instant!

[463] PN 32, st 1.

[464] PN 17, st 3.

Again, in the play she wrote two months later for the Christmas festivities, she makes the Angel of the Holy Face say what she herself said to the Lord in the chapel, "Jesus, in the Host I see the splendor of Your face shine forth…Your ravishing charms are not at all hidden from me…I see Your ineffable look penetrating pure souls, inviting them to receive You." [465] So that she wouldn't forget the Lord's loving gaze, Thérèse placed an image of the Holy Face in her breviary. When she was sick, she attached it to her bed curtains.

We will benefit much more from the Masses we attend if we take a few minutes to rejoice in and be illuminated by the smile Jesus is giving every one of us, if we say to Him, "Here I am Lord. I am happy at the thought that you are smiling at me and that I can make you smile even more by making the most of this loving encounter with you!"

The Curé of Ars liked to repeat the exchange he had had one day with Louis Chaffangeon, the village blacksmith. Let us listen to the Curé recounting it himself: "In the parish there was a man who died some years ago. Entering the church one morning to pray before going out into the fields, he left his pickaxe at the door and forgot himself, before God. A neighbor who worked in the same place and who was used to seeing him there, was surprised by his absence. Going back, he went into the church thinking he would find him there. And there he did find him.

He asked him, "What are you doing here for so long?"
"I am looking at God and He is looking at me."

---

[465] RP2 5v.

As a matter of fact, old Mr. Chaffangeon had used the word *aveuse*, speaking in his native dialect and not *avise*. To *aveuse* a field is to regard it with love, perceiving and appreciating its full value.

Each time the Curé of Ars repeated this story—always with tears in his eyes—he added: "He looked at God and God looked at him. Everything is in that, my children."

Jesus answers me

Heaven for me is to be able to draw down on souls,
On the Church my mother and on all my sisters
Jesus' graces and his Divine flames
That can enkindle and rejoice hearts.
I can obtain everything when mysteriously
 I speak heart to heart with my Divine King.
That sweet prayer so near the Sanctuary,
That is Heaven for me!...[466]

Thoroughly convinced of the apostolic fruitfulness of her contemplative prayer, Thérèse believed that simply by being in the Lord's presence a flood of graces waiting to be poured on the world would flow out. We will benefit more from attending Mass if we live out the epiclesis which follows the consecration prayers: "Father, having been fed with the Body and Blood of Christ, may we be filled with the Holy Spirit and gathered into one by Him into a single body." We should be happy that we can bring into the world the floods of love and joy overflowing from God's heart, by uniting ourselves intimately to the prayer of the Eucharist.

[466] PN 32, st 2.

CHARLES DE FOUCAULD: *ALL YOU NEED*

Peace will also increase…by God's grace, I find it before the tabernacle…He is there, what more do you need? And He is perfectly happy there; shouldn't I be perfectly happy too? And though I am not, since those I love on earth are suffering or are anxious and sad…well, then I pray to Him for them, very poorly, very badly, but with everything in my heart. Praying to Our Lord for those I love is the great occupation of the hours I spend before Him; it is doing what I can do, both for Him and for them…That is everything one needs.[467]

Jesus is transforming me

Heaven for me is hidden in a little Host
Where Jesus, my Spouse, is veiled for love.
I go to that Divine Furnace to draw out life,
And there my Sweet Savior listens to me night and day.

Oh! what a happy moment
when in your tenderness You come,
my Beloved, to transform me into yourself.
That union of love, that ineffable intoxication,
that is Heaven for me!…[468]

Thérèse realized very well that the Mass is a divine banquet wherein Jesus desires to give Himself to us even more than we desire to receive Him. However, unlike what happens during our human

---

[467] Charles de Foucauld, *Pere de Foucauld-Abbe Huvelin, Correspondance Inédite*, ed. Fr. J. and Fr. Six, (Tournai: Desclee et Cie, 1957), 20.
[468] PN 32, st 3.

meals, there we don't assimilate the food we eat; instead, Jesus "assimilates" us, making us like Himself, transforming us into Himself.

At the end of the above stanza, when Thérèse uses the word intoxication, she is referring to the "sober inebriation" the Fathers of the Church used to describe the joy with which the Holy Spirit fills our hearts. This joy is compatible with aridity in thanksgiving after communion; Thérèse experienced this. It can also coexist with the spiritual night; she was immersed in this for two months.

May every one of our communions be the "blessed moment" in which we give Jesus the joy of transforming us, of fashioning us into His image and likeness, so that we can love the hidden life as He did, and so that we can become "meek and humble of heart," as He was. What does it matter if we don't always feel fervent at these meetings? Thérèse believed that *the essential thing was that Jesus is happy* to come to me and accomplish His work in me as Savior.

If I am in a state of grace so I can receive Him worthily, it's enough for me to invite the saints and angels to come into my soul and offer Him a "magnificent concert." This was the Carmelite's method:

> I can't say that I frequently received consolations when making my thanksgivings after Mass; perhaps it is the time when I receive the least. However, I find this very understandable since I have offered myself to Jesus not as one desirous of her own consolation in His visit but simply to please Him who is giving Himself to me. When I am preparing for Holy Communion, I picture my soul as a piece of open/cleared land and I beg the Blessed Virgin to remove from it any *rubbish* that would prevent it from being *free*; then I ask her to set up a huge tent worthy of *heaven*, adorning it with *her own* jewelry; finally, I invite all the angels and saints to come and conduct a magnificent concert there. It seems to me that when Jesus

descends into my heart. He is content to find Himself so well received and I, too, am content. All this, however, does not prevent both distractions and sleepiness from visiting me, but at the end of the thanksgiving when I see that I've made it so badly I make a resolution to be thankful all through the rest of the day.[469]

St. John Vianney

Like fragrant oil spreading throughout a piece of cloth and expanding to the last thread, to the very edge, so the Holy Eucharist spreads into our soul when it is pure. It diffuses and penetrates it completely, but only in the pure soul, aflame with love.[470]

Jesus embraces me

Heaven for me is feeling within myself the resemblance
Of the God who created me with his Powerful Breath.
Heaven for me is remaining always in his presence,
calling him my Father and being his child.
In his Divine arms, I don't fear the storm.
Total abandonment is my only law.
Sleeping on his Heart, right next to his Face,
That is Heaven for me!...[471]

---

[469] A 79v–80r; see also PN 54, st 5.
[470] Bernard Nodet, *Jean-Marie Vianney, Cure of Ars* (Paris: Xavier Mappus, 1959), 118.
[471] PN 32, st 4.

There is a very ancient iconographic tradition that shows the apostle John resting on the Savior's breast on the evening of the Last Supper. This is a beautiful way of representing the fruits of Eucharistic communion. This is how Jesus Himself spoke about it in the bread of life discourse, which echoed powerfully in the ears and the heart of this very apostle John. "He who eats my flesh and drinks my blood abides in me, and I in him."[472] While Thérèse didn't really care for images depicting Jesus simply showing His Heart, she loved the image in her collection which portrayed the beloved apostle resting peacefully in Jesus' arms and on His Heart. This image surely inspired the four last lines of this stanza.

BROTHER MARCEL VAN: *IN THE ARMS OF JESUS*

One evening in June 1945, before the end of WWII, Brother Marcel Van was adoring the Blessed Sacrament along with his community. During benediction, Jesus suddenly appeared to him:

> I saw Jesus who, coming from far away, was walking towards me. He advanced with an unmoving face, but it was filled with an exceptional gentleness. His hair came down to his shoulders. Oh! but the most striking feature was primarily the kindness of his face, that face was truly the reflection of his heart overflowing with an infinite love. And I believe that a single glance from him would be enough to cast every soul into ecstasy. The color of his clothes was no different than the representations you see in pictures. He wore

---

[472] Jn 6:56.

> a pale rose robe which reached his ankles, a red belt
> and cloak, just as in the image of Jesus the Savior.
> Jesus came near me, and I saw myself then changed
> to a little child of two or three. Before I had even the
> time to be surprised by this, I saw Jesus sit down on
> a stone seat, and he took me in his arms and pressed
> me to his heart. Then we began talking together.[473]

In her poem, Thérèse also tells us about her way of praying after communion: she surrendered herself to Jesus' arms and rested on His Heart. In her collection of images, Thérèse had some showing Jesus embracing a communicant approaching the holy table for the first time. She would have been happy to hear that the first apparition of Jesus to St. Margaret Mary at Paray-le-Monial took place on December 27 1673, the feast of St. John. Jesus invited the Visitandine nun to rest on His heart just as He had done with the beloved apostle at the Last Supper. This is truly the Savior's desire: that we will have the courage to abandon ourselves to Him, the Bridegroom; He is just waiting to enfold each of the members of the Church, His Bride, in His wonderful embrace.

However, this is on condition that we never forget that the hands holding us then are the same ones which were bound in the Garden of Gethsemane and nailed to the wood of the Cross. It's by His allowing them to be bound and pierced that we have been freed from every form of slavery. Likewise, it's on condition that we remember on leaving the church building that we abide "in Christ." Indeed, it is so that we may dwell more and more in Him that Jesus literally takes hold of us at the time of communion.

---

[473] Marcel Van, *Autobiographie* (Paris: Editions St. Paul, 2000), 414.

The Trinity dwells in my soul

I've found my Heaven in the Blessed Trinity
That dwells in my heart, my prisoner of love.
There, contemplating my God, I fearlessly tell Him
That I want to serve Him and love Him forever.
Heaven for me is smiling at this God whom I adore
When He wants to hide to try my faith.
To suffer while waiting for Him to look at me again
That is Heaven for me!...[474]

If Jesus is the "divine prisoner" of the tabernacle, the Blessed Trinity is the continual guest of our souls. Jesus promised this to us.[475] By loving Him, with the help of the Spirit of Love who surrounds us with His flames, we draw the Father into our hearts. The whole Trinity becomes our "prisoner of love." (Thérèse used this phrase in her poem Living on Love; she found it in St. John of the Cross.) Thérèse frequently marveled at the continual presence of the Blessed Trinity in the souls of the baptized. She wrote to Céline on July 7, 1894: "How great must a soul be to contain a God!...And yet the *soul of a child* one day old is a Paradise of delights for Him."

We need to recall the ongoing presence of the Blessed Trinity in the depth of our soul so that the fervor of our holy communions isn't a mere flash in the pan. When Jesus gives Himself to us in communion it's so that He may remain with us. He comes to us—and He dwells in us—with the two other Persons of the Holy Trinity. It's up to us to join them as often as possible throughout the day in our hearts. And if God seems to hide, to slip away from our faith—Thérèse was speaking from experience in her poem—as she did, we can continue smiling at Him...to please Him!

---

[474] PN 32, st 5.
[475] Jn 14:23.

St. Elizabeth of the Trinity:
Your soul is God's temple

"Realize that your soul is the temple of God," it is St Paul who says this; at every moment of the day and night the three Divine Persons abide within you. You do not possess the sacred Humanity [of Christ] as you do when you receive Communion; but the Divinity, that essence the blessed adore in Heaven, is in your soul; there is a wholly adorable intimacy when you realize that you are never alone again.[476]

Our communions will be much more fruitful when we genuinely believe that we are always "in Christ Jesus"—this expression appears more than fifty times in the writings of St. Paul—and that we are truly "in His hands" at every hour of the day and night. In view of that, let's go to communion and ask Jesus to take hold of us, so that on leaving Mass we dwell more and more in Him.

And let us live the whole of our lives as an anticipation of the heavenly banquet which will bring us into the arms of our Bridegroom eternally. This is what Thérèse recommended to her beloved novice, Marie of the Trinity, when she bid her farewell; she wrote on the back of the image she gave her on August 12, 1897: "May your life be all of humility and love in order that you may come to where I am going: into the arms of Jesus!..."[477]

---

[476] St. Elizabeth of the Trinity, Letter 273, to her mother, *Complete Works*, (ICS Publications, Washington DC, 1995), vol. 2, p. 271.
[477] LT 264.

20

Trouble Reciting the Rosary
Praying the rosary is difficult

*"I love the Blessed Virgin so much that it should be
easy for me to recite in her honor prayers which
are so pleasing to her...I think that the Queen of
heaven, since she is my MOTHER, must see my
good will and she is satisfied with it."*[478]

Trouble praying the rosary: this is a confession Thérèse made
in the last pages of her second autobiographical manuscript.
Although she liked the prayers she recited with her community, "I feel
that the fervor of my sisters makes up for mine." She acknowledged
that "when alone, the recitation of the rosary is more difficult for
me than the wearing of an instrument of penance."[479] Immediately
afterward she gives the reason for this: "I feel I have said this so
poorly! I force myself in vain to meditate on the mysteries of the
rosary; I don't succeed in fixing my mind on them."

---

[478] C 25v.
[479] C 25v. She repeated this a month later: "When I think of how much trouble
I've had all my life trying to recite the rosary!" (YN August 20, n. 12).

Poor Thérèse! Someone should have explained to her that there are many ways of praying to the Blessed Virgin and addressing her with the Archangel Gabriel's salutation. It wasn't until the 15th century that Christians began the custom of associating the litany-meditation of the *Ave Maria* with meditation on the fifteen mysteries of the rosary. Nonetheless, there are still many Catholics who prefer to gaze on the Virgin Mary and tell her of their trust and love without assuming they are obligated to meditate on this or that mystery of the life of Christ. For example, Pope John XXIII recited his rosary every day but preferred to tell his beads while thinking about the great intentions of the world and the Church.

Still, Thérèse eventually understood that she shouldn't feel guilty about encountering this problem. "For a long time, I was desolate about this lack of devotion that astonished me, *for I love the Blessed Virgin so much* that it should be easy for me to recite in her honor prayers which are so pleasing to her. Now I am less desolate; I think that the Queen of heaven, since she is my MOTHER, must see my good will and she is satisfied with it."[480]

"The Queen of Heaven is my mother"

This statement is central in Thérèse's Marian devotion. To appreciate it, we should bear in mind that Thérèse lived in an era when, for the sake of exalting Mary's greatness—the dogma of the Immaculate Conception had been defined in 1854—preachers had a tendency to present her as an exceptional being, as someone absolutely inimitable. Thérèse was annoyed by this. Six weeks before her death she said: "It is good to speak about her privileges, but we must not discuss only these, and when, in a sermon, one is obliged from beginning to end to exclaim and say 'Oh! Ah!'—we've had enough of that."

---

[480] C 25v.

That's why on the same day she stated:

We know very well that the Blessed Virgin is Queen of heaven and earth, but she is more Mother than Queen; and we should not say, on account of her prerogatives, that she surpasses all the saints in glory just as the sun at its rising makes the stars disappear from sight. My God! How strange that would be! A mother who makes her children's glory vanish! I myself think just the opposite. I believe she'll increase the splendor of the elect very much.[481]

In reading the Gospel Thérèse realized that Mary lived a life like ours, very simple, and that as a result all her children could be like her. What kind of mother would it be whom her children couldn't imitate? To develop this idea, in May 1897 Thérèse composed her last poem, as her final homage to her heavenly mother: "Why I love you, Mary!"

In the second stanza she responds to the title as a question: she loves Mary so much because she is a mother who lived and suffered just like each one of her children does.

> If a child is to cherish his mother,
> She has to cry with him and share his sorrows.
> …
> In pondering your life in the holy Gospels,
> I dare look at you and come near you.
> It's not difficult for me to believe I'm your child,
> For I see you human and suffering like me…[482]

---

[481] YN August 21, n. 3.
[482] PN 54, st 2.

Whether it's hard or easy for us to recite the rosary, let's see how Thérèse's Marian vision can help us to benefit from Mary's presence in our lives.

Her presence is that of a true mother. Faithful to the longstanding tradition of the Church, Thérèse took seriously the word Jesus spoke to His beloved apostle before His death. Indicating the Virgin Mary, He said, "Here is your mother." "And from that hour, he took her to his own home."[483] What joy we could have if, like St. John, like Thérèse, we had the boldness to fully welcome Mary as our mother, during our days…and our sleepless nights too!

A mother's smile, full of tenderness

For Thérèse, Mary was never a mother who was content to regard her children "from the heights of heaven." Mary was really spending her heaven "on earth." Through the mystery of her Assumption, when she was exalted to the highest place in heaven as queen and intercessor, the Blessed Virgin's activity no longer has physical limits: it extends to all the members of Jesus' mystical body, reaching everywhere. It is *here*. So, we can call on Mary as a mother who is personally present in our lives.

With this in mind, Thérèse was faithful to a resolution she made on May 8, 1884, the day of her first communion: to recite the *Memorare* every day. A year earlier on May 13, 1883, the feast of Pentecost, in a room of their house, Les Buissonnets, Thérèse had been healed by Mary's smile. That smile "penetrated to the depths" of her soul and healed her instantly. "All of a sudden the Blessed Virgin appeared beautiful to me, so beautiful that never had I seen anything so attractive; her face was suffused with an ineffable benevolence and tenderness, but what penetrated to the very depths of my soul

---

[483] Jn 19:27.

was the 'ravishing smile of the Blessed Virgin.'"[484] It's evident that Thérèse's Marian devotion was profoundly affected by this experience. She allowed her whole life to be permeated with that maternal tenderness, the sweetness of which she had perceived in a moment.

Thérèse calls us to reflect regularly that this maternal gaze is on us. Before saying a "Hail Mary" we should remember to let ourselves be greeted by her. At every hour of the day and night our heavenly Mother is bending over us with love and illuminating us with her smile. It's a smile we don't see but is more beautiful than anything we can imagine. This smile should transform our lives. As one child said to his mother, "Mommy, we do everything better when we know you are there!"

Her virginal mantle surrounds us

Present to us, Mary doesn't simply look at us with love. She is a mother who truly produces her Son's divine life in us: we are in her as in a maternal womb surrounding and carrying us such that Jesus' life never stops growing in our hearts. Karol Wojtyla discovered this important truth in his youth while reading *True Devotion to the Blessed Virgin Mary* by St. Louis-Marie de Montfort. This book reconciled him to Polish Marian devotion, which had seemed to him exaggerated up until then.

Without having ever read the works of St. Louis-Marie de Montfort, Thérèse early on learned to consider Mary as a mother to whom she could go and find refuge under her virginal mantle. She knew that the scapular worn by the Carmelites is the symbol of this mantle, and the Blessed Virgin is happy to protect her children with it. The feast of Our Lady of Mount Carmel, which was then very important in parishes—and called at that time the Feast of the Scapular—commemorated this each year.

---

[484] A 30r.

Before starting her pilgrimage to Rome, she went to Paris and before the statue of Our Lady of Victories, asked the Virgin to keep her far from anything that might harm her purity. She also asked her to accomplish as soon as possible her dream: to go and be hidden "underneath her virginal mantle…. This was one of my first desires as a child. Growing up, I understood it was at Carmel I would truly find the Blessed Virgin's mantle, and toward this fertile Mount I directed all my desires." [485]

And it so happened that six months after her reception of the Carmelite habit Thérèse experienced, through an exceptional mystical grace, that she was being protected by the Virgin's mantle. One day in July 1889, perhaps the 16th, the feast of Our Lady of Mt. Carmel, Thérèse walked to the grotto in the garden, dedicated to St. Mary Magdalene. Having begun her prayer there, an astonishing sense of recollection overcame her. Thérèse described it eight years after it occurred (July 1897), in a conversation with Mother Agnes, in which she described the most striking graces she had received in her life.

> It was as if a veil was thrown for me over all things on earth…I was completely hidden under the veil of the Blessed Virgin. At that time, I had been put in charge of the refectory and I remember that I did things as if not doing them, it was as if I had been lent a body. I stayed like that for a whole week… This is a supernatural state that is very difficult to explain. God alone can place us in it and sometimes it's enough to detach a soul forever from the things of earth. [486]

She admitted that she experienced then what Teresa of Avila calls in *The Interior Castle* the "flight of the spirit." St. Teresa says: "It operates

---

[485] A 57r.
[486] NV and YN July 11, n. 2.

in such a way that the spirit truly seems to have left the body...It seems to her that her whole being is found in a region entirely different from that in which we live, that there it was shown her, without mentioning other things, a light so superior to that of the one here below that she could not, despite the efforts of an interior life, have imagined it."[487] Thérèse's Marian devotion retained the imprint of this experience. She lived her contemplative life in Mary, under her virginal mantle.

In the first stanza of her first poem (February 2, 1893), a Marian poem, she expressed her joy in living under Mary's mantle.

> Ah! let me hide myself under the veil
> Concealing you from all mortal eyes,
> And near you, O Morning Star!
> I shall find a foretaste of Heaven.[488]

The same image occurs in a poem the following year, "My song for Today." Thérèse wrote:

> O Immaculate Virgin! You are my Sweet Star
> Giving Jesus to me and uniting me to Him.
> O Mother! Let me rest under your veil
> Just for today.

And in a Marian poem she gave to Céline for her first Christmas in Carmel (1894), Thérèse makes the Queen of Heaven say:

> I will hide you under the veil
> Where the King of Heaven takes refuge.
> From now on my Son will be the only star
> That shines for you.

---

[487] *Sixièmes Demeures*, trans. Fr. Gregoire de St. Joseph, (Paris: Ed. du Seuil, 1949), 970–71.
[488] PN 1, st 1.

But to shelter you always
Under my veil beside Jesus,
You must stay little,
Adorned with childlike virtues.[489]

The sign of the Scapular points to an effective synthesis of Marian spirituality, which nourishes the devotion of believers and makes them sensitive to the Virgin Mother's loving presence in their lives. The Scapular is essentially a "habit." Those who receive it are associated more or less closely with the Order of Carmel and dedicate themselves to the service of Our Lady for the good of the whole Church. Those who wear the Scapular are thus brought into the land of Carmel, so that they may "eat its fruits and its good things" (cf. Jer 2:7), and experience the loving and motherly presence of Mary in their daily commitment to be clothed in Jesus Christ and to manifest him in their life for the good of the Church and the whole of humanity.

Therefore two truths are evoked by the sign of the Scapular: on the one hand, the constant protection of the Blessed Virgin, not only on life's journey, but also at the moment of passing into the fullness of eternal glory; on the other, the awareness that devotion to her cannot be limited to prayers and tributes in her honor on certain occasions, but must become a "habit," that is, a permanent orientation of one's own Christian conduct, woven of prayer and interior life, through frequent reception of the sacraments and the concrete practice of the spiritual and corporal works of mercy. In this way the

---

[489] PN 13, st 4–5.

Scapular becomes a sign of the "covenant" and reciprocal communion between Mary and the faithful: indeed, it concretely translates the gift of His Mother, which Jesus gave on the Cross to John and, through him, to all of us, and the entrustment of the beloved Apostle and of us to her, who became our spiritual Mother.

A splendid example of this Marian spirituality, which inwardly molds individuals and conforms them to Christ, the firstborn of many brethren, is the witness to holiness and wisdom given by so many Carmelite saints, all of whom grew up in the shadow and under the protection of their Mother.

I, too, have worn the Scapular of Carmel over my heart for a long time![490]

By the same token, Thérèse invites us to take refuge under Mary's veil as she did, so we can be protected from the evil one's temptations, especially when he tries to assault our chastity. This was the advice Thérèse gave to Céline when the latter was about to depart for Lourdes on pilgrimage. On May 10, 1890 she wrote: "And the Blessed Virgin! Ah, Céline, hide yourself well in the shadow of her virginal mantle in order that she may virginize you!…"[491] And four years later in April 1864, on the occasion of her sister's twenty-fifth birthday, she again invited her to take refuge under Mary's veil and under the wings of her guardian angel.[492]

---

[490] John Paul II, Message to the Carmelite Order, for the 750th anniversary of the giving of the Scapular, March 25, 2001.
[491] LT 105.
[492] LT 161.

We can take refuge in Mary the more we live "in Jesus." In the collection of images Thérèse liked, there is one in which we see Mary holding the child Jesus on her knees, and He is holding a very small child. Thérèse understood that, far from distracting us from Jesus, Marian devotion leads us to Him. As Thérèse sings in her poem "Just for Today," Mary is truly the sweet star who gives us Jesus and unites us with Him.

A mother who is always ready to listen to us

Thérèse prayed to the Blessed Virgin with great simplicity. She knew that a child can tell their mother anything. She recognized that she need not "tidy up" her prayer, especially when addressing the Virgin Mary. She expressed a similar idea the next year in August. "I was asking the Blessed Virgin yesterday evening to stop me from coughing in order that Sister Geneviève would be able to sleep, but I added: 'If you don't do it, I'll love you even more.'"[493]

A mother we can imitate

A final way of loving one's mother and pleasing her is trying to be like her. If Thérèse found meditation on the mysteries of the rosary difficult, nevertheless she really loved to reflect on the simple life Mary certainly led in Nazareth and about the model to be found in it. She dedicated almost all the stanzas of her poem "Why I love you Mary" to this reflection. She especially liked to contemplate the humility of the Lord's little handmaid, the silence of her hidden life, the faith with which she accepted "unforeseen events from God," the depth of her contemplative prayer, and the love with which she offered her Son on Calvary for the salvation of all.

[493] YN August 15, n. 4.

Thérèse knew that in striving to imitate her heavenly mother she pleased her as much as by reciting the "prayers which are pleasing to her." That was always her great desire: to love her heavenly mother, to make her happy; that she be pleased with her child![494]

Thérèse loved the Blessed Virgin so much that she said often she was luckier than Mary, because Mary did not have the Blessed Virgin to love! "No doubt, the Blessed Virgin must laugh at my simplicity, and nevertheless what I am telling her is really true!..."[495]

That's why, on September 8, 1897, she wrote on the back of the image of Our Lady of Victories on which she had glued the little white flower given to her by her father, ten years earlier, "O Mary, if I was the Queen of Heaven and you were Thérèse, I would want to be Thérèse so that you could be the Queen of Heaven!"[496] These were the last lines she wrote.

---

[494] Thérèse always took care not to displease her heavenly mother. As a child, after having recited her prayers with the family before the statue of Our Lady before which her mother had taught her to pray, she asked Pauline: "Is God happy with me? Is the Blessed Virgin happy with me?" (note from M. Agnes, p. 65 in the first of the two notebooks in which she recopied Thérèse's manuscripts). Later, when Pauline, as prioress of the convent, asked her to write down her memories from childhood, she knelt before this same statue and asked the Virgin to guide her hand "so that she would not write a single line which was not agreeable to her" (A 2r).

[495] LT 137; the same reflection is found in YN August 21, n. 3 and August 31, n. 10.

[496] Pr 21.

21

The Haunting Desire for Authentic Love
I want to be sure of truly loving God

"I want to love you like a little child.
I want to fight like a brave warrior."[497]

There are many Catholics who are sad because they don't really grasp what they need do to live the great Commandment of Deuteronomy,[498] which Jesus Himself repeated. "Hear, O Israel: The Lord our God is one Lord; and you shall love the Lord your God with all your heart, and with all your soul, and with all your might." The sadness of these souls often comes from the fact that on the subject of the great commandment, the "first" commandment,[499] they hear sermons which seem to them completely contradictory.

Certain preachers insist a great deal on the importance of generosity to succeed in the Christian life: one must love God "with all one's strength"; we should have no hesitation about loving Him to the point of folly, just as Jesus did "foolish" things for us. Conversely,

[497] PN 36, st 3.
[498] Dt 6:4–5.
[499] Mt 22:37.

others say that it's especially important to "let go," to leave things alone, to allow the Lord to act in us and that the great sin of mankind is not abandoning self trustingly to the Lord's care. Who should we believe? Which approach is correct?

Let's enroll in St. Thérèse's school once more. She understood perfectly that these two ways of loving God are both important, and both are equally valid. They are the expression of two elements of the love we should have for the Lord—one more active, the other more contemplative.

Sometimes the soul has only one desire, that of "abiding in the Lord's love"; sometimes it wants to generously fulfill all His commands.[500] With two successive statements, Jesus summed up the two complementary ways by which we can love God: abiding in His love and keeping His commandments. We should never separate these two verbs, for fear that we might fall either into Pelagianism or quietism. (Pelagians forget that God is the source of the good works we do. Quietists forget that combat is an essential component of the Christian life.)

The desire to lose oneself in the divine ocean depends on a more "maternal" view of God, seen as a bosom, so to speak, into which one desires to sink. A spirituality that emphasizes this way of going toward God in an exclusive way would eventually transform prayer into a pantheistic fusion with the great All. The desire to offer or give something to God relies on a more "paternal" view of God: God is the wholly Other who requires and expects something from His children.

In the Bible God is presented in both ways: as an infinitely tender mother who wants to take us on her lap[501] and as a demanding father who expects His children's independence. By using both of these im-

---

[500] Jn 15:9-10.
[501] Is 66:11–33.

ages the Bible reminds us that, while being a Fire by which we wish to be consumed, God remains wholly other…Let's consider how Thérèse lived these two complementary aspects of authentic love for God.

The desire to be one with God

To love God is to desire to be one with Him. Thérèse expressed this desire sometimes by saying she wanted to let herself be more and more permeated with Him and sometimes by saying she wanted to be lost in God. These two movements of prayer have often been compared with the two phases of breathing.

Breathing in

When our prayer resembles an intake of breath, we desire God as the one who comes to fill the void in our souls. With trust, we are opening ourselves to the outpouring of His Spirit. Thérèse often approached God this way: *with a beggar's heart and with hands open before Him*, to allow the Holy Spirit to flood her soul. She is taking up here all the Biblical prayers which invite us to receive the Lord's infinite treasures like a parched land longing for rain or the deer longing for flowing streams.[502]

Thérèse understood at once that these confident calls are also acts of love, since what we desire is God Himself. We should find joy in the idea that He comes to dwell in our hearts, as Jesus promised us: "If a man loves me, he will keep my word, and my Father will love him, and we will come to him and make our home with him."[503]

When Thérèse wished to express what it meant for her to "live on love," the first idea that came to her mind was the marvelous opportunity we have of possessing God in our souls:

---

[502] Ps 63:2 and 42:2.
[503] Jn 14:23.

Living on Love is holding You Yourself.
Uncreated Word, Word of my God,
Ah! Divine Jesus, you know I love you.
The Spirit of Love sets me aflame with his fire.
In loving you I attract the Father.
My weak heart holds him forever.
O Trinity! You are Prisoner
Of my Love!...[504]

Thérèse has contributed a great deal to the Catholic rediscovery that the primary thing—and in one sense the only thing—God wants of us, is to believe in His love and allow ourselves to be transformed by Him. The reason for this is that nothing pleases God more than pouring out on us the torrents of His infinite love. Thérèse's great insights were always directed to a deeper discovery that the Lord was an *inexhaustible fountain* of graces and that this fountain is just waiting to be poured out on us. To open oneself to God isn't only the means to be transformed by Him, and achieve the holiness to which He is calling us, it's also *the best means of loving Him, and pleasing Him, since His sole desire is to come to us.*

Two years before her Act of Offering to Merciful Love, Thérèse had already written: "Merit does not consist in doing or in giving much, but rather in receiving, in loving much...It is said, it is much sweeter to give than to receive, and it is true. But when Jesus wills to take *for Himself the sweetness of giving*, it would not be gracious to refuse."[505]

On June 9, 1895, Thérèse would comprehend in a dazzling way how true it is that the Lord is a burning furnace of charity and

---

[504] PN 17, st 2.
[505] LT 142.

mercy which seeks only to set souls ablaze who offer themselves to Him.

> O my God! Is Your disdained Love going to remain closed up within Your Heart? It seems to me that if You were to find souls offering themselves as victims of holocaust to Your Love, You would consume them rapidly; it seems to me, too, that You would be happy not to hold back the waves of infinite tenderness within You…O my Jesus, let me be this happy victim; consume Your holocaust with the fire of Your Divine Love![506]

In other words, Thérèse discovered what Psalm 147 had already announced: "The Lord delights in those who hope in His love."[507] Loving God is pleasing Him by opening our soul to Him in absolute trust, allowing Him to accomplish in us His eternal desire of giving Himself to mankind. Conversely, sin is "pouring concrete" with regard to Him, hardening our heart. That's why the first beatitude is "blessed are the poor in spirit"; blessedness is found by having a soul sufficiently *empty* that it can receive the kingdom of God.

When Thérèse received the grace to go deeper into the commandment relating to fraternal charity, she understood that the Lord so much wants to take possession of our lives that His will is to love in us everyone He commands us to love. Accordingly, as she advanced, Thérèse understood more and more that the Lord is a torrent of love just waiting to inundate us…in proportion to our confidence in Him: "Let thy steadfast love, O Lord, be upon us, even as we hope in thee."[508] She also realized that the more she opened her heart to

---

[506] A 84r.
[507] See Ps 147:11.
[508] Ps 33:22.

the floods of divine mercy, the more she was allowing that mercy to reach the Church and the world.

However, this desire of letting the Lord reign more and more in her heart and in the hearts of others for Thérèse could often take a different form.

The movement of breathing out

When our prayer resembles exhalation, we desire to lose ourselves in God as a droplet of water is lost in the ocean, or better yet, the way a child throws himself into his father's arms.

There was already a desire for union with God in Thérèse's heart at her first communion: "Jesus and poor little Thérèse...were no longer two, Thérèse had vanished as a drop of water is lost in the immensity of the ocean."[509] Later, in meditating on some texts from the Old Testament copied into a notebook by Céline, Thérèse discovered that to rise to heaven it isn't necessary to grow, but instead remain very little, the more easily to be carried to the Father in Jesus' arms; He is our "divine elevator."[510]

In her poetry Thérèse frequently describes this attitude of abandonment to the arms of Jesus or the Father; for her it's an act of both trust and love:

> In his Divine arms, I don't fear the storm.
> Total abandonment is my only law.
> Sleeping on his Heart, right next to his Face,
> That is Heaven for me!...[511]

We know that this movement of abandonment into God's arms is psychologically suspect in certain circles. Some have the idea that

[509] A 35r.
[510] C 3r.
[511] PN 32, st 4.

it contains an infantile mindset, a fear and flight from reality. It's true that there are false religious attitudes, and that prayer for some Christians is simply a way of escaping from reality and turning their backs on their neighbor. However, we would have to remove entire pages from the Bible if we decide we have no right to surrender ourselves to God's embrace and remain there in peace and silence, "like a child in its mother's arms."[512]

The Bible insists on the importance of this self-surrender—both body and soul—into God's hands. "Cast your burden on the Lord, and He will sustain you."[513] Catholic tradition has always seen in this prayer of abandonment an authentic act of love. Consider the well-known prayer of Charles de Foucauld, written in 1896:

> Father, I abandon myself into your hands,
> do with me what you will.
> Whatever you may do, I thank you:
> I am ready for all, I accept all.
> Let only your will be done in me and in all your creatures.
> I wish no more than this, O Lord.
> Into your hands, I commend my soul;
> I offer it to you with all the love of my heart;
> For I love you, Lord, and so need to give myself:
> To surrender myself into your hands without reserve
>   and with boundless confidence.
> For you are my Father.

From this vantage, to love God is to cast ourselves into Him with the force of a river flowing into the sea; it is letting ourselves be drawn by Him the way iron filings are attracted by the pole of

---

[512] Ps 131:2.
[513] Ps 55:22.

a magnet. And at the end of her life Thérèse understood fully that by letting herself be attracted in this way, captivated by the Lord, she was helping all her brothers and sisters to allow themselves to be drawn by Him in turn, to hasten towards God all the more. The Bride in the Song of Songs simply says, "Draw me!" And then a great number of souls begin to run towards the Beloved too! It's not even necessary to think about them for them to be drawn toward the Lord. Thérèse observes: "this is done without constraint, without effort, it is a natural consequence of her attraction for You."[514]

The desire to render God love for love

While Thérèse's expression of her love for God frequently had the character of a contemplative repose in Him, at other times it was expressed in the form of a desire to give Him love for love—as the saying was at that time—the desire not to let any opportunity for sacrifice be lost and thus to save many souls for Him.

In this approach, God is not seen as the One who gives but as the One who receives, as the One who awaits our response, as "the little divine beggar of Christmas." The soul recalls that "The greatest honor God may bestow on a soul is not to give it much but to ask much from it."[515]

We know the place this desire had in Thérèse's heart, both as a child and as a young woman: she increased her sacrifices as she prepared for her first communion; her desire to obtain the conversion of sinners beginning in 1887; her sacrifices in preparation for her entry into Carmel at the beginning of 1888.

Moreover, reading Fr. Arminjon's *Conferences* reinforced in her heart the desire to be generous on earth so that on the last day the

---

[514] C 34r.
[515] LT 172.

Lord could say to her, "Now it is my turn" to be generous! An echo of this reading appeared in a letter to Céline: "Eternity is advancing in great strides...Soon we shall live the very life of Jesus...After having drunk at the fountain of all sorrows, we shall be deified at the very fountain of all joys, all delights..."[516]

Several months later, after describing the sorrow one experiences when the soul is plunged into an aridity that only Jesus understands, she dared to say that such suffering was equivalent to a true martyrdom—a martyrdom without honor and glory—but she didn't neglect to mention the reward Jesus promised to those who had loved Him in this way: "God will cry out: 'Now, my turn.' Oh, what will we see then?...What is this life which will no more have an end?...God will be the soul of our soul."[517]

She also expressed the desire to render God love for love in a letter to her godmother in September 1896. She understood that it was sufficient to put much love into life's simplest actions to increase the level of love in the whole Church, and at the same time, in all of its members. At this time, Thérèse isn't coming before the Lord with "empty hands", but with a heart full of love, so that apostles might preach the Gospel well and martyrs might not refuse to shed their blood.[518]

How did she demonstrate her love since "love is demonstrated by actions"? Well! Thérèse resolved more firmly than ever not to let any opportunity slip away for offering Jesus the sacrifices along her

---

[516] LT 85.

[517] LT 94.

[518] Fr. Conrad de Meester, author of *With Empty Hands*, does not dispute this idea, correctly observing that Thérèse showed herself truly to be the daughter of a business entrepreneur when she said to Jesus at the end of her life: "God will have to carry out my will in heaven because I have never done my own will here on earth" (YN July 13, n. 2).

path and singing while offering Him these "rose petals." Then she added, her "song would be all the more melodious in proportion to the length and sharpness of the thorns" in the midst of which she would sometimes be obliged to gather those roses![519]

St. Elizabeth of the Trinity:
TWO MOVEMENTS OF PRAYER

In her well-known prayer from November 21, 1904, St. Elizabeth of the Trinity expresses in a single paragraph the two complementary ways of loving the Lord. She begins by telling Him her desire to render Him love for love: "O my beloved Christ, crucified for love, would that I might be for You a spouse of Your heart! I would anoint You with glory, I would love You—even unto death!" Then she admits that it is impossible to live up to this ideal unless Jesus comes to "adorn me with Yourself; submerge me—expiration—identify my soul with all the movements of Your soul; substitute Yourself in me—inspiration."

"Yet I sense my frailty and ask You to adorn me with Yourself; identify my soul with all the movements of Your soul, submerge me, overwhelm me, substitute Yourself in me that my life may become but a reflection of Your life. Come into me as Adorer, Redeemer and Savior."

With marvelous suppleness, Thérèse repeatedly moved from one form of love to the other. For example, for her the child is sometimes

---

[519] B 4v.

the one who expects everything from his father, who surrenders, who lets himself be loved and forgiven with absolute trust. Sometimes the child is the one who doesn't let an opportunity pass of offering his father another bouquet of flowers, new smiles, in order to make him happy.[520] Yet she never forgot that such offerings, such flowers, while being the fruit of her efforts, are also the Lord's free gift: it was He who put the bouquet into the child's hands. As St. Augustine put it, she understood that in crowning our merits, God is crowning His own gifts.

In one of her poems, "Jesus Alone," Thérèse quite correctly expresses the two complementary elements of her love for the Lord:

> It's to you alone, Jesus, that I'm attached.
> It's into your arms that I run and hide.
> I want to love you like a little child.
> I want to fight like a brave warrior.
> Like a child full of little attentions,
> Lord, I want to overwhelm you with caresses,
> And in the field of my apostolate,
> Like a warrior I throw myself into the fight!...[521]

Yes, we can be sure of pleasing the Lord by being both the child who joyfully throws himself into His arms and the valiant warrior who bravely sets off into the field of battle to "win" souls for Him.

---

[520] YN August 6, n. 8.
[521] PN 36, st 3.

22

God's Apparent Silence
God doesn't answer my prayers

*"When we pray to the Blessed Virgin and she doesn't
answer, that's a sign she doesn't want to. Then it's better
to leave her alone and not torment ourselves."*[522]

It's a fact—many of our petitionary prayers aren't answered
positively, even those which seem to be entirely legitimate and
addressed to God with a child's trust and a beggar's perseverance,
like the man pounding on his neighbor's door to obtain something
to give his friend who is on a journey.[523] The saints all experienced
this trial at one time or another. The Curé of Ars prayed night
and day for the conversion of his parish but suffered until the
end of his life seeing that certain parishioners chatted during his
sermons...or didn't make their Easter duties. A year before his
death, he rejoiced at the idea that the parish mission preached by
Fr. Descôtes might make the village recalcitrants abandon their
religious indifference.

522 YN August 23, n. 8.
523 See Lk 11:5–8.

Thérèse was no exception to this. She died before seeing the conversion of acquaintances for whom she had prayed confidently. During the spiritual night of the last eighteen months of her life, she offered all her acts of faith for the conversion of René Tostain, an agnostic judge who had married her distant cousin, Marguerite-Marie Maudelonde. This judge, a man who was also very upstanding, died, as he had lived, an agnostic. Thérèse had prayed that Jeanne Guérin, her first cousin, married to Dr. Francis La Neele, would become a mother, and yet that couple remained childless.

She wrote to Jeanne more than once about her hopes on this subject. On October 17, 1891, she penned the following: "My poor prayers undoubtedly are not worth much, however, I hope that Jesus will answer them, and, instead of looking at her who is addressing them to Him, He will rest His eyes on those who are their object, and thus He will be obliged to grant me all my requests. I hope that soon God will send a little Isidore as perfect as his Papa or else a little Jeanne resembling exactly her Mamma..." Two years later, October 22, 1893, she wrote again, "So, without leaving aside good Saint Anne, I am praying to St. Teresa to obtain through her intercession the favor of being an aunt myself. I do not doubt that she will answer me by sending to my dear little Jeanne a blessed family that will give to the Church some great saints."[524]

How can St. Thérèse help us to avoid sadness in the face of the apparent uselessness of our prayers, and especially when confronted with the religious indifference of young people or adults for whom we have fasted and prayed for years? If we aren't answered, it's not necessarily because we haven't obeyed the Lord's advice to His disciples about how to conquer the evil one: "And He said to them, 'This kind cannot be driven out by anything but prayer and

---

[524] LT 150.

fasting.'"[525] Rather than feeling guilty, let's allow Thérèse to show us how to profit from this trial. We can grow in faith, hope, charity, and gratitude.

My faith deepens

Our certainty about being loved by God unceasingly doesn't depend on the number of favors He grants us, but on His word. In Psalm 119, He tells us in thirty-six different ways that His love for us is "without measure."[526] He is a Father who knows His children's smallest needs, even before they present them to Him.[527] He demonstrated His love for us in the most dazzling way by giving us His Son as our Savior. After such proofs of love, will we act like temperamental children—never satisfied with the gifts their parents give them?

Thérèse loved Job's exclamation: "Though He slay me, yet will I trust Him."[528] She quoted this Scripture verse frequently to reaffirm before the Lord her resolute faith in His loving presence. Repeating it on her sick bed, experiencing her night of faith, she admitted that this statement had "fascinated her from childhood."[529] (As a matter of fact, a book containing this verse was awarded to her as a prize by the Abbey school, when she was about eleven years old.[530])

Similarly, this is the reason she was so fond of the image representing Jesus sleeping in St. Peter's boat as it is tossed by the storm.[531]

---

[525] Mk 9:29.
[526] See Ps 119, 156.
[527] Mt 6:8.
[528] Job 13:5 NKJV.
[529] YN July 7, n. 3.
[530] Awarded on August 4, 1884, the book was about natural science: *La Théologie des plantes ou histoire intime du monde vegetale*, by Fr. Chaudé (see BT, 17).
[531] DLVI 401.

If Jesus wishes to keep sleeping, we should not wake Him, she said, because He knows what to do. This idea appears in a stanza of her poem, "Living on Love": "Oh! Lord, don't fear that I'll wake you./ I'm waiting in peace for Heaven's shore...[532]

Thérèse frequently used nautical vocabulary to express her complete trust in Jesus' presence amid her sufferings. Even if Jesus seemed to be sleeping, His heart was awake.[533] As a result, she should continue her voyage to eternity's shores in profound peace.

> Divine Pilot! whose hand guides me,
> I'm soon to see you on the eternal shore.
> Guide my little boat over the stormy waves in peace
> Just for today.[534]

And so, we should never interpret the fact that we haven't been answered as a sign that God is displeased with us, that He is reproaching us for a lack of fervor in prayer or a failure of generosity in some area of our lives. Rather than assuming we are failing in trust or love, let's remain His trusting children. That's how we should always go to Him, calling to Him, "*Abba!*" If He doesn't grant our desires as quickly as we would like, we should remember that God isn't deaf, even when He appears mute. "Behold, he who keeps Israel will neither slumber nor sleep."[535]

Here is the marvelous answer one child gave when asked about this state of affairs: "Doesn't God hear you?" "He listens to me, but He says, 'Not yet!'" How true this is! When God postpones answering us, it's because His schedule doesn't match ours. "The Lord waits to be gracious to you."[536]

---

[532] PN 17, st 9.
[533] Song 5:2.
[534] PN 5, st 5.
[535] Ps 121:4.
[536] Is 30:18.

My hope grows

Let's remember that God's apparent delays in answering our prayers may be due to the bad will of men, to hardened hearts. God's grace doesn't override human freedom. Sinners for whom we increase our prayers and fasting remain free beings. Besides, they can repair in a few moments years and years of depravity since, in God's eyes "One day is as a thousand years, and a thousand years as one day."[537] This is why we should never give up hope for anyone.

We should take into account that we can benefit by all these delays to deepen our trust. Or rather, God wishes, on this occasion, to make our hope increase. This is certainly the reason why Jesus didn't immediately answer the prayers of the Canaanite woman who was begging Him for her daughter's healing. "A Canaanite woman from that region came out and cried, 'Have mercy on me, O Lord, Son of David; my daughter is severely possessed by a demon.' But He did not answer her a word." The apostles intervened in their turn so that the woman wouldn't come after them with her cries. Far from satisfying the woman's desire, Jesus answered rather dryly, "It is not fair to take the children's bread and throw it to the dogs." With a marvelous confidence, the woman replied: "Yes, Lord, yet even the dogs eat the crumbs that fall from their master's table." Then Jesus proclaimed His admiration and answered the mother, "O woman, great is your faith! Be it done for you as you desire."[538]

It's likely that Jesus purposely didn't answer the woman's request immediately in order to oblige her in some fashion to take her audacity further—or more precisely, to allow her to open up to the grace of a greater hope.

537 2 Pt 3:8.
538 Mt 15:21–28.

For, let's remember, hope is a theological virtue; we can't acquire it through our own efforts. It would be an accomplishment if someone could boast about trusting the Lord, but it's a grace which prepares us for all others. Consequently, when we feel very poor in trust, let's ask God to transform our thimbleful of hope into an immense vessel, so that He can pour out on us all His various blessings. The Bible affirms, His mercy is "upon us, even as we hope" in Him.[539]

This was how St. Thérèse encouraged Céline to persevere in prayer for the conversion of Hyacinthe Loyson: "Let us not grow tired of prayer; confidence works miracles. And Jesus said to Blessed Margaret Mary: 'One just soul has so much power over my Heart that it can obtain pardon for a thousand criminals.'"[540]

As a matter of fact, Fr. Loyson never rejoined the Catholic Church he had chosen to renounce in 1870. He thanked the Lisieux Carmel for sending him in 1911, a copy of *The Story of a Soul*, saying that he was very touched by what he had read. Beginning in 1897 he benefited from the friendship of Fr. Huvelin, the outstanding priest who helped Fr. Charles de Foucauld in his conversion and accompanied him in his vocational search. However, Fr. Loyson's *curriculum vitae*, engraved on his funerary monument ends with the words: He rose above all churches and ending his life as a freethinking monotheist. Yet we must mention that at the moment of his death, on February 9, 1912, he kissed his crucifix and whispered, "My sweet Jesus!"

However, it's true that Thérèse experienced the joy of seeing her prayers miraculously answered more than once. Some examples include: Pranzini's conversion *in extremis*, on August 31, 1887; the permission to enter Carmel granted by her uncle Guérin on October 22, 1887; Bishop Hugonin's permission to receive the veil at

---

[539] Ps 33:22.
[540] LT 129.

age 15, given January 1, 1888; the snowfall for her reception of the habit, January 9, 1888; the permission given by Sr. Aimée de Jesus in September 1894 for Céline's entry into Carmel; Sr. Marie of the Trinity's profession, April 30, 1894 and so forth. Yet, as we described at the beginning of this chapter, this wasn't always so.

My love is purified

Thérèse believed that if we continue loving the Lord when He doesn't grant the favors we ask for, we make Him very happy, since we are then demonstrating that we love Him far more than the gifts He gives us. As she wrote to Céline, "He does not will that we love Him for His gifts, He Himself must be our reward."[541]

By not granting our desires immediately, God clearly wants to correct them, harmonizing them with His loving plan for us. "Truly, truly, I say to you, if you ask anything of the Father, He will give it to you in my name."[542] To pray in Jesus' name isn't simply to ask Him to intercede for us before the Father; it's to pray as He has taught us, by asking His Spirit to *purify our hearts of all desires not in conformity with the Father's will.*

My gratitude becomes stronger

St. Paul repeats many times the importance of giving thanks and the close connection this has with Christian joy. In his first letter to the Thessalonians, he writes: "Rejoice always, pray constantly, give thanks in all circumstances; for this is the will of God in Christ Jesus for you."[543] A few years later he repeats this to the Philippians: "Rejoice in the Lord always; again I will say, Rejoice…Have no anxiety

---

[541] LT 145.
[542] Jn 16:23.
[543] 1 Thess 5:16–18.

about anything, but in everything by prayer and supplication with thanksgiving let your requests be made known to God." The Apostle stresses: prayer should be permeated with thanksgiving.[544]

Thérèse also emphasized the place thanksgiving ought to have in our prayer. She told Céline: "It is the spirit of gratitude which draws down upon us the overflow of God's grace, for no sooner have we thanked Him for one blessing than He hastens to send us ten additional favors in return. Then, when we show our gratitude for these new gifts, He multiplies His benedictions to such a degree that there seems to be a constant stream of divine grace ever coming our way."[545]

Similarly, when Céline asked her sister to write a poem honoring all the sacrifices she had had to accept to enter Carmel, Thérèse did not fulfill her sister's wish. She turned the topic upside down. The twenty-three stanzas of the poem she gave Céline don't commemorate Céline's sacrifices for Jesus, but all of Jesus' gifts to Céline: "Remember all the proofs Jesus has given you of His spousal love."[546]

Yes, what we have already received from God—His infinite love, all the blessings He has granted us throughout our lives, and especially our faith in His love—all this is infinitely more important than our requests to Him, however legitimate they may be. That is why the Apostle says our prayers of supplication should always be accompanied by thanksgiving.[547]

But please note! This doesn't mean petitionary prayers are less beautiful, less pure, less pleasing to God than prayers of thanksgiving. God is delighted to see that we believe in His omnipotence

---

[544] Ph 4:4–7.
[545] MSST 64.
[546] See PN 24.
[547] Ph 4:6.

and His infinite love, and that consequently we are bold enough to ask Him to accomplish great things for us and through us. A good father is happy to arrange surprises for His children, to offer them gifts that are completely unexpected. Much more so, our heavenly Father has prepared from all eternity truly astonishing graces for His cherished children.[548]

Let's remember that the two greatest saints who were not answered were Mary and Joseph. While giving Nazareth an extraordinary witness of fraternal charity, they must have prayed a great deal for the people of their town, many of whom were their relatives. Yet the gospel tells us that Jesus couldn't do any miracles there because of their lack of faith.[549] Surely Mary suffered very much on account of this.[550] However, in maintaining her faith, she merited many graces of conversion for her contemporaries…and for all her children! What's more, we know from ancient graffiti that a Jewish-Christian community developed some years later in the town of Nazareth.[551]

ABBA AGATHON: *PERSEVERANCE IN PRAYER*

In their sayings, the Desert Fathers frequently return to the topic of the struggle required to persevere in prayer.

---

[548] See Lk 11:13.

[549] Mk 6:5–6.

[550] It's quite likely that Joseph had left this world before the beginning of Jesus's public ministry, for there is no mention of him in the account of the wedding at Cana.

[551] On the walls of Nazareth is found the oldest *Kairé Maria* (*Ave Maria*) known.

> The brethren asked Abba Agathon, "Amongst all good works, which is the virtue that requires the greatest effort?" He answered, "Forgive me, but I think there is no labor as great as prayer. For every time a man wants to pray, his spiritual enemies, the demons, want to prevent him. They know that it is only by turning him from prayer that they can hinder his journey. Whatever good work a man undertakes, if he perseveres in it, he will attain rest. But prayer is warfare to the last breath."[552]

We, too, merit many graces for the Church and the world by offering smiles to the Lord when we are faced with disappointments caused by what appears to be His deafness to our pleas. All the same, we can be sure of this—He is not asleep. Thérèse liked to "hear" Jesus repeating to her the verse from the Song of Songs, the one which Céline wrote on the sail of the little boat she had given her in December 1887, to encourage her to wait peacefully for the Bishop's permission: "I sleep, but my heart is awake."[553]

As Thérèse liked to say to Sr. Marie of the Trinity: "One can never have too much confidence in the good God, so powerful and so merciful! We obtain from Him as much as we hope for."[554] This is why we have the right and the duty to remain joyful when the Lord doesn't answer our prayers as quickly as we would like.

---

[552] Benedicta Ward, *The Sayings of the Desert Fathers* (Kalamazoo: Cistercian Publications, 1975), 21–22.
[553] Song 5:2 NKJV.
[554] TLMT 133–34.

23

The Issue of Heaven
I ask myself if heaven is real

*"When I sing of the happiness of heaven and of
the eternal possession of God, I feel no joy in this,
for I sing simply what I want to believe."*[555]

What if there is nothing after death? What proves that those who have died still exist, that they are aware of us, that they love us? How can we remain at peace when these questions suddenly grip our minds and become entrenched? A fundamental doubt about the existence of heaven is all the more painful since up until this point we had a serene certainty about it: when we attended a funeral Mass, it was almost self-evident for us that the deceased knew we were there, near him: he was praying for us and asking us to pray for him so that he could have the quickest possible entry into heaven's full light.

Thérèse can help us remain peaceful when we are in the grip of this dreadful anxiety. She went through this very trial and responded to it in an exemplary way.

[555] C 7v.

The trial

In the wee hours of Good Friday 1896, Thérèse checked her handkerchief to see that it was really blood she had coughed up the night before. Seeing it, Thérèse was elated. "At this time, I was enjoying such a living faith, such a clear faith, that the thought of heaven made up all my happiness, and I was unable to believe there were really impious people who had no faith. I believed they were actually speaking against their own inner convictions when they denied the existence of heaven."[556]

However, at the start of the next week, "on the joyous day of Easter," Jesus allowed her soul to be invaded with thick darkness. She had the sense that in progressing towards death, she was advancing towards nothingness. Thérèse experienced this night of faith for a long time. In 1891 as well she had faced "great interior trials even to the point of asking myself whether heaven really existed."[557] But the affliction now was on an entirely different scale. It was no longer "a veil" which hid heaven from her but "a wall": "It seems to me that the darkness, borrowing the voice of sinners, says mockingly to me:… 'Advance, advance; rejoice in death which will give you not what you hope for but a night still more profound, the night of nothingness.'" Thérèse added: "I don't want to write any longer about it; I fear I might blaspheme; I fear even that I have already said too much."[558]

The fact that there had been no miracle at Mother Genevieve's tomb (she was foundress of the Lisieux Carmel), as Thérèse had hoped, also didn't help her to believe in the existence of heaven.

As strange as it may seem, Thérèse's doubts weren't about the existence of God or Jesus' presence in her life, but about the reality of a future life. Unlike the agnostic who doubts everything or the believer

---

[556] C 5r.
[557] A 80v.
[558] C 6v–7r.

who questions his faith outright, Thérèse was horribly tempted to doubt the existence of heaven, even though she was continually in conversation with Jesus. *She recognized the incoherence of these trials.* "It's upon heaven that everything bears," she told Mother Agnes on July 3, adding, "How strange and incomprehensible it is!"[559] A month later she emphasized again the incoherence by telling Mother Agnes: "Must one love God and the Blessed Virgin so much and have these thoughts!"[560]

Sometimes there were flashes of light, such as the visit she received in a dream, from Venerable Anne of Jesus, but these were short.[561] "It is true that at times a very small ray of the sun comes to illumine my darkness, and then the trial ceases for an instant, but afterward the memory of this ray, instead of causing me joy, makes my darkness even more dense."[562]

The response

How did Thérèse respond to this awful ordeal? Unable to refute arguments trying to convince her there was no heaven, *she simply countered it with the word of Jesus:* "If it were not so, would I have told you that I go to prepare a place for you?...I will come again and will take you to myself, that where I am you may be also."[563] She quoted this Gospel verse specially in a prayer filled with the image of Joan of Arc and composed during her night of faith:

O my Jesus, I will fight then, for your Love, until the evening of my life. As you did not wish to rest on earth, I want to

[559] YN July 3, n. 3.
[560] YN July 10, n.7.
[561] B 2r–v.
[562] C 7v.
[563] Jn 14:2–3.

follow your example. I hope this promise that fell from your Divine lips will find fulfillment in me: "If anyone follow Me, where I am, there also will my servant be. Whoever serves me, my Father will honor."[564]

She re-read the account of the resurrected Christ's appearances and attempted to harmonize them into a genuine Paschal concordance.

On the advice of Fr. Godefroid Madeleine to whom she confided her temptations, she resolved always to wear over her heart the text of the Creed. She copied it onto a sheet which she then glued to the front page of her pocket Gospel. Moreover, she wrote it with a pen dipped in her own blood as ink, the better to show Jesus she was ready to shed her blood for each of the articles of the Apostle's Creed. (The retreat preacher never suggested this to her!)[565]

In other words, though her mind was overrun by doubts, Thérèse didn't give in to the temptation to doubt. She believed wholeheartedly in the existence of heaven, despite all the objections endeavoring to show it didn't exist. Far from doubting, she made more acts of faith. She wrote in her last manuscript:

> I believe I have made more acts of faith in this past year than all through my whole life. At each new occasion of combat, when my enemies provoke me, I conduct myself bravely. Knowing it is cowardly to enter into a duel, I turn my back on my adversaries without deigning to look them in the face; but I run toward my Jesus. I tell Him I am ready to shed my blood to the last drop to profess my faith in the existence of heaven.[566]

---

[564] PR 17.
[565] See Prayer 19: "I believe in…eternal life" (DLTH 259).
[566] C 7r.

The offering

As she had always done before, Thérèse offered this new trial for the salvation of her brethren. Up till then, she had prayed for the conversion of sinners and the holiness of priests. She discovered at the beginning of April 1896 that there really were "souls who do not have faith."

Having lived her entire life in a Catholic atmosphere, she had had trouble imagining that there could be unbelievers with good will. She was probably thinking of René Tostain, a judge in Lisieux, who had married her cousin, Marguerite-Marie Maudelonde, and who was the model of a sincere agnostic.[567] Perhaps she was thinking of Henri Chéron whom she had met in the back office of her uncle's pharmacy—she remembered also the accordion tunes he played to entertain her. He filled the columns of the *Progrés Lexovian* (a newspaper for Lisieux) with his virulent anti-clericalism. (He had started it to oppose Mr. Guérin, formerly a patron.)

Does this mean that Thérèse from that time on regarded all unbelievers as sincere? Not at all! She said later, "Jesus made me feel that there were really souls who have no faith, and who, through the abuse of grace, lost this precious treasure, the source of the only real and pure joys."[568] Thérèse was surely thinking of Leo Taxil, the man blessed with a Christian education in youth and who later indulged in a heinous deception. Besides, later in this passage, she again speaks about her unbelieving brethren as "sinners." She is seated at their table and partakes with them the bread of sorrow, that is, while having faith, she doesn't experience its joys.

However, she was happy to offer this sacrifice to Jesus to obtain the salvation of her unbelieving brethren:

---

[567] See YN September 2, n. 7.
[568] C 5v.

I tell Him I am ready to shed my blood to the last drop to profess my faith in the existence of heaven. I tell Him, too, I am happy not to enjoy this beautiful heaven on this earth so that He will open it for all eternity to poor unbelievers. Also, in spite of this trial which has taken away all my joy, I can nevertheless cry out: "You have given me DELIGHT, O Lord, in ALL your doings."[569]

Thérèse wrote this psalm verse at the end of her pocket Gospel, before the text of the creed which she had penned with her blood.

The example of Mary

Thérèse also liked to ponder Mary's unwavering faith during the darkness she experienced. She dedicated four stanzas of her last poem to meditation on the terrible agony the Blessed Virgin felt when she set out to search for Jesus, when He had remained behind in Jerusalem to converse with the teachers of the law.[570] The Virgin "lived by faith, as we do" Thérèse liked to repeat.[571]

> No rapture, miracle, or ecstasy
> Embellish your life, O Queen of the Elect!...[572]

Complete abandonment

To the end of her life, Thérèse remained plunged in darkness. In the course of a poem or reflection, she describes her trial.

> Heaven for me is smiling at this God whom I adore
> When He wants to hide to try my faith.[573]

---

[569] C 7r.
[570] PN 54, st 13–16.
[571] YN August 21, n. 3.
[572] PN 54, st 17.
[573] PN 32, st 5.

When the blue Sky becomes somber
And begins to abandon me,
My joy is to stay in the shadow...
I love the night as much as the day...

And I'm twice as tender
When He slips away from my faith.[574]

Still, Thérèse abandoned herself trustingly into God's hands. He had never disappointed her hopes. He could truly cause her to live forever with Him even if she didn't see how the mysterious passage would be accomplished. More than ever, death appeared to her as an immense leap which would cause her to land "on the good God's lap."[575]

She was conscious that this ordeal was causing her faith to grow, "Since the time He permitted me to suffer temptations against the faith, He has greatly increased the spirit of faith in my heart."[576] Yet she didn't rely simply on her own strength to resist the temptation to doubt. "If I said to myself: 'O my God, You know very well I love You too much to dwell upon one single thought against the faith,' my temptations would become more violent and I would certainly succumb to them."[577]

MOTHER TERESA'S NIGHT OF FAITH

We might think that Mother Teresa of Calcutta lived life like a long, tranquil river. A life of inner joy crowned with dazzling successes. But this isn't the case.

---

[574] PN 45, st 3, 4.
[575] DE/G 3.9.2.
[576] C 11r.
[577] YN August 7, n. 4.

"My smile is a great cloak that covers a multitude of pains," she wrote in July 1958. "I smile all the time. The Sisters and the people think that my faith, my hope, my love fill me deeply, and that intimacy with God and union with His will permeate my heart. If only they could know."

Only today do we know, from the documentation gathered for her beatification process, what this dramatic confidence was all about. We now have her unpublished correspondence with her confessors, with her archbishop. She reveals to us her secret, hidden even from her closest collaborators who never suspected anything: eighteen months of uninterrupted dialogue with Jesus, an interior voice that inspired her, and even more, that commanded her to create a new order to go with Him and for Him to the poorest.

And then, half a century of dark night, with only one month of light in October 1958 when, in the oppression of her spiritual abandonment, she obtained a sign of His hidden presence. The rest of the time, and this was half a century, she lived faith amid trial, like Thérèse of Lisieux whose name she wanted to take: "I feel that God is not God, that He does not really exist. There is a terrible darkness in me. It is as if everything in me is dead, because everything is frozen. It's only the blind faith that carries me, because, in truth, everything is darkness for me. Sometimes the agony of desolation is so great and at the same time the lively hope of the Absent One so deep, that the only prayer that I still manage to recite is: 'Sacred Heart of Jesus, I entrust myself to You. I will fill your thirst for souls.' Today I felt a deep joy: because Jesus can no longer experience the agony directly, He desires to live it through me. I surrender myself more than ever to Him."

She begged her bishop, "Pray for me, pray for me that I may never become like Judas."

Like St. Thérèse of Lisieux, the Carmelite whose little way she wished to follow, she is a sign of hope for us today. She said, "If I ever become a saint, I will be absent from heaven all the time to go to earth to light the light of those who are in darkness." Both suffered much, the suffering of the dark night, and physical sufferings too. For Mother Teresa a chronic, stabbing headache. For both, participation in Christ's cross, in the silence of Carmel or in the confusion of the cities. And Mother Teresa never stopped saying that her strength came to her from a single source: Jesus. Following her example, let us allow Jesus to enter our lives and abandon ourselves completely to his love. This is what she did; this is following Thérèse of Lisieux's little way of love. Mother Teresa took her name in religious life: "I chose her as my patron saint because she did ordinary things with an extraordinary love."[578]

We can't simply be content to admire Thérèse—we must imitate her! If we are tempted to call an article of the Creed into question, like Thérèse we must wield the sword of God's Word to conquer temptation. This is the offensive weapon to employ for conquering the evil one, as St. Paul tells us.[579]

[578] Cardinal Paul Poupard, Conference at Notre Dame, Paris, March 16, 2003.
[579] Eph 6:17.

With John Henry Newman, let us keep in mind that "a thousand difficulties do not make a single doubt."[580] We can affirm with conviction that eternal life is real, even if we don't see how the human soul can exist and think without being united to the body it's normally meant to animate.

---

[580] This well-known aphorism from Newman is quoted in the *Catechism of the Catholic Church* 157. It is found at the beginning of Chapter 5 of his *Apologia Pro Vita Sua*.

24

Fear of God's Judgement
I fear the judgement of God

"[Fr. Prou] told me that my faults caused God no pain,
and that holding as he did God's place, he was telling me in
His name that God was very much pleased with me."[581]

Could there be a greater sorrow for a disciple of Christ than the issue of whether or not he will be able to join Him in heaven? Here it's not a question of doubt about the existence of heaven, but about the possibility of attaining it. It isn't a matter of temptation against the virtue of faith, as we contemplated in the last chapter, but against the virtue of hope: "Am I pleasing to God now? Will I make the right choice at the hour of death?"

By pondering how Thérèse responded to this temptation we will see again how we can and should remain joyful in every situation, and particularly in the terrible battle that we will all experience "at the hour of our death," and for which every day we ask the Blessed Virgin's assistance.

[581] A 80v.

For the sake of precision, we are making a distinction between the fear of being damned and the fear of having to spend time in purgatory, treating each separately.

Fear of damnation

As a child, Thérèse frequently asked her parents or older sisters if God was happy with her. The sacrifices she made and that she kept track of on her "chaplet of good deeds" were done for the sake of pleasing Jesus. When she confessed to Fr. Domin on the day before her first communion, she asked him, "Father, do you think that Jesus is pleased with me?"[582]

This desire to please Jesus was the fundamental motivation of her life, as we have shown.[583] It accounts for the intense suffering she experienced at the beginning of her adolescence during the fifteen months her scruples lasted (July 1885 to October 1886). When she was freed from it, this desire was more serene. However, in the last eighteen months of her life, an anxiety of the same type unsettled her once more. It wasn't attacks of scruples per se—she no longer saw sins where there were none—but she was haunted by a question: was the "little way" which she had taught her novices correct? Was it truly pleasing to the Lord?

The spiritual night into which she entered in April 1896, a few days after her first hemoptysis, consequently, wasn't only about the existence of heaven. She told Mother Agnes one day in May: "Yesterday evening, I was seized with a real agony and my darkness increased. Some cursed voice said to me: 'Are you sure of being loved by God? Did He come and tell you?' It is not the opinion of creatures which will justify you before Him."[584]

---

582 PA 395.
583 See Chapter 2, p 17.
584 21–26.5.11, *Last Conversations*.

In fact, Thérèse was asking herself if God was as kind, as merciful as she had believed up to then. Was her entire little way of trust and love merely an illusion? Fr. Godefroid Madelaine who heard Thérèse's confessions in 1896 testified that she was suffering from extremely intense temptations "concerning her eternal salvation." "Her soul went through a crisis of spiritual darkness in which she believed she was damned."[585]

Fortunately, Thérèse occasionally received genuine reassurances from heaven. During the night of May 10, 1896, Venerable Anne of Jesus[586] appeared to her in a dream. She told Thérèse she would die soon and that God was very pleased with her. A year later, a note from Mother Agnes arrived to console her. In that note her "little mother" reminded her of all the favors Jesus had granted her and assured her she was "deeply cherished by God and soon to receive from His hand her eternal crown."

She then opened her Gospel and her eyes fell upon a passage which she hadn't noticed particularly until then: "For he whom God has sent utters the words of God."[587] Thérèse went to sleep entirely at peace: this Gospel verse showed her that she should take the consoling words her sister had written as God's words…It was true that God was very pleased with her.[588]

We have seen previously[589] that Thérèse had a deep awareness of being intensely affected by pride, so much so that she didn't hesitate,

---

[585] PA, 559.
[586] A companion of St. Teresa of Avila, Anne de Lobera was the nun for whom St. John of the Cross wrote the commentary on his *Spiritual Canticle*. In 1604, she brought the Teresian reform to Paris and a few years later to Belgium. She died at the Brussels Carmel in 1621.
[587] Jn 3:34.
[588] DE 434.
[589] See Chapter 4.

a few weeks before her death, to say that she was praying not to yield to temptations of pride which might surface in her soul. As Fr. Molinié (a great disciple of, and commentator on St. Thérèse) put it: she had "the courage to be afraid."[590] She truly understood that the only way of getting by, of being saved, was to abandon herself utterly into Jesus' arms—He is the only one who can save us. As Thérèse describes it in poem 32:

> In his divine arms I do not fear the storm
> Total abandonment is my only law.

The Curé of Ars: *I will not be confounded forever*

We have much need of grace. It's like that night, I didn't sleep; I wept over my poor life. All of a sudden, I heard a voice which said to me, "*In te Domine speravi; non confundar in aeternum*" ("In thee, O Lord, have I hoped; I will not be confounded forever.") I looked around me and I saw no one. The same voice repeated these words again more distinctly. I got up and opening my breviary, my eyes fell on the same passage and I was greatly consoled.[591]

We shouldn't fear the storm of the temptation to despair because *in Jesus we have an absolutely sure refuge*: He is our stronghold and our savior. Following Thérèse, this is the same method we should use when we ask ourselves if we will have to make a more or less lengthy stay in purgatory before we finally enter into God's glory.

---

[590] This is the title of one of his books (Paris: Cerf, 1975).
[591] Bernard Nodet, *Jean-Marie Vianney*, 71.

Fear of purgatory

Thérèse's attitude toward the possibility of going to purgatory seems to us to be an example of the one all Catholics should have when thinking about their future in the next life.

Thérèse believed in purgatory

Thérèse learned from the catechism that the *Church militant*, still on earth, mustn't forget the *Church suffering*, the souls in purgatory who are finishing their purification in the fire of love before joining all the members of the *Church triumphant* in heaven. She mentioned the Church's three parts when she described her desire to offer Jesus the flowers of her sacrifices, so that the Church triumphant may drop them on "the Church suffering in order to extinguish its flames" and "on the Church militant in order to gain the victory for it."[592]

Thérèse prayed for the souls in purgatory

Throughout her life, Thérèse prayed for the Church suffering. On the days of her profession and vestition, she asked for the deliverance of "all the souls in purgatory."[593] At the beginning of her Act of Offering to Merciful Love, written in 1895, she expressed her desire to "work for the glory of the Church by saving souls on earth, and by delivering those who are suffering in purgatory." Every day she recited indulgenced prayers for this intention.

Following the custom of the day, she prayed the Office of the Dead every time she heard of another Carmelite's death. On May 18, 1897, when she was already extremely sick, she resolutely asked Mother Agnes not to be dispensed from this recitation. She told her: "It's the only thing I can do for the Sisters who are in purgatory,

---

[592] B 4v.
[593] LT 74; A 76v; Pr 2.

and it doesn't tire me out in the least."[594] At the start of August she was too exhausted to continue it any longer. So, she asked the Lord to pay her debts. She said to Him: "I beg You, pay the debt that I have acquired with regard to the souls in purgatory, but do it as God, so that it be infinitely better than if I had said my Offices for the Dead."[595]

The following month she asked to be given her crucifix in order to gain a plenary indulgence for the benefit of the souls in purgatory. "I can give them no more than that!"[596] Like St. Teresa of Avila, her patron saint, she would have accepted staying in purgatory till the end of time if she would thus save a single soul through her prayers.[597]

She hoped to go straight to heaven

Thérèse prayed earnestly for the souls in purgatory. She hoped to go directly to heaven as Mother Geneviève had herself hoped. One day Thérèse had said to her, "Mother! You will not go to purgatory." The holy Carmelite foundress had replied gently, "I hope so!"[598]

From the time she made her Act of Offering to Merciful Love, Thérèse felt that this love was purifying her soul profoundly and left in it no trace of sin. "The Fire of Love is more sanctifying than is the fire of purgatory," she explained at the end of her first manuscript.[599] This idea also appears in her poem addressed to the Sacred Heart:

> To be able to gaze on your glory,
> I know we have to pass through fire.

[594] YN May 18, n. 2.
[595] YN August 6, n. 4.
[596] YN September 11, n. 5.
[597] LT 221; see YN July 8, n. 15.
[598] A 78v.
[599] A 84.

So I, for my purgatory,
Choose your burning love, O heart of my God![600]

In the letter from May 9, 1897, in which she described to Fr. Roulland her idea of God's justice, she expressed again her hope on this subject: "How would He purify in the flames of purgatory souls consumed in the fires of divine love?"[601]

One condition: count only on God's mercy

This boundless trust of St. Thérèse is an essential aspect of her "little way": the child who expects *everything* from God's mercy will receive everything from Him. Yet it will always be necessary to come before Him with empty hands, not relying on our own merits. Thérèse had a keen awareness of her life's imperfections: "All of our justice is stained in your eyes."[602] In particular, she didn't want to be judged on the value of her poor love. She counted exclusively on God's mercy for admittance to heaven, and for entering immediately.

Here is the well-known response Thérèse one day gave to Sr. Fevronia of the Holy Childhood, who thought that by exalting God's mercy Thérèse was forgetting His justice too much: "Sister, what you want from God's justice, you will receive from God's justice. A soul receives exactly what she expects from God."[603]

Again, we must truly count *exclusively* on God's mercy. *The fact that we believe in His mercy doesn't give us any right to benefit from it.*

---

[600] PN 23, st 8.
[601] LT 226.
[602] Pr 6.
[603] NPPA, Sr. Marie of the Angels. Sr. Fevronia was subprioress, and was solicitous to see her sisters follow the Carmelite Rule as perfectly as possible, which she herself followed strictly. Thérèse did so as well. But she wasn't counting on that fidelity for going immediately to heaven. She knew that "all our justices are stained" in God's eyes.

God is not in any way obliged to be merciful to us from the simple fact that we believe in it. Relying on one's faith is also appealing to God's justice to avoid purgatory; it's imagining that such faith *merits* us immediate entry into heaven.

The genuinely poor person holds out his hand without demanding anything, without claiming anything. He seeks only one thing: to soften the heart of the person from whom he hopes for alms. "Of the kindness of your heart, sir!"

However, to espouse this attitude, we need to have a heart in harmony with God's mercy, not a hard heart, always ready to expect rigorously just judgement for others. It requires a genuinely merciful heart. And such a heart is given by God's Spirit and He will give it if we ask Him for it "nicely," like beggars hoping for alms.

At the end of this final chapter, we wish to underline the uniqueness of the Catholic approach toward heaven. A Catholic believes in the existence of hell and knows he is proud enough to be in danger of going there; he believes in the existence of purgatory and knows too that he is so attached to his idols that he could indeed require purification there. Yet his is not a panicked fear, since it's accompanied by a boundless hope in God's mercy.

All the same, we shouldn't confuse this hope with the casual attitude of someone who has eliminated all fear about his eternal destiny because he realized once and for all "with his head" that God is so good that after death all His children will immediately enter paradise. No. While loving all His children infinitely, the Creator definitely cannot force His creatures to love Him above everything else. While drawing them to Himself in many ways, He cannot oblige them to allow themselves to be drawn. Even if the gates of heaven remained completely open forever, it might happen that certain souls prefer to remain outside rather than cast themselves, under the Holy Spirit's influence, into the arms of Jesus, so that they could go through Him, with Him and in Him, into the Father's bosom.

This is why the saints—our models—lived to the end of their days in a healthy filial fear with regard to their Creator and never stopped asking Him for the grace of perseverance. This is the ultimate grace which we ask the Blessed Virgin to obtain for us every day, "Pray for us sinners, now and at the hour of our death, Amen."

As St. Francis de Sales correctly stated, "Humility and trust are the two crutches we need to make our way to God…" We need these both right up to the day we can toss them away because we have definitively arrived in God's arms.

> On the threshold of his home
> Our father is awaiting you
> And the arms of God
> Will open for you.
>
> As on your first morning
> The sun will shine
> And you will enter into
> The joy of God.

Conclusion

We have been able to substantiate throughout these chapters the verities—*incredible but true*—that God has been pleased to reveal to us through His prophets and especially through His beloved Son, that allowed the saints to remain always joyful whatever might be happening in their lives. The Gospel is truly *good news*, a set of good things to enjoy. And these good things profoundly transform our view of our life, the world, and God.

Still, we must *believe with all our hearts*. That's why at the beginning and end of the Gospel proclamation two beatitudes announce clearly the happiness faith produces. First, there is the blessing proclaimed by Elizabeth when she welcomed the visit of her cousin, the Blessed Virgin Mary, "Blessed is she who believed what was spoken to her by the Lord!" And eight days after the Resurrection, Jesus said to Thomas the Apostle: "Blessed are those who will believe, though they have not seen me as you see me now!"[604]

Hence, it's essential to do everything we can to make our faith stronger and more enlightened; we must beg the Lord to make it

---

[604] Jn 20:29.

grow in our hearts, since it is and will always be a gift from His hand, the first of His gifts, an inestimable grace.

Yet it isn't enough to have faith—we must take the time to savor every facet of the Good News, since these are all indispensable if joy is to permeate our life. In particular, the practice of daily prayer is essential. In our regular, loving meetings with the Lord, we acquire good "reflexes" for the rest of our day. When an unexpected problem occurs, along with the inevitable pain it brings, we quickly recall the Lord's presence. He has permitted this difficulty and is always ready to give us the grace to accept it with a smile. And if prayer itself is difficult, we don't panic because we have the habit of frequently reflecting on how normal such aridity is and that the complete absence of consolation is fruitful.

Finally, we considered the place Jesus Himself had in Thérèse's joy. It was through living continually *with* and *in* Jesus that Thérèse always remained so peaceful. She wholeheartedly believed in the promise Jesus made to His disciples before His Ascension: "These things I have spoken to you, that in me you may have peace."[605] Yes, to remain at peace, we must remain *in Jesus*, surrendering ourselves to His hands...Just as He invited us to do: "Remain in me...remain in my love."[606] What does it mean to remain in Him if not to live as if we really were being held by God? That's why, as we saw, Thérèse collected images in which she could picture herself in the arms of Jesus, as lamb in the shepherd's arms, *as a child in his father's arms*, a bride in her husband's embrace, or better yet, as St. John at the Last Supper resting in the arms and on the Heart of his Master.

She also frequently contemplated the image of the Holy Face; it was her favorite image. And even though Jesus was depicted in it

605 Jn 16:33 NKJV.
606 Jn 15:4, 9.

with His eyes closed, she happily used this image to ponder Jesus' continual gaze, His *smile* at her. That smile gave her joy and she genuinely hoped to make it grow by responding to it with her most beautiful smile.

We must keep returning to this reality: the saints are lovers of Jesus. They are so entranced by the Lord's mad love for them that they desire to do something mad for Him in return. They are so captivated by His smile and His happiness, that they want to smile too, simply to make Him happier!

This is what Thérèse expressed well in the poem she composed a few months before her death, "My Joy." When she gave it to Mother Agnes for her feast day, she told her: "My whole soul is there."

> Oh! how many charms there are in suffering
> When one knows how to hide it with flowers!
> I truly want to suffer without saying so
> That Jesus may be consoled.
> My joy is to see him smile
> When my heart is exiled...
>
> My only joy on earth
> Is to be able to please you.[607]

---

[607] PN 45, st 5–6.

About The Cenacle Press
at Silverstream Priory

An apostolate of the Benedictine monastery of Silverstream Priory in Ireland, the mission of The Cenacle Press can be summed up in four words: *Quis ostendit nobis bona*—who will show us good things (Psalm 4:6)? In an age of confusion, ugliness, and sin, our aim is to show something of the Highest Good to every reader who picks up our books. More specifically, we believe that the treasury of the centuries-old Benedictine tradition and the beauty of holiness which has characterized so many of its followers through the ages has something beneficial, worthwhile, and encouraging in it for every believer.

cenaclepress.com

Also available from The Cenacle Press at Silverstream Priory

Robert Hugh Benson
The King's Achievement
By What Authority
The Friendship of Christ
Papers of a Pariah
Confessions of a Convert
Christ in the Church

Blessed Columba Marmion
OSB
Christ the Ideal of the Monk
Christ in His Mysteries
Words of Life On the
Margin of the Missal

Dom Pius De Hemptinne OSB
A Benedictine Soul: Biography,
Letters, and Spiritual Writings
of Dom Pius De Hemptinne

Dom Eugene Vandeur OSB
Hail Mary

Dom Hubert Van Zeller OSB
Letters to A Soul
We Work While the Light Lasts
The Yoke of Divine Love
Approach to Monasticism
Approach to Penance
Approach to Prayer
Approach to Spirituality

Fr Willie Doyle, SJ
Pamphlets for the Faithful

Father Ryan T Sliwa
New Nazareth's In Us

St John Henry Newman
(ed. Melinda Nielsen)
Festivals of Faith

Monks of Silverstream Priory
Dawn Tears, Spring Light, Rood
Peace: Poems

cenaclepress.com